Java Applets
Interactive Programming

by Elizabeth Sugar Boese

ISBN: 978-0-6152-0453-6

Copyright Year: 2008
Copyright Notice: by Elizabeth Sugar Boese. All rights reserved.

Preface

This book is a gentle introduction to the art of programming, focusing on giving you the tools to create sophisticated programs fast. It assumes you have never programmed before, and explains the necessary concepts to get up and running but segregates the advanced material into "Advanced Concept" sections. It is intended to motivate and excite you to the fun of programming. Everything is based on graphics and specifically applets, which enable you to put all of your work up on the Internet. There's also a chapter that explains how and where to put your applets on the Internet. This edition is updated for Java 6.0.

Why choose this book?
- The examples are all graphical Java applets, which can be put directly on to the Internet.
- The book is updated based on Java 6 using the capabilities of Swing components.
- You learn how to create applets and put them on the Internet, to show off to your family and friends.
- The material is all based on the standard Java API, enabling you to understand examples from other books and the Internet and without relying on custom libraries specific to a particular book.
- The book explains the essentials but puts the nitty gritty detail into separate "Advanced Concept" sections. This gives the strength of learning more of the neat stuff that can be done in applets and less time worrying about memory structures and parameter passing details unless your course requires it.
- The examples are creative, giving you a chance to think outside-the-box. For example, learn how to create your own fonts, how to have an image as a backdrop with your components on top, how to create a slideshow by either using buttons or an automated rotation. There are also many business-focused examples.
- Each chapter contains summaries and exercises to practice.
- A workbook is also available with lab exercises and slides with fill-in-the-blanks. Instructors can receive the slides with blanks filled in. The fill-in-the-blank style has been more successful in gaining students' attention during lectures as well as helps them learn how to study for what's important.
- This material has been used successfully for over 5 years in a non-majors course at Colorado State University in addition to several other universities. Students are able to produce sophisticated and very creative projects by the end of the semester. For example, student projects include a "Where's Waldo" game, football statistics and details for every team, "Stephanie's Closet" where you can rotate her shirts and/or pants to select what to wear, word search, sound mixer, Jeopardy game, hangman, photo albums, memory game and much more. To see some examples of what students have produced recently, go to:
  http://www.cs.colostate.edu/~boese/JavaApplets/studentProjects.html

Object or Procedural?
Teaching Objects-first vs. procedural programming is currently a huge debate for introductory courses. This book follows a natural approach - procedural with emphasis on using methods, and creating classes when necessary (e.g., extending the JPanel class to create a custom component). It is presented in an as-needed basis; when we need to create our own custom font, we need this separate class. The Advanced Sections enable students to go into more detail of the concepts, covering core curriculum requirements for CS1.

Topics
Chapter 1 introduces the programming process.
Chapter 2 explains how to draw shapes, text and images on the applet.
Chapter 3 covers some basics of variables and how to segment the code into methods.
Chapter 4 introduces components such as labels, buttons, lists and text boxes.

Chapter 5 explores the different layout managers to display components and discusses design strategies.
Chapter 6 revisits data types and variables in more detail and mathematical operations.
Chapter 7 discusses conditional structures such as the if, if-else and switch statements.
Chapter 8 introduces events and method stubs.
Chapter 9 explains repetition statements (loops).
Chapter 10 details the use of classes and how to extend the JPanel class to create custom components.
Chapter 11 explores some additional useful components and enhancements on components.
Chapter 12 discusses arrays, tables and ArrayList.
Chapter 13 explains threads and timers for slideshows and animation.
Chapter 14 introduces some basics to game programming, including Breakout and dungeon games.
Chapter 15 talks about Internet applications including JEditorPane, hosting applets on the Internet, emailing and reading/writing files on the server with CGI programs.
Chapter 16 concludes with a discussion about Java and compares it to other languages, what object-oriented is, and some additional third-party libraries, Graphics2D and Jar files.
Appendix has a listing of the Java API and a section on debugging techniques.

AWT vs. Swing

AWT (Abstract Windowing Toolkit) contains the original classes for creating graphics. Swing is a newer set of graphics that replace many of the old classes in the awt package. Although we still use some classes from awt (e.g. layout managers, Graphics), we should not mix and match awt components with Swing components. For example, putting TextFields (instead of Swing JTextFields) on JTabbedPanes do not display properly. This is a heads-up to those of you who have programmed with AWT components; by following this book you won't have any problems.

Instance Variables

Sometimes it is incorrect to initialize instance variables at the top of the program (e.g., Image with the call to getImage. However, it is necessary to declare variables as instance variables in order to access them in multiple methods throughout our programs. To minimize confusion, we take the approach that variables should only be declared at the top, and initialized within a method. We follow this approach for *all* variables to avoid the confusion. There's no harm done in this approach and students find it much easier to follow.

Supplemental materials

Supplemental materials are available on the website: http://java.frogandthefly.com and instructor slides/exam questions/homework and lab solutions from the author: boese@cs.colostate.edu.

Suggestions?

If you have suggestions on how to improve this book, or features you'd like added in the next edition, please contact me and let me know!   boese@cs.colostate.edu

Acknowledgements

Huge thanks go out to the students who helped with their creative ideas and suggestions, to the publishers for accepting this book and to you for buying it!

Credit goes to Luke Scanlon for the ski tuning photo. All other photos were taken by me.

Elizabeth Sugar Boese

Table of Contents

CHAPTER 1 11
INTRODUCTION TO PROGRAMMING 11
WHY LEARN TO PROGRAM? 12
PROGRAMMING LANGUAGES 12
HOW JAVA WORKS 13
Where did Java come from? 14
The Internet and World-Wide-Web 14
WHY PROGRAM IN JAVA? 15
THE JAVA APPLET 15
Import Statements 16
Header Comments 16
Class Declaration 17
Paint Method 17
HTML file 17
Running an example – Windows machine 18
Running an example – Linux machine 20

CHAPTER 2 25
DRAWING SHAPES AND TEXT 25
Drawing Basics 26
Coordinate System 26
Drawing Text 26
DRAWING SHAPES 31
Lines 31
Ovals and Circles 31
Rectangles and Squares 32
Filling shapes 32
Arcs 33
Polygons 34
IMAGES 35
IMAGES IN JAVA 37
Putting it Together 40

CHAPTER 3 45
VARIABLES AND METHODS 45
VARIABLES 46
Declaration 46
Initialization 47
Assignment 47
Reference 47
Locations and Scope 48
METHODS 49
Method Structure 50
Why have methods? 51

CHAPTER 4 57
SWING COMPONENTS 57
SWING 58

ADDING COMPONENTS TO THE APPLET	59
JLABEL	61
Images	*63*
JBUTTON	66
TEXT COMPONENTS	69
JTextField	*70*
JPasswordField	*70*
JTextArea	*71*
JCHECKBOX	72
JRADIOBUTTON	74
JCOMBOBOX	75
JLIST	75
COMPONENTS	78

CHAPTER 5 86

GUI DESIGN	86
LAYOUT MANAGERS	87
FlowLayout	*87*
BorderLayout	*90*
GridLayout	*93*
BoxLayout	*95*
WARNINGS!	97
STRUCTURING WITH METHODS	98
DESIGN	99
Design Guidelines	*101*
CASE STUDY	101

CHAPTER 6 109

DATA TYPES AND OPERATORS	109
VARIABLES	110
Rules:	*110*
Java Reserved Words	*110*
Data Types	*111*
Instance Variables	*112*
MATH	113
Math Class Methods	*113*
Arithmetic Operators	*114*
Relational Operators	*115*
Conditional Operators	*117*
ORDER OF OPERATIONS	118
INSTANCEOF OPERATOR	118
CONVERTING TYPES	119
Converting int to String	*119*
Converting String to int or double	*119*
Converting Object to String or component	*120*

CHAPTER 7 124

CONDITIONALS	124
IF STRUCTURE	125
If-else Structure	*126*
Comparing Data Types	*129*
Nesting if Statements	*130*

Switch Statements	130
Comparing if and switch	132
Example: Seasonal Weather	133

CHAPTER 8 142

Events	142
ActionEvents	*144*
ItemEvents	*148*
ListSelectionEvents	*150*
KeyEvents	*151*
MouseEvents	*153*
Method Stubs	155
Case Study	161
Summary	164

CHAPTER 9 166

Loops	166
Repeating Statements	167
While Loop	*167*
For Loop	*168*
Do Loop	*172*
Animation	172
Which loop to use?	173
Careful!	173

CHAPTER 10 179

Classes	179
Using Classes	180
Extending JPanel	180
Customizing our Class	*182*
Font Fun	*187*
Background Image	*190*
Customized Field Set	*191*

CHAPTER 11 197

Swing Components II	197
JTabbedPane	198
ToolTips	201
Borders	202
Etched Border	*203*
Bevel Border	*203*
Titled Border	*204*
Matte Border	*204*
Audio	205
JFrame	207
MediaTracker	211

CHAPTER 12 215

Collections	215
List Data Structures	216
Arrays	216
Array Declaration	*216*

Array Initialization	*216*
Array Element Initialization	*217*
Short-cut Initializer List	*217*
Length	*217*
ARRAYS AND JTABLE	224
2-D Arrays	*224*
JTABLE	225
Coloring	*227*
ARRAYLIST	228
CASE STUDY	231

CHAPTER 13 237

THREADS AND TIMER	237
THREADS	238
Animation	*242*
TIMERS	243

CHAPTER 14 249

GAME PROGRAMMING	249
OVERVIEW	250
Game World	*250*
Player Control	*250*
Brains	*250*
Flicker	*251*
BREAKOUT GAME	252
DUNGEON GAMES	258

CHAPTER 15 272

INTERNET APPLICATIONS	272
INTERNET	273
JEDITORPANE	273
HOSTING YOUR APPLET ON THE WEB	277
APPLET PARAMETERS	278
CONFIGURATION FILES	279
APPLETS AND EMAIL	281
WRITING TO A FILE	283

CHAPTER 16 287

JAVA	287
Simplicity	*288*
Small language – or is it?	*288*
Graphics	*288*
Object-Oriented	*288*
Platform Independent	*288*
Multi-Threading	*289*
Security	*289*
MODIFYING AND USING FREE APPLETS	289
OTHER FEATURES THROUGH 3RD-PARTY LIBRARIES	289

APPENDIX A 295

DEBUGGING	295
ERRORS	296

Printing Designators *297*
Printing Values *299*
Color-Coding Components *300*
Debuggers *300*

APPENDIX B 303
Java API 303

Chapter 1

Introduction to Programming

"I think there is a world market for maybe five computers."
  - *Thomas Watson, chairman of IBM, 1943*

Objectives:

- Why learn to program?
- Programming languages
- How Java works
- Where did Java come from?
- The Internet and World Wide Web
- Why program in Java?
- The Java applet
- Running an example – Windows machine
- Running an example – Linux machine

Why learn to program?

We have all learned the basics of computation, such as: 2 + 2 = 4. We learned how to compute more complex mathematical expressions, such as: 5 * (3 + 7) / 2. We also learned how to describe a calculation, such as: *the area is the width multiplied by the height.*

Learning how to program is learning how to solve problems. First we have to figure out what the problem is, then design a solution, implement, test and fix errors. This takes a lot of practice and patience. Sometimes we'll get error messages that tell us explicitly what the problem is, and sometimes we won't get any error messages at all – and it doesn't work! This process can be somewhat frustrating, but also can be very rewarding when we figure out the problem.

Programming helps us develop critical thinking and problem solving skills. By learning how to program, we learn how to formulate problems, think creatively about solutions and express a solution clearly and accurately. Problem solving is important for all disciplines; for example

- Mathematics — use of formal languages, calculation of formulae
- Engineering — designing, assembling components, evaluating between solutions
- Natural Science — observing behavior of humans/animals/plants/weather
    - forming hypotheses and testing
    - analyzing results from experiments
- Art — digital image/video/sound/movie manipulation
- History — recording, storing, indexing, searching, analyzing and retrieving historical documents and information
- All fields — process of discovering something new
    - exploration of data and analysis

Programming Languages

When working with computers, computers cannot understand the complexity of the English language. Instead, we need to write a computer program. A **program** is a set of instructions for the computer to execute. Programs are written in a programming language. A **programming language** is a grammar to designate information and instructions that a computer understands. Programming languages are a lot less descriptive than English, but they do use English words (aren't you glad you speak English?). The grammar is also referred to as the **syntax**.

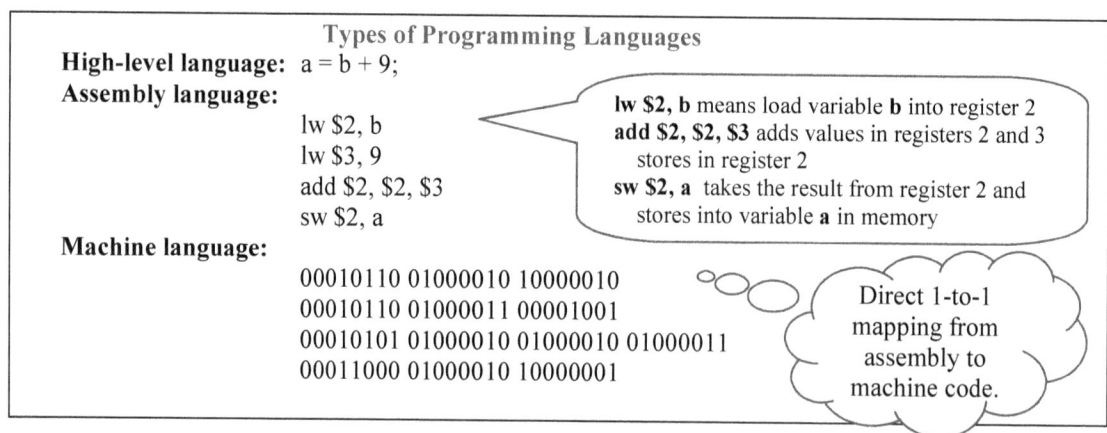

There are three main types of languages that we're going to look at: machine, assembly, and high-level languages. **Machine code** is the lowest level of programming languages; it is the only encoding that the computer understands – 0's and 1's. Computers today store all information in a binary representation –

as groups of 0's and 1's. Machine code differs for different machine types: the machine code to add two values together will be different groups of 0's and 1's on an Intel system vs. a SPARC station, etc. **Assembly language** is a mapping of the machine code to something more readable. For example, "lw $2, b" will load the value in a variable named b into register 2. **High-level language** allows us to simplify the program code with a higher level of abstraction than assembly code. An example of high-level code would be: "x = y + 2;". Java is an example of a high-level language.

When we write in a high-level language, we still need to decompose it into machine code before the computer can execute its instructions. To do this, we take the **source code** which is the program that we wrote and either run it through a compiler or an interpreter. A **compiler** translates source code into a target language. Sometimes compilers translate source code into machine code, and sometimes it translates to another type of code. Programming languages like C and C++ are run through compilers which translate the source code into machine code. This is important because it means the compiled C program can only be executed on machine types that it was compiled on. Other languages like HTML and JavaScript are not compiled but interpreted. The source code for these programs is run through an interpreter. An **interpreter** translates the code into machine code and then executes the machine code

How Java works

Java source code (.java file)

```
public class Fun extends JApplet
{
    public void paint( Graphics g )
    {
        g.drawString( "Hi!", 0, 20 );
    }
}
```

Java Compiler

Java bytecode (.class file)

```
ljsdf@!lj dsfljk#9sdf03
sdf9021f9080dfs098
09f09d8sdf 3209fsd 90s09
```

Java bytecode is platform independent

→ pc → Interpreter → 0100110 1010101

→ workstation → Interpreter → 1110101 0111010

→ Macintosh → Interpreter → 0000101 0001010

The interpreter translates bytecode to machine code and executes the program

Machine code is different for each machine

Java works a little differently than these other languages. Java source code is first compiled into **bytecode**. This bytecode can be distributed to any type of system: Macintosh, Windows, UNIX, etc. This bytecode is then run through an interpreter, the JVM (Java Virtual Machine), which translate the bytecode into machine code for the particular machine for it to run. This is where the buzzwords "platform independent" and "write once, run anywhere" concepts are derived.

These are two important catch-phrases associated with Java: "**platform independent**" and "**write once, run anywhere**". It is important to understand these phrases when talking about Java. Java is platform independent because the source code is compiled to bytecode, and it's the bytecode that can be used on any platform. This works because each platform has an interpreter that can translate the bytecode to the machine code for that particular platform. So platform independence is assuming the use of an interpreter, but the source code doesn't need to be re-compiled on these machines. This leads into the phrase, "write once, run anywhere". Java bytecode works on any platform. Other languages require the program to be modified so it can be compiled for each platform.

The advantage of using interpreters is that we don't need a specific compiler for each machine; the code is platform-independent allowing the code to be run on different machines. However, there are some disadvantages to using interpreters. Code is slower to execute, between 10 to 100 times slower than code compiled straight to machine code. It still requires an interpreter to be on the machine in order to execute the code. And it also limits the abilities that could be programmed, since the code should be able to execute on all types of machines. Therefore, a special machine such as SGIs which are known for extra graphics abilities would not be exploited when programming in an interpreted language.

Where did Java come from?

Java was originally intended to make smart appliances, such as toasters and TVs. The idea was to create a small language that is easy to learn (unlike machine code) that could run on any kind of computer chip. This would enable a manufacturer of a smart appliance to upgrade the computer chip without having to re-write the software to run it. However, Java never took off for electronic appliances, but then along came the World-Wide-Web.

The Internet and World-Wide-Web

A common misconception is that the World-Wide-Web (WWW) *is* the Internet, but in fact the Internet was around long before the WWW came into existence. In 1969, the US Department of Defense connected four universities together to form the first Internet. They wanted to make it easier to share information between researchers. By 1970, e-mail was invented to communicate between people via computers on the Internet. In the 80's and early 90's, programs such as Gopher and WAIS were developed to navigate text files on the Internet.

The WWW came about in 1993 with the first Web browsers that could display text and images from files on computers connected to the Internet. The WWW relies on the HTTP protocol (HyperText Transfer Protocol). A **protocol** is a set of rules, so HTTP is the set of rules governing how to handle Web pages.

Web pages are identified by the **URL** (Uniform Resource Locator) which contains the protocol (e.g. http), the internet address, and a path to the file. The internet address usually starts with *www*. Part of the internet address is the **domain name**, which can be bought and registered for a Web site. The domain name ends with a **top-level domain**, to identify its overall purpose and/or country of origin. For example, let's look at the URL below and dissect it:

URL: http://www.cs.colostate.edu/~boese/Research/index.html

                                            domain name   file name

Web pages are intended to work on any computer platform, similar to Java programs. Java became an ideal language to adapt to the WWW as Java applets embedded within a Web page.

Top-Level Domains:	
.com	-- commercial sites
.org	-- non-profit organization
.net	-- network organization
.edu	-- educational institution

Country TLDs	
.org.nz	-- non-profit in New Zealand
.co.uk	-- commercial in the UK
.co.ca	-- commercial in Canada
.jp	-- Japanese sites
.eu	-- European Union sites

Why program in Java?

Java provides a programming tool for web pages that has graphics capabilities, is machine independent (as described above), and is a relatively easy language to learn (compared to others). It can also be used to program over networks.

So why wouldn't we use Java? Java is undergoing constant change which requires learning and upgrading tools and software, the language is growing in size adding complexity, and it's slower to execute than languages like C and C++.

Deciding the appropriate language for a program is based on many factors. Sometimes the decision is based on which languages the programmers already know, the efficiency and speed of a language, the graphics capabilities, platform independence, etc. For this course, we choose Java because it is still relatively simpler than other languages, it has graphics capabilities which makes it a bit more fun, and allows us to create applets that we can put up on the Internet.

There are two different types of Java programs that we can create: applets and applications. Applets are Java programs embedded in a web page. Applications are stand-alone programs that can be run by themselves. In this course, we'll be writing applets so that we can display our applets on the Internet. In order to create an applet, there are three different files that we will work with: the Java program (also called source code) which is what we will write, the bytecode which is what the output from the compiler, and the HTML file to display the applet. The source code is in a file with a **.java** file extension. The bytecode is in a file with a **.class** file extension. HTML files end with either **.htm** or **.html** file extensions.

The Java Applet

Java programs come in two forms: applications and applets. Applications run on their own, similar to MS Word or the Netscape browser. Applets run inside a web page.
Our focus is on applets, so let's look at a simple example of an applet.

```java
import javax.swing.*;
import java.awt.*;
/** first program
 * @author  E.S.Boese
 * @version fall 2005
 */
public class MyFirstProgram extends JApplet
{
   public void paint( Graphics g )
   {
        super.paint( g );
        g.drawString( "Hello World", 30, 20 );
   }
}
```

Let's break this program down into each part for discussion.
There are four main parts in this program.

- Import statements
- Header comments
- class declaration
- paint method

Import Statements

The two import statements

    import javax.swing.*;
    import java.awt.*;

Import statements allow us to re-use code that has already been written. There are classes that we can use so that we don't have to re-invent the wheel again. There are many standard classes that come with every Java distribution. For example, we want to create an applet and want the text to appear on the screen. Someone else has already written the code to make the screen draw things for us. We can use that class by referencing it: the JApplet class in our example. But when the compiler looks for this JApplet.class file, it needs to know where it is. We can tell the compiler where to look by specifying that it is in the javax.swing package. The star (*) designates to the compiler to look at all the classes in that package, as the package may contain many different classes. We could also be more specific and state exactly which class, by the following import statement:

    import javax.swing.JApplet;

Both ways work, and neither is more efficient than the other.

The second import statement tells the compiler to look for classes in the java.awt package. This is where it will find the Graphics class. The Graphics class works with the browser to draw things on the screen. All we need to do is add instructions on exactly what we want drawn and where we want it.

Import statements need to go at the very top of our program.

Header Comments

    /** first program
     * @author E.S.Boese
     * @version fall 2007
     */

The top of our program should always begin with a header comment. This comment area should include a description of the program, your name as the author, the date you created it. Comments are not executed as part of the program, but are used as a documented record about the program for us humans to read. There is more information we could provide here, but for now, we will keep it to these basics.

There are two types of comments in Java programs: multi-line comments and in-line comments. The example above used a multi-line comment, designated with a slash-star (/*) to begin the comment and a star-slash (*/) to end the comment. Everything between the /* and */ is ignored when the program is executed. This format allows for the comment to extend over multiple lines, as we see in this example.

Another type of comment is an in-line comment, designated with two forward slashes (//). We will see this in our future examples. The // designates that the rest of the line (everything after the //) is to be ignored as a comment. The // can only apply to a single-line.

Class Declaration

```
public class MyFirstProgram extends JApplet
{

}
```

Each class we create needs a class declaration. Here we define the name of the class. In our example, the name of the class is `MyFirstProgram`. This also means that the class is located in a file called `MyFirstProgram.java`. It is important to note that the class name and the filename must match exactly - including upper/lower case letters.

Because we are developing applets, we want to specify that our class is an applet. To do so, we say that our class **extends** the `JApplet` class. This way we *inherit* the functionality of an applet without re-writing the code to make an applet an applet!

We start out our class declaration with the word `public`, to ensure that we can run the program directly. We're not going to go into much more depth about this at the moment.

Paint Method

```
public void paint( Graphics g )
  {
        super.paint( g );
        g.drawString ( "Hello World", 30, 20 );
  }
```

The `paint` method is where the meat of the program occurs. In our example, we want to draw the text for "Hello World" inside our applet. The `Graphics` class helps us accomplish this. We can call a *method* on the `Graphics` object. The method we call is the `drawString` method, which prints text.

To use the `Graphics` class, we have a *variable* reference: in our example, we used the name `g`. Now we can call *methods* on this object, by calling **g.<method>** where **<method>** is the name of a method such as `drawString`.

When we call this method, we need to send it some *parameters*. Each parameter is separated with a comma. In our example, there are three parameters: "Hello World", 30, and 20. The first parameter, "Hello World", is the text that we want to print. The second parameter 30 designates the x-coordinate of where to draw the text, and the third parameter 20 designates the y-coordinate of where to draw the text.

We'll be talking more about methods later.

HTML file

The HTML file is essential for displaying applets – applets are intended to be embedded within web pages. This needs to be in a separate file than our .java file with our source code. HTML files should also have an extension of .html. This book is not about writing HTML, so we will only present the essential HTML code to get an applet to display.

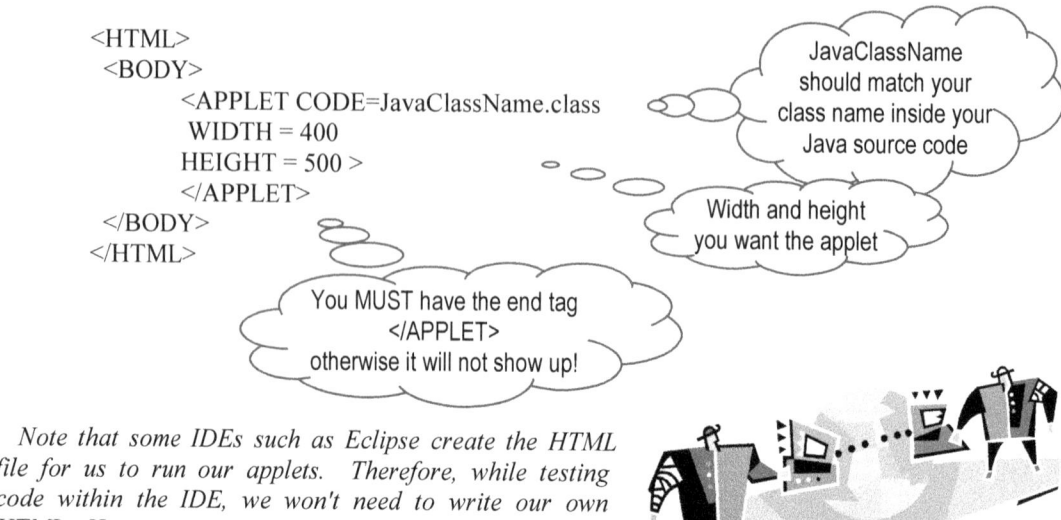

```
<HTML>
  <BODY>
    <APPLET CODE=JavaClassName.class
    WIDTH = 400
    HEIGHT = 500 >
    </APPLET>
  </BODY>
</HTML>
```

JavaClassName should match your class name inside your Java source code

Width and height you want the applet

You MUST have the end tag </APPLET> otherwise it will not show up!

Note that some IDEs such as Eclipse create the HTML file for us to run our applets. Therefore, while testing code within the IDE, we won't need to write our own HTML. However, once we want to put our applet up on the Internet, we will have to create an HTML file.

Running an example – Windows machine

To set up our first applet, follow the steps below on a computer running Windows.
1. Open a "Command Prompt".
   (Select start → All Programs → Accessories → Command Prompt)
2. We're going to use the basic editor, Notepad to write our first program. If we want a program named **FirstProgram**, we need to add the .java extension to the filename, so we would type:

   notepad FirstProgram.java

   Filenames cannot have spaces.

3. Type in the following code below, exactly how it appears:

```
/** First program with Java
 * @author: your name
 */
import javax.swing.*;
import java.awt.*;

public class FirstProgram extends JApplet
{
    String text = "Cookie Monster";
    public void paint ( Graphics g )
    {
        g.drawString ( text, 15, 20 );
    }
}
```

4. To save the file, make sure Notepad doesn't add a .txt extension. Change the box that says "Save as Type:" to "All Files", and make sure the filename includes the .java extension.
5. Close Notepad, and return to the Command Prompt window.

6. Now we want to compile the program. The java compiler is called **javac** Type:

   javac FirstProgram.java

   If there are any syntax errors, they will be listed in the terminal window. If there are errors, we need to go pack to step 2 and correct the code until there are no errors when we compile the program.

7. When we run the source code through the compiler without errors, we get a bytecode file. If we get a listing of the directory, we should see the .class file listed:

   dir

   There should be the two files listed: FirstProgram.java and FirstProgram.class

8. Now we need to create the HTML file to embed the applet. Using Notepad, open a new file named FirstProgram.html

   notepad FirstProgram.html

9. Enter the following code exactly in this file:

```
<HTML>
<BODY>
 <APPLET CODE="FirstProgram.class"  WIDTH=500  HEIGHT=400>
 </APPLET>
</BODY></HTML>
```

      Java is case sensitive, so ensure that FirstProgram has a capital F and capital P, just as it is inside the java file.

10. Save this file as we did before, this time with the .html extension. Close Notepad.
To view the applet, we use the program named: **appletviewer**

   appletviewer FirstProgram.html

A window should appear with Cookie Monster typed in it.

Running an example – Linux machine

To set up our first applet, follow the steps below on a Linux machine.
1. Open a term window.
2. We're going to use the basic editor, pico to write our first program. If we want a program named **FirstProgram**, we need to add the .java extension, so we would type:

    pico FirstProgram.java

3. This editor is similar to Notepad on Windows. Type in the following code below, exactly how it appears:

```
/** First program with Java
 * @author: your name
 */
import javax.swing.*;
import java.awt.*;

public class FirstProgram extends JApplet
{
        String  text = "Cookie Monster";
        public void paint ( Graphics g )
        {
                g.drawString ( text, 15, 20 );
        }
}
```

4. To save the file, hold down the control key (cntrl) and press the letter O key.
5. To exit the pico environment, press cntrl-x
6. Now we want to compile the program. The java compiler is called **javac** Type:

    javac FirstProgram.java

    If there are any syntax errors, they will be listed in the terminal window. If there are errors, go back to step 2 and correct the code until you get no errors when you compile the program.

7. When we run the source code through the compiler without errors, we get a bytecode file. If we get a listing of the directory, we should see the .class file listed:

    ls

    (the lower-case letter L and the lower-case letter s)
    There should be two files listed: FirstProgram.java and FirstProgram.class

8. Now we need to create the HTML file to embed the applet. Using pico, open a new file named FirstProgram.html

    pico FirstProgram.html

9. Enter the following code exactly in this file:

```
<HTML>
<BODY>
 <APPLET CODE="FirstProgram.class" WIDTH=500 HEIGHT=400>
 </APPLET>
</BODY></HTML>
```

Java is case sensitive, so ensure that FirstProgram has a capital F and capital P, just as it is inside the java file.

10. Save this file as we did before.

11. To view the applet, we use the program named: **appletviewer**

   appletviewer FirstProgram.html

A window should appear with Cookie Monster typed in it.

Summary

- A **program** is a set of instructions for the computer to execute.
- The **syntax** is the grammar used by a programming language.
- A **programming language** is a grammar to designate information and instructions that a computer understands.
- **Machine code** is made up of 0's and 1's and is the only language a computer understands. Programs in other languages need to be converted to machine language before a computer can execute it.
- **Assembly language** is a mapping of the machine code to something more readable, based on English words such as "load" and "add".
- **High-level language** allows us to simplify the program code with a higher level of abstraction than assembly code, such as "x = x + 2".
- **Source code** is the program that we write, usually in a high-level language such as Java.
- A **compiler** translates source code into a target language.
- An **interpreter** translates the code into machine code and then executes the machine code.
- When Java is compiled, the compiler creates an intermediate coding called **bytecode.**
- A programming language is considered to be **platform-independent** if it can be interpreted/executed on different machine types (e.g., SunOS, MacOS, Linux, Windows) without changes.
- Applets are embedded within web pages. The .java file is the source code, the .class file is the bytecode, and the .html file (web page) specifies the .class file.
- Import statements are placed at the top of a program to designate the packages where other classes used by the program can be found.
- Header comments are listed at the beginning of a program to specify the author and date.
- Comments are not executed as part of the program, and are used to explain things about the code. They can either be two forward slashes // to designate the rest of the line is a comment, or across multiple lines by beginning with /* and ending with */
- The class header starts all programs. This needs to include
    public class nameOfProgram extends JApplet
- The paint method is where we can draw things on the applet.

Exercises

1. True or False. A Java compiler translates source code to machine code.
2. True or False. Java is an object-oriented language.
3. Java is considered to be **platform-independent** because
   a. the source code can be compiled to machine code on any machine
   b. the bytecode can be interpreted on any machine
   c. the source code is the same independent of the machine it is developed on
   d. the bytecode gets translated to source code on any machine
4. Approximately when did the Internet begin? the WWW? computers?
5. What is the difference between the Internet and the World Wide Web?
6. Why do we use the import statement?
7. True or False: Java source code gets compiled into a .class file which is machine code.
8. True or False: Computers store all information using decimal representation.
9. What is bytecode? How does it differ from machine code?
10. What is the definition of syntax?
11. How is the use of an IDE such as Eclipse useful for programming?
12. What's the difference between running Java programs vs. C programs on different computer types? What more do we need to do with a C program?
13. What is a program?
14. What is an algorithm?
15. How do programs differ from algorithms?
16. There are three major programming language types: machine languages, assembly languages, and high-level languages. Give an example of each. How are they inter-related?
17. Match the following terms to their best fitting definitions
    a. grammar   ____ program
    b. data in context   ____ package
    c. made up of 0's and 1's   ____ algorithm
    d. steps to solve a problem   ____ syntax
    e. what Java compiles to   ____ machine language
    f. a mathematical computation   ____ compiler
    g. type of programming language   ____ byte code
    h. set of instructions for a computer   ____ assembly
    i. referenced using the import statement
    j. process of viewing the source code
    k. translates the source code into another

18. True/False: Computers store all information using binary representation.

19. True/False: Import statements can be listed anywhere in the program.

20. True/False: Comments are used by the interpreter to determine the instruction set.

21. What does it mean for a language to be portable? Define "platform-independent" and what the Java motto "write once, run anywhere" means.

22. Explain the process of a Java program: source code, interpreter, compiler, bytecode, machine code. Draw a diagram.

23. If the name of our class is called **CurrencyConverter**, what is the name of the source code file? What is the name of the bytecode file?

24. What is the difference between in-line comments and block comments?

25. What class do applets need to inherit from? What package is it in?

26. Put the following in order of when they came into existence.

    a. _____ Java

    b. _____ WWW

    c. _____ computers

    d. _____ Internet

27. Write a program that displays your name, date, and a fun fact about yourself. Put each entry on a separate line.

Chapter 2

Drawing Shapes and Text

Roses are #FF0000
Violets are #0000FF...

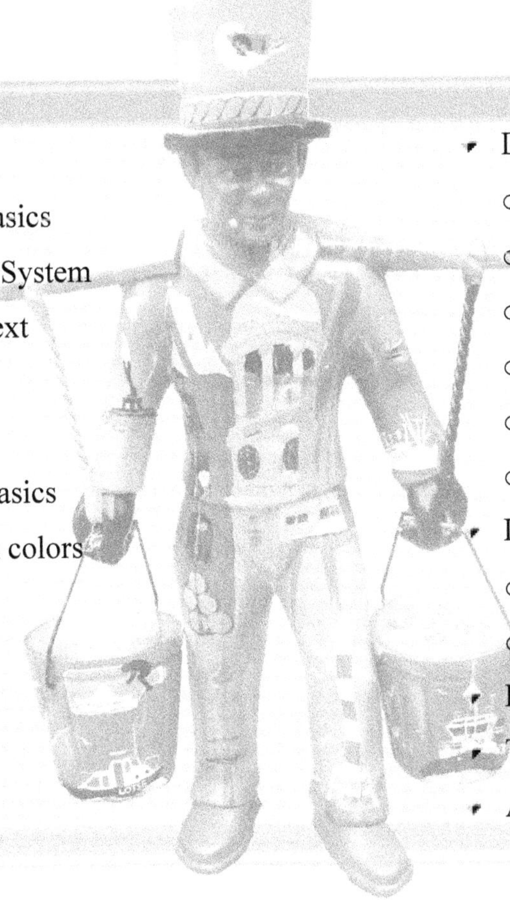

Objectives:

- Drawing Basics
- Coordinate System
- Drawing Text
    o Text
    o Fonts
    o Color basics
    o Custom colors
- Drawing Shapes
    o Lines
    o Ovals and Circles
    o Rectangles and Squares
    o Filling Shapes
    o Arcs
    o Polygons
- Images
    o File type
    o File size
- Pixels
- Transparency
- Anti-aliasing

Drawing Basics

We can draw things on an applet by writing a `paint` method. The `paint` method allows us access to a `Graphics` object, which is how we can specify what to draw and where to draw it. The paint method gets automatically called by the browser when it needs to draw the applet or re-draw the screen if it has changed. An outline of a program with a paint method is listed below:

```java
import java.awt.*;          // access the Graphics object
import javax.swing.*;       // access to JApplet

public class DrawEx extends JApplet
{
    public void paint( Graphics g )
    {
        // put your code here!
    }
}
```

The `Graphics` object allows us to call *methods* for drawing. We can draw circles, ellipses, squares, rectangles and polygons, as well as write text.

Coordinate System

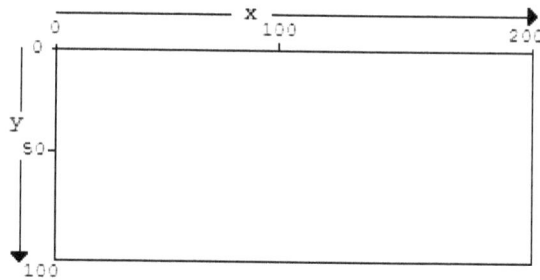

For all of these drawing methods, we will need to specify where to draw using an x and y coordinate system.

The Java x-y coordinate system starts in the upper-left corner at (0,0).

As we go right along the x-axis, the x-coordinate value goes up. As we go down along the y-axis, the y-coordinate value goes up.

Drawing Text

We can draw text on an applet by using the `drawString` method inside our `paint` method. The `drawString` method requires the text and x and y coordinates to specify where the text should begin.

```
graphicsObj.drawString( String, x-coordinate, y-coordinate );
```

Example inside the paint method:

*The name of the Graphics object must match: e.g. **grp***

```java
public void paint( Graphics grp )
{
    grp.drawString( "Some text to display", x, y );
}
```

26

Our first example draws text in various locations in our applet. Notice what happens when we specify a location of (0,0) for our x and y coordinates:

```java
import java.awt.*;            // access the Graphics object
import javax.swing.*;         // access to JApplet

public class Text1 extends JApplet
{
   public void paint ( Graphics gr )
   {
          gr.drawString ( "Hello Worldling", 0, 0 );
          gr.drawString ( "Java rocks", 0, 50 );
          gr.drawString ( "Skiing is fun", 50, 50 );
          gr.drawString( "To be, or not 2 B", 50, 65 );
   }
}
```

Notice the 'g' from "Worldling" hanging in view...

Applet output shows: Java rocks/Skiing is fun, To be, or not 2 B

The "Hello Worldling" is not visible in the applet because the x and y coordinates specify the bottom-left of where the text begins. So, if we are using 12-point font, our text begins at 0,0 and the top of our letters are at -12 in the y direction - not in the visible area for the applet! So, how would we fix this so that the text appeared at the top of the applet?

Also notice how the text can be written on top of other text. If we don't want this overlap, it is up to us to place them such that they don't overlap.

In the next example we show where various coordinates display on the applet.

```java
import java.awt.*;
import javax.swing.*;
public class Coords extends JApplet
{
        public void paint( Graphics g )
        {
                g.drawString( "(0,0)",    0,  0 );
                g.drawString( "(100,10)", 100, 10 );
                g.drawString( "(20,50)",  20, 50 );
                g.drawString( "(190,90)", 190, 90 );
        }
}
```

(0,0) bottom-left is at top of applet and text above it

Applet shows: (100,10), (20,50), (190,90)

To draw text beneath text we've already drawn, we keep the x value the same and increase the y value. The default font size is 12 pt, which means 12 pixels. Add 12 (or a little more for nice spacing between the two lines) to the y value and we'll draw text beneath our other text.

Fonts

We can change the *font* of our text by specifying a particular font name, style, and size. The structure for creating a font appears below:

```
Font fnt = new Font( type, style, size );
g.setFont( fnt );
```

OR

```
g.setFont( new Font( type, style, size ) );
```

Although we can try to reference some fancy fonts, they may not be available on other systems that run our applet! The main fonts we can always depend on are: "Serif", "SansSerif", "Monospaced", and "Dialog" (Dialog is the default font).

There are four styles that are available:

- Font.PLAIN
- Font.BOLD
- Font.ITALIC
- Font.BOLD + Font.ITALIC

This last one is a combination of both **bold** and *italic* to get ***boldItalic***.

A range of sizes are available, but regular text is usually either 10-pt or 12-pt font. Anything below size 8 is nearly impossible to read.

So now we can create fonts, such as the following:

```
Font small = new Font( "Serif", Font.PLAIN, 8 );
Font big = new Font( "SanSerif", Font.BOLD + Font.ITALIC, 36 );
```

To use these fonts, we can apply them to our components. So far, we have only been working with the `Graphics` component. To apply a particular font, we call the method `setFont` on the object.

```
import java.awt.*;
import javax.swing.*;

public class TextFonts extends JApplet
{
   public void paint ( Graphics g )
   {
      g.drawString ("Hello World",0,10 );
      Font small = new Font( "Serif", Font.PLAIN, 8 );
      g.setFont( small );
      g.drawString ("Java rocks", 0,50 );
      g.drawString ( "Hiya", 60, 15 );        // font stays the same until we call setFont again
      Font big = new Font( "SanSerif", Font.BOLD + Font.ITALIC, 36 );
      g.setFont( big );
      g.drawString ( "Skiing is fun", 50, 50 );
   }
}
```

This next example shows the differences between the font types. Monospaced is similar to Courier – they are both fixed-width fonts. This means that each letter has the same amount of spacing, therefore lower-case 'i' has a lot of space on either side. The others are all *variable-width* fonts, such that the letter 'i' only takes up as much space as necessary. Variable-width fonts tend to be easier to read, but if we want to ensure the spacing then a fixed-width font may be desired.

```
import java.awt.*;
import javax.swing.*;
public class FontTypes extends JApplet
{
  public void paint ( Graphics g )
  {
    Font serf = new Font( "Serif", Font.PLAIN, 14 );
    g.setFont( serf );
    g.drawString ( "Serif", 10, 15 );
    g.setFont( new Font ( "Sans-Serif", Font.PLAIN, 14 ) );
    g.drawString ( "Sans-Serif", 10, 30 );
    g.setFont( new Font ( "Dialog", Font.PLAIN, 14 ) );
    g.drawString ( "Dialog", 10, 45 );
    g.setFont( new Font ( "Monospaced", Font.PLAIN, 14 ) );
    g.drawString ( "Monospaced", 10, 60 );
  }
}
```

Color Basics

We can change the color when we draw shapes and text by creating `Color` objects. The simplest way to use colors is to reference one of the colors already created for Java programs.

The following colors are available:

Color.BLACK	**Color.BLUE**	Color.CYAN	Color.DARK_GRAY
Color.GRAY	Color.GREEN	Color.LIGHT_GRAY	Color.MAGENTA
Color.ORANGE	Color.PINK	Color.RED	**Color.WHITE**

If we want to use a color, we use the method `setColor( color )` on the component we wish to change colors.

```
import java.awt.*;
import javax.swing.*;
public class ColorEx extends JApplet
{
  public void paint ( Graphics g )
  {
    g.setColor( Color.RED );
    g.drawString ( "Hello World", 0,12 );
    g.setColor( Color.BLUE );
    g.drawString ( "Java rocks", 0,50 );
    g.setColor( Color.CYAN );
    g.fillRect ( 50,60,40,20 );
  }
}
```

A good way to think about how this **setColor** method works is to imagine we're using a marker. By default, we're holding on to a black marker, and anything we're asked to draw we do with the black marker. As soon as we call **setColor** to change the color, for example to red, then we put down the black marker and now pick up the red marker. Now, anything we're asked to draw will be in red, until we call **setColor** to change to another color.

Creating Custom Colors

We can also create our own custom colors. We do so by specifying how much red, green and blue we want in our color.

> Color mycolor = new Color(red, green, blue);

The max number for these values is 255, which means we want a lot of that color. Therefore, we can analyze some colors:

> Color red = new Color(255, 0, 0);
> Color gray = new Color(128, 128, 128);
> Color yellow = new Color(255, 255, 0);
> Color white = new Color(255, 255, 255);
> Color black = new Color(0, 0, 0);

```java
import java.awt.*;
import javax.swing.*;
public class ColorEx2 extends JApplet
{
  public void paint ( Graphics g )
  {
    g.setColor( new Color( 130, 130, 80 ) );
    g.drawString ( "Hello World", 0,12 );
    g.setColor( new Color( 128, 0, 128 ) );
    g.drawString ( "Java rocks", 0,50 );
    g.drawString ( "Rockin' to the music", 10,70 );
  }
}
```

Notice that the color stays the same until setColor is called again.

There are several ways to figure out the RGB colors for the color we want. We could do the trial-and-error method of trying different values until we figure it out. An easier way would be to look for a color wheel on the Internet with the RGB values given. We can also use any graphics program such as Microsoft Paint to tell us as well.

In MS Paint, select "Colors" then "Edit Colors..." then click on the button "Define Custom Colors..." It should display a whole spectrum of colors. When we click on a color, it shows us the RGB values in the lower right-hand corner of the dialog box.

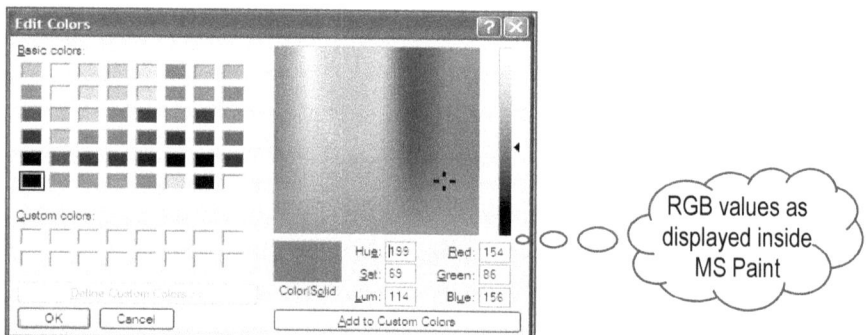

RGB values as displayed inside MS Paint

Drawing Shapes

Lines

We use the coordinate system to specify the x and y coordinates of where our line should start and x and y coordinates for where the line should end. Since we are drawing on the applet, we need to reference our Graphics variable again.

The specification for the `drawLine` method follows:

```
drawLine( x, y,  x2, y2 );
```

Our first example draws a diagonal line from the upper-left corner (0,0) to (50,50).

```java
import java.awt.*;        // access the Graphics object
import javax.swing.*;     // access to JApplet
public class LineDiagonal extends JApplet
{
        public void paint( Graphics g )
        {
                g.drawLine( 0,0, 50, 50 );
        }
}
```

To draw a horizontal line, the **y** values need to stay the same. For example:

```
g.drawLine( 10, 40, 70, 40 ); // draws horizontal line 40 pixels down
g.drawLine( 30, 10, 50, 10 ); // draws horizontal line 10 pixels down
```

To draw a vertical line, the **x** values need to stay the same.

```
g.drawLine( 40, 10, 40, 30 ); // draws vertical line 40 pixels right
g.drawLine( 30, 10, 30, 50 ); // draws vertical line 30 pixels right
```

Experiment with different values to see what type of lines you can draw. Remember that we can draw lines on top of other lines and other shapes or text.

Ovals and Circles

Let's start off by drawing an oval/ellipse. Ellipses are created using the method: `drawOval`
We need to send some *parameters* to the method, to designate where we want our ellipse drawn and the width and height. Again, we will need to call our methods on the Graphics variable. The specification for the `drawOval` method follows:

drawOval(x, y, width, height);

The **x** and **y** coordinates specify the location of the upper-left corner of the ellipse. Note that it does not specify the middle of the ellipse! If we place our ellipse in the top-left corner of the applet, we could use an **x** and **y** coordinate of zero. Let's make a really wide oval with a width of 100 and a height of 10. The following code and example run is depicted below:

```
import java.awt.*;           // access the Graphics object
import javax.swing.*;        // access to JApplet
public class Ellipse extends JApplet
{
        public void paint( Graphics g )
        {
                g.drawOval( 0,0, 100, 10 );
        }
}
```

Now, if we wanted to draw a circle, how would we change the above code? There is no method called `drawCircle`, so we have to use the `drawOval` method. But that's ok, because we know that circles are ovals with the same width and height. Modify the above program to make it draw a circle.

Rectangles and Squares

In a similar way, we can draw rectangles and squares. The method we use is called `drawRect` and we specify the x and y coordinates for the upper-left corner of the rectangle, and a width and height to specify the dimensions.

> drawRect (x, y, width, height);

Like the circle, we can draw a square by specify a rectangle with the same width and height. The following code and example run shows how to draw a square:

```
import java.awt.*;           // access the Graphics object
import javax.swing.*;        // access to JApplet

public class Square extends JApplet
{
        public void paint ( Graphics g )
        {
                g.drawRect ( 0,0, 20, 20 );
        }
}
```

We can also draw a rounded rectangle by calling the `drawRoundRect` method.

Filling shapes

Sometimes we want our shapes to be filled in with color. It is easy to fill in our shapes, by simply changing the method call from *draw* to *fill*. *This does not work on lines.*
For example, instead of `drawRect` we can call `fillRect`. The rest of the code is the same.
Examples:

> g.drawRect(0, 0, 20, 20);   →   g.fillRect(0, 0, 20, 20);
> g.drawOval(0, 0, 100, 10);   →   g.fillOval(0, 0, 100, 10);

We can draw multiple objects on the same applet by making multiple calls to these methods. In the following example, we change the location of each shape that we draw.

```
import java.awt.*;        // access the Graphics object
import javax.swing.*;     // access to JApplet

public class Shapes extends JApplet
{
    public void paint ( Graphics g )
    {
        g.setColor( Color.GREEN );
        g.fillOval( 0,0, 100, 10 );
        g.setColor( Color.BLUE );
        g.drawRect( 0,0, 20, 20 );
        g.drawRect ( 10,10, 20, 20 );
        g.drawRect ( 20,20, 20, 20 );
        g.drawOval ( 30, 30, 20, 20 );
    }
}
```

Arcs

Arcs are a bit more difficult to get your head around. When drawing an arc, we still need to specify the **x** and **y** coordinates and a width and height. But we also need to specify the starting angle and arching angle of the arc. The starting angle is based from the center of our x-y coordinates and width/height dimensions, with the angle of zero extending horizontally to the right. See the diagrams below for examples of starting angles:

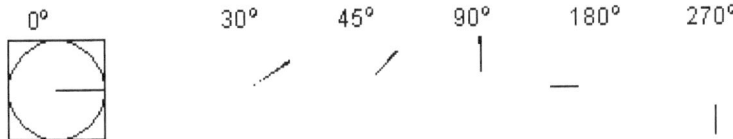

Then we also define the angle for the arc. The following images depict different arc angles:

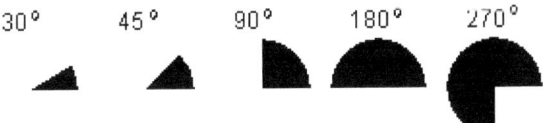

The code to create an arc is as follows:

```
drawArc( x, y, width, height, startingAngle, archingAngle );
```

OR, filled in

```
fillArc( x, y, width, height, startingAngle, archingAngle );
```

The width and height are based on the concept that an arc of 360 degree angle is a full oval, like the ones we draw with drawOval.

```
import javax.swing.*;
import java.awt.*;
public class PieChart extends JApplet
{
   public void paint( Graphics g )
   {
      // pie
      g.setColor( Color.RED );
      g.fillArc( 20,20, 300, 300, 20, 90 );
      g.setColor( Color.YELLOW );
      g.fillArc( 20,20, 300,300, 110,45 );
      g.setColor( Color.BLUE );
      g.fillArc( 20,20, 300,300, 155, 180 );
         // outline
         g.setColor( Color.BLACK );
         g.drawArc( 20,20, 300, 300, 0, 360 );
   }
}
```

drawing the outline has to be done last – Why?
To overlay it on **top** of color pies

Polygons

Polygons can include any number of points. To create a polygon, first we declare and instantiate a Polygon object:

```
Polygon  poly;
poly = new Polygon( );
```

Now we can add as many points we want to our polygon. Keep in mind that the order in which we add points to the polygon is important – think of it like connect-the-dots. The polygon will be created by drawing lines from one point to the next. We add points to the polygon by calling the **addPoint** method:

```
poly.addPoint( x, y );
```

where **x** and **y** are our **x** and **y** coordinates for the point.

When we're ready to draw a polygon, we can use either the draw or fill methods from the Graphics class:

```
drawPolygon( poly );
fillPolygon( poly );
```

The following two examples show the same points in the polygon, but in different order:

```
import javax.swing.*;
import java.awt.*;

public class PolyEx1 extends JApplet
{
   public void paint( Graphics g )
   {
     Polygon pg = new Polygon( );
     pg.addPoint( 10, 10 );
     pg.addPoint( 50, 10 );
     pg.addPoint( 70, 80 );
     pg.addPoint( 50, 100 );
     pg.addPoint( 10, 30 );
     g.drawPolygon( pg );
   }
}
```

```
import javax.swing.*;
import java.awt.*;

public class PolyEx2 extends JApplet
{
   public void paint( Graphics g )
   {
     Polygon pg = new Polygon( );
     pg.addPoint( 10, 10 );
     pg.addPoint( 50, 100 );
     pg.addPoint( 10, 30 );
     pg.addPoint( 50, 10 );
     pg.addPoint( 70, 80 );
     g.drawPolygon( pg );
   }
}
```

Images

Images can be painted on to our applet with a call to the **drawImage** method. But first we need to load the image into the applet. To load the image, we call the method **getImage** and specify the location of where we're running the applet, which is obtained through a call to **getCodeBase( )** and then the name of the image file.

```
Image imageVariable = getImage( getCodeBase( ), filename );
```

To draw the image on to our applet, we call **drawImage** specifying the image variable from above, the x, y coordinates of 0,0 (top-left corner) of where to draw it, and the keyword **this**.

```
g.drawImage( imageVariable, 0, 0, this );
```

```
import javax.swing.*;
import java.awt.*;
public class ImageEx extends JApplet
{
   public void paint( Graphics g )
   {
     Image img = getImage( getCodeBase( ), "Lion.jpg" );
     g.drawImage( img, 0,0, this );
   }
}
```

img is the variable we declared in the previous line

To scale the image to a different size, we call the method **drawImage** and send it additional information. This extra information includes: the coordinates for where to draw the image (xd1, yd1), the coordinates of the bottom-right corner of where we want to draw the image (xd2, yd2) which defines the size to stretch the image, the coordinates of the top-left corner of the actual image where you want to start (xs1, ys1) and the coordinates of bottom-right corner of the actual image (xs2, ys2). The coordinates on the source image allow you to crop the image. If you want the full source image, then use coordinates (0,0) for (xs1, ys2) and the width and height for (xs2, ys2).

```
g.drawImage( imageVariable, xd1, yd1, xd2, yd2, xs1, ys1, xs2, ys2, this );
```

```
import javax.swing.*;
import java.awt.*;
public class ImageEx extends JApplet
{
   public void paint( Graphics g )
   {
      Image img = getImage( getCodeBase( ), "Lion.jpg" );
      g.drawImage( img, 0,0, 500, 500, 0, 10, 1200, 1200,  this );
   }
}
```

Now we can draw a picture of a photo and then call our drawing methods to draw on top of it. For example, in the program below I added some callouts to a photo I took while dining in China.

```
import java.awt.*;
import javax.swing.*;
public class DrawOnImage extends JApplet
{
   public void paint( Graphics g )
   {
      Image breakfast = getImage( getCodeBase( ), "China_Foods.jpg" );
      g.drawImage( breakfast, 0,0, this );
      Font bold16font = new Font( "Serif", Font.BOLD, 16 );   // font for all text
      g.setFont( bold16font );
      g.setColor( Color.green );              // eggs
      g.drawOval( 21, 180, 40, 40 );
      g.drawOval( 22, 181, 38, 38 );          // thicken the drawing
      g.drawLine( 42, 180, 50, 95 );   // line from eggs
      g.drawString( "Eggs for breakfast", 50, 95 );     // drawn at top of line pointing to eggs
      g.setColor( Color.blue );               // noodles
      g.drawOval( 35, 245, 90, 75 );
      g.drawLine( 120, 255, 190, 240 );
      g.drawString( "Noodles for every meal", 190, 245 );
      g.setColor( Color.YELLOW );             // sauces
      g.drawRect( 70,180, 90, 40 );
      g.drawLine( 115, 180, 130, 145 );
      g.drawString( "Amazing sauces", 130, 140 );
   }
}
```

Images in Java

A picture says a thousand words.
How much is that in pixels?

Creating for the Web requires the use of images, and creating Java applets is no exception. Images are an important part of portraying ideas and presenting our web site. There is a lot we can do with image processing software and we will cover some of the necessary basics. We can also do a lot of image processing by programming Java code, but it adds complexity that is unnecessary when it is easier to use an image processing software package like Microsoft's Paint program, GIMP, Jasc's Paint Shop Pro or Adobe's Photoshop.

Java supports three major formats for images: .jpg, .gif and .png.

.jpg JPEG stands for Joint Photographic Experts Group and has file extensions of either .jpg or .jpeg (both work the same). It supports 24-bit colors, which is 2^{24} number of colors. JPG format is best for pictures of naturalistic artwork and photographs. It doesn't work so well on lettering, simple cartoons and black-and-white line drawings. JPG uses a compression algorithm to save the file as a smaller size, but can cause a loss of detail.

.gif GIF stands for Graphics Interchange Format and is a proprietary image encoding format. It supports only 8-bit colors, which amounts to only 256 colors. Therefore, it is not optimal for photographs or realistic artwork. It does work well on lettering and simple sketches, but most importantly it also supports transparency and animation. Transparency allows part of the image to be clear, such that the background shows through parts of the image. We can create transparent images in sophisticated programs such as GIMP, Paint Shop Pro and Photoshop, as well as Web online sites such as http://stuff.mit.edu/tweb/map.html. For animation, the specific format is GIF89a and can also support interlacing. Animated images can be created through some graphics programs and other downloading software.

.png PNG stands for Portable Network Graphics. It was created as a free compression algorithm once GIF became patented. It has better compression than .gif so usually results in smaller file sizes, and supports millions of colors. It also supports transparency but not animation.

Why do we care about the file type?

There are several reasons why we should choose different file formats for different image types. As discussed above, some support transparency and animation, while others don't. Some can handle millions of colors while others are restricted in the number of colors. Some of the compression algorithms can reduce the size of the file drastically, which can increase the loading speed of the image as well as decrease the amount of space required on the web server to store the image.

Changing the file size

When we get images back from digital cameras or photo CDs, the images are huge and fill our screens! The standard resolution for camera images is 1600x1200 pixels – which is usually bigger than the resolution of our screens (standard computer screen resolution is 1280x1024). This is too big to display on the Internet. The best way to shrink the size of the photo which also shrinks the size of the file is to do so inside an image processing program.

To see the size of our image in Microsoft's Paint program, open our image and

Click on **Image**
then **Attributes**

We should see a dialog box similar to the following:

640x400 pixels is probably the biggest size we'd want, or even smaller.
To resize an image in MS Paint,

Click on **Image** then **Stretch/Skew…**

Change the **Stretch** only,

and keep the % for width and height the same (This keeps the image proportionally correct).
For a 1600x1200 photo, go to either 30% or 20%

In our software program, we sometimes see different terms such as dpi and ppi. DPI stands for "dots per inch" and is used for printing purposes. PPI stands for "pixels per inch" and is referenced for screen display.

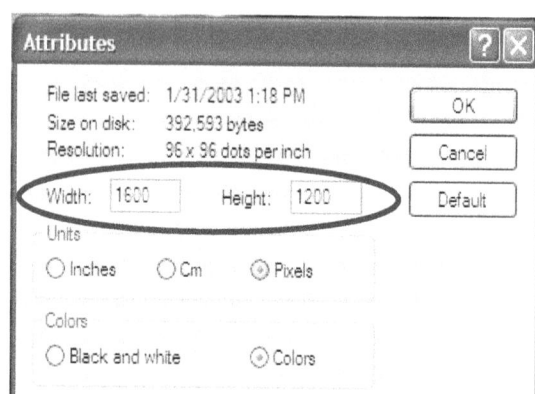

Image Orientation

Some photos from digital cameras appear sideways on our computer. We can rotate them in any image processing program. For example, in Microsoft Paint:

Click on **Image**
then select **Flip/Rotate…**
then **Rotate by angle…**
select either **90** to rotate right or **270** to rotate left

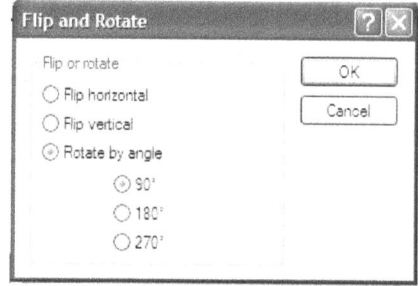

Pixels

We've been talking about pixels a lot – what exactly is a pixel? The easiest way to understand pixels is to see one up close. If we take an image and zoom in on it, we'll see each individual pixel as a rectangle of one color. For example, if we zoom in on the image to the left below we can see the individual pixels in the image:

You can do this yourself in any paint program. We can see that each pixel is one solid color. The more pixels we use to display an image, the better the quality – because the pixel rectangles take up less space of the image.

This also explains why our drawings are ragged – we are seeing the rectangular pixels attempting to form curves. The anti-aliasing helps dither the colors between the curve color and the surrounding colors.

Antialiasing

When we write text and draw on our applet, you might notice the drawing is rather ragged and not smooth. We can fix this by turning anti-aliasing on when we're drawing. To see the difference with antialiasing, look at the two spaceship graphics below:

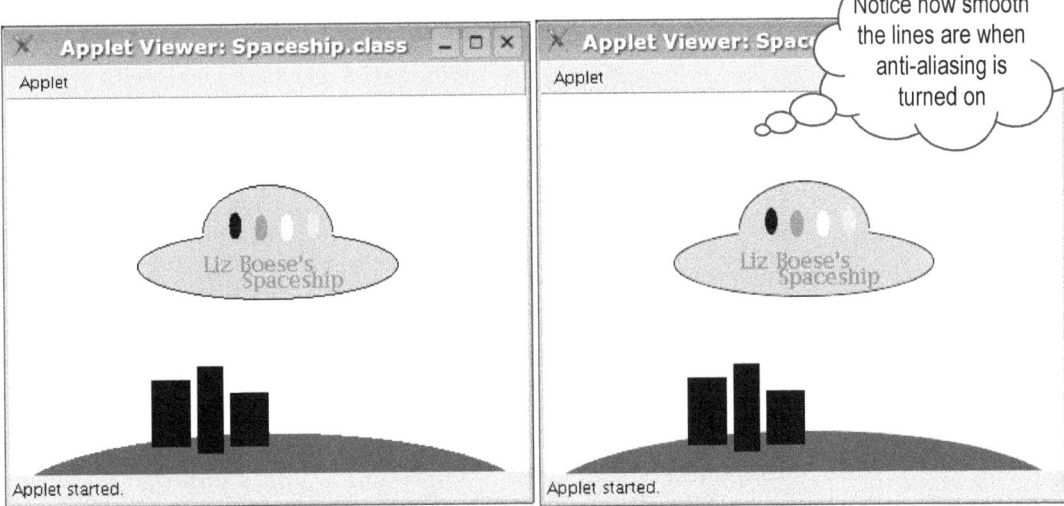

Notice how smooth the lines are when anti-aliasing is turned on

To achieve anti-aliasing, we need to work with a **Graphics2D** object instead of a plain **Graphics** object. We do this by *casting* our Graphics object to Graphics2D:

```
public void paint( Graphics grph )
{
        Graphics2D  g2d = (Graphics2d )grph;
}
```

Now we want to tell the program to turn anti-aliasing on:

```
g2d.setRenderingHint( RenderingHints.KEY_ANTIALIASING,
       RenderingHints, VALUE_ANTIALIAS_ON );
```

then continue to add your drawing code, using the **g2d** variable we defined.

Image Transparency

There are different ways to make our images transparent. Transparent images must be saved as either .gif or .png. If you're familiar with a paint program, you can make your images transparent using it (MS Paint does not do transparency).

One easy way to make images transparent is to use an online program. The only caveat is that you must have your image uploaded and available on the Internet. You can read about this in the last chapter if you're not familiar with setting it up. One website that I have used throughout the years is at: http://stuff.mit.edu/tweb/map.html or try searching on the Internet. If you find an image you want to use on the Internet, copy the URL of the image and feed it to the online website. If you have your own image you want to make transparent, use either a graphics program or upload the image to a website where it has a URL to access it.

Putting it Together

The following lists the types of drawing we can do:

Lines	drawLine(x, y, x2, y2)
Rectangles	drawRect(x, y, width, height) fillRect(x, y, width, height) clearRect(x, y, width, height)
Rounded rectangles	drawRoundRect(x, y, width, height, arcWidth, arcHeight) fillRoundRect(x, y, width, height, arcWidth, arcHeight)
3-D Raised or lowered rectangles	**Raised:** draw3DRect(x, y, width, height, true) **Lowered:** draw3DRect(x, y, width, height, false) **Raised:** fill3DRect(x, y, width, height, true) **Lowered:** fill3DRect(x, y, width, height, false)
Ovals	drawOval(x, y, width, height) fillOval(x, y, width, height)
Arcs	drawArc(x, y, width, height, startAngle, arcAngle) fillArc(x, y, width, height, startAngle, arcAngle)
Polygons	drawPolygon(Polygon) fillPolygon(Polygon)
Images	drawImage(Image, x, y, this) drawImage(Image, xd1, yd1, xd2, yd2, xs1, ys1, xs2, ys2, this)

The figure to the right depicts a grid view of the Java coordinate system. Each point along the x-axis (horizontal) and y-axis (vertical) is labeled at 10-pixel segments. To draw the rectangle, we specify the x and y coordinates of where it begins (10, 20) then specify the width of 20 pixels and height of 40 pixels. The red rectangle can be drawn using the fill method fillRect as:

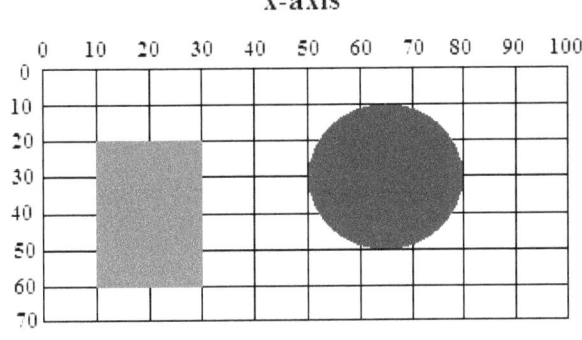

```
g.setColor( Color.RED );
g.fillRect ( 10, 20, 20, 40 );      // x, y, width, height
```

The blue circle is drawn similarly, with the x-coordinate as the top-left corner of where we want to begin the circle (50), and the y-coordinate at the top-left corner as well (10). The width of the circle is 30 pixels, and height is 40 pixels.

```
g.setColor( Color.BLUE );
g.fillOval( 50, 10, 30, 40 );       // x, y, width, height
```

We can create our own coordinated shapes by drawing two or more shapes on top of each other in the same color. When displayed, it appears as if it is one shape.

```
import java.awt.*;
import javax.swing.*;
public class Overlap extends JApplet
{
        public void paint ( Graphics g )
        {
                g.setColor( Color.BLUE );
                g.fillOval( 10,10, 50, 50 );
                g.fillRect( 50,10, 50, 50 );
        }
}
```

Summary

- Coordinate system starts in the upper left corner with (0,0).
- Drawing shapes is accomplished by calling methods on the Graphics object inside the paint method.
- Lines are drawn using **drawLine.** drawLine(x, y, x2, y2)
- Horizontal lines are drawn with two different x values and the y values unchanged.
- Vertical lines are drawn with the x values unchanged and different y values.
- Circles and ellipses are drawn using **drawOval**. drawOval(x, y, width, height)
- Circles have the same value for the width and height of the oval.
- Rectangles and squares are drawn using **drawRect**. drawRect(x, y, width, height)
- Squares have the same value for both the width and height.
- Arcs are drawn using **drawArc**. drawArc(x, y, width, height, startAngle, arcAngle)
- Polygons are drawn by creating a **Polygon** object, adding points to the Polygon object with **addPoint**, then drawn by calling **drawPolygon** on the Graphics object.
- Draw/fill methods on the Graphics object are drawn in order of the program, where subsequent drawings are drawn on top of the previously drawn ones.
- Colors can be set by calling the method **setColor** on the Graphics object. setColor(Color)
- There is a set of colors that can be referenced as Color.name (e.g. Color.RED).
- Custom colors can be created by specifying the amount of red, green and blue. **Color newColor = new Color(red, green, blue);**
- Text can be drawn by calling **drawString** on the Graphics object.
  drawString(string, x, y)
- Fonts are created by specifying the type (e.g., "Serif"), style (e.g., Font.BOLD or Font.PLAIN) and the size in pixels. Font fnt = new Font("Serif", Font.PLAIN, 12);
- Font of bold and italic can be specified with a style of **Font.BOLD + Font.ITALIC**.
- Set the font for drawing by calling the **setFont** method on the Graphics object.
- Java supports 3 main image formats: .jpg, .gif and .png.
- .jpg is a good image format for photographs and naturistic artwork.
- .gif is used for simple line/cartoon drawings and animation and transparency.
- .png is good for both photographs and simple drawings and can do transparency.
- File size of images is important to minimize the download time of the applet.
- Pixels are individual rectangular regions of the screen that displays one color.
- The more pixels used to represent an image, the better the quality.
- Anti-aliasing helps smooth out curves.
- To use anti-aliasing, we need to make use of the Graphics2D class.
- PPI stands for pixels per inch and is referenced for screen viewing.
- DPI stands for dots per inch and is referenced for printing.

Exercises

1. In a window that is 100x100 pixels, position 95,95 is nearest to the _____ corner.
2. If we draw a rectangle with the same value for width and height, what did we draw?
    a. parallelogram   b. square
    c. rounded square   d. rounded rectangle
    e. polygon   f. hexagon
3. What two steps are necessary to paint an image?
4. True or False: The paint method is called automatically by the browser whenever it needs to redraw the screen
5. How do we create a new font that is both bold and italic?
6. In what package is the Graphics object?
7. True/False: To draw a circle, call the method drawCirc and send the x,y coordinates and the radius of the circle?
8. Take the Hello World example and center the text.
9. Draw a car. Draw a house. Draw a self-portrait. Draw Pac-Man. Draw a spaceship.
10. Draw a smiley face or a pirate face. Draw a farm house with animals.
11. Draw a bar graph (histogram). Draw different chart types on the same data values.
12. Write out a multi-line blog. If you're unsure what a blog is, Google it.
13. True/False: We can create colors by specifying the amount of red, blue and yellow.
14. In the arc example, what would happen if we draw the outline before filling in each of the pie sections?
15. What colors do the following statements produce?
    Color mycolor = new Color(255, 0, 255);
    Color mycolor = new Color(0, 0, 255);
    Color mycolor = new Color(128, 128, 128);
16. Write a program that displays a photo of yourself and display your name in large text on top of the image.
17. Write a program that is your own personal logo. Make use of several shapes, both filled and outlined in your design.
18. Correct the errors in the following program: (best to rewrite it to the right) about 15 errors. Find as many as you can =)
    ```
    //  ****************************
    My First Applet – I'm so proud!   ***/
    Import java.swing;

    Public class MyfirstApplet
    {
       private void paint ( graphics theGraphics );
       {
          graphics.drawstring( 'chocolate', 20 )
    }
    ```

19. Which of the image formats is best for photographs?
20. Which of the image formats supports animated images?
21. Which of the image formats supports transparency?
22. Why do we care what type the image should be saved as?
23. What are two ways to decrease the size of an image?
24. Which three major image formats does the Web fully support?
25. True or False. ppi is used for printing, dpi is used for screen display.
26. True or False. We cannot change the size of an image within the Java code.
27. True or False. Anti-aliasing makes the text in an image appear smoother.
28. True or False: Images with transparency can be saved as .JPG.
29. What is the purpose of using anti-aliasing on images?
30. Does anti-aliasing work on text?
31. True or False: Photographs are best saved as .GIF
32. Find a simple image (not a photograph) and make one of the colors transparent. Draw it on an applet in two areas with different backgrounds.

Chapter 3

Variables and Methods

Variables vary...
After all, change is the status quo.

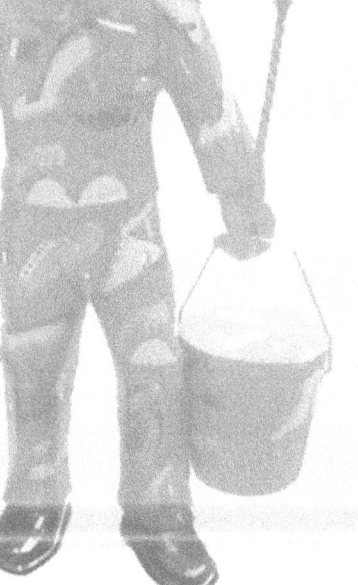

Objectives:

- Variables
  - Declaration
  - Initialization
  - Assignment
  - Reference
  - Location and Scope
- Methods
  - Structure
  - Why have methods?

Variables

A variable is a name for a spot in memory. We can store values in memory by referencing a variable name. But first we need to *declare* the variable.

Declaration

We declare a variable by specify a *data type* and *variable name*. We have already used a variable when we referenced a `Graphics` object.

```
Graphics g
```

`Graphics` is the data type and `g` is our variable name.

There are other data types we can use in our programs. There are 8 *primitive* data types in Java:

<u>Integers:</u>	byte, short, int, long
<u>Real values:</u>	float, double
<u>Boolean:</u>	boolean
<u>Characters:</u>	char

These are considered to be *primitive* because these are the only things that are *not* objects.

Integers are whole numbers that could be either negative or positive or 0. We cannot use commas when declaring our numbers.
Integer examples: -528, 0, 12973, -2.
Although there are four data types for integers, we usually work with the `int` data type.

Real values are floating-point numbers that are either negative or positive.
Real number examples: -41.238, 0, 12.34447, 9.234e102
Although there are two data types for real values, we usually work with the `double` data type.

Boolean values can only contain one of two values: either `true` or `false`. Note that when we assign either `true` or `false`, we do *not* put the value in quotes! `true` and `false` are *reserved words* in Java, which means they have special meaning in the Java syntax.

Characters are represented inside single-quotes. We can only store one character inside a `char` data type.

So, let's see some examples of declaring primitive data types:

```
int numPeople;
int age, numCredits, yearInSchool;
boolean isHappy;
char middleInitial;
double gpa;
```

Declaration includes the data type then a variable name.

We can declare variables together as in the second example, where age, numCredits and yearInSchool are all declared to be of type `int`. Each declaration needs to end with a semi-colon.

When we're not using a primitive data type, we'll be using an object data type. The most common object data types is the String. We can declare Strings as follows:

```
String str;
```

We will work with many other objects besides Graphics and String once we get to chapter 4.

For choosing variable names, we can use any combination of letters, numbers, the underscore _ character or the dollar sign $. However, we cannot begin a variable name with number. There isn't really a limit on how many characters we use for a variable name (within reason). It is best to be as descriptive as possible for the name, so that you and anyone helping or maintaining the code you wrote can figure it out easily. Usually variable names begin with a lower case letter, and any word we add to create a phrase would start with a capital letter to make it easier to read. Since we cannot use spaces in our variable names, we could instead use the underscore character to separate the words.

Initialization

Initializing a variable is when we assign a variable a value for the first time. This is usually done at the same time as we declare our variables. Instead of just declaring them, we also assign them an initial value.

Examples:

```
int numPeople = 17;
boolean isHappy = true;
char middleInitial = 'S';
int age = 21, numCredits = 15, yearInSchool=1;
double gpa = 3.6;
```

> **Initialization** is an assignment of a variable for the first time

We can create strings in one of two ways:

```
String str = "Cookie Monster likes cookies";
String str = new String( "Cookie Monster likes cookies" );
```

Both of the preceeding lines have the same affect – creates a String object with the characters: "Cookie Monster likes cookies".

Assignment

An assignment is when we change the value of a variable. This is similar to *variable initialization* except that we do not declare the variable's type.

Examples:

```
numPeople = 22;
age = 25;
gpa=3.3
isHappy = false;
middleInitial = 'E';
str = "I like cookies too";
str = new String( "Life is a bowl of chocolate" );
```

> **Assignment** changes the value of a variable. Note that the variable is always left of the equals sign.

Reference

We can refer to our variables that we create by referencing them with the name we declared. Be sure to not put the variable name in double quotes, otherwise it will print the variable name instead of the value that the variable is referencing!

```
String name = "Elizabeth S. Boese";
g.drawString ( name, 0,12 );   // prints Elizabeth S. Boese
g.drawString ( "name", 0,12 ); // prints name
```

We can also reference our variables inside equations:

```
gpa = gradeValue * numCredits / 100;
```

Strings are very common to programs and there are some methods that we may want to call on our String variables. When we call a method on a String, we need to refer to the variable.

> String str = "Something";
> str.toUpperCase( ) returns a copy of the string in all upper-case letters (e.g. "SOMETHING")
> str.toLowerCase( ) returns a copy of the string in all lower-case letters (e.g. "something")
> str.length returns the number of characters in the string (e.g. 9)
> str.charAt(index) returns the character at position index in the string
> where the first character is at index 0

Locations and Scope

When we write our programs, there are two ways we can *declare* our variables: as instance variables or local variables. **Instance variables** are declared at the top of the program just after the class header and open squiggly-bracket. **Local variables** are declared inside methods, such as the `paint` method. Local variables consist of variables declared inside the method as well as those declared in the **parameters** for the method. In the example below, x and y are instance variables and text and grph are local variables.

```java
import javax.swing.*;
import java.awt.*;
public class HiWorld extends JApplet
{           // declare instance variables here
    int x;
    int y;
    public void paint ( Graphics grph )
    {
        x = 0;              // initialize the instance variables
        y = 12;
        String text = "Hello World";   // local variable
        grph.drawString ( text, x, y );
    }
}
```

We'll want to declare most of our variables as *instance variables*. This allows us to reference those variables throughout the entire class. Variables that we declare inside a method can only be referenced inside that method. This will become essential once we get to the chapter on events.

```java
import javax.swing.*;
import java.awt.*;
public class HiWorldWithMethods extends JApplet
{
    // declare instance variables here
    int x = 0;
    int y = 12;
    public void paint ( Graphics grph )
    {
        String text = "Hello World";   // local variable
        grph.drawString ( text, x, y );
        anotherMethod( grph );
    }
    public void anotherMethod( Graphics g )
    {
        g.drawString ( text, x, 50 );  // won't work!
    }
}
```

Cannot reference the variable `text` because its scope is only within the paint method!

We cannot access the variable **text** inside the `anotherMethod` method because `text` was declared inside the paint method and is only accessible inside that paint method. However, we can access the variable `x` inside `anotherMethod` because `x` is an instance variable.

Methods

We can create multiple methods in our program, as we saw in the last example. A method is a set of statements grouped together which can be called or *invoked* by the program. The statements within the method are designated inside the squiggly-brackets. Each method needs its own set of squiggly-brackets to designate the beginning and ending of that method.

In the previous example, we *invoked* the `anotherMethod` method inside the `paint` method. We do so by specifying the name of the method being called, in this case `anotherMethod`, placing the parenthesis, and sending any data as *parameters*. In our example, there was one parameter that was sent: `grph`. A copy of `grph` is copied into the method's parameter's variable name: `g`. This allows the `anotherMethod` method to also call the `drawString` method on the `Graphics` object.

Our example also shows two different type of method calls:

- within a class
- in another class

The method call to `anotherMethod` called a method inside the same class. We can see the definition of the method `anotherMethod` in this class. The `drawString` method, on the other hand, was a call to a method inside a different class - the `Graphics` class. This time we do not see the definition of the `drawString` method in this class. We can only invoke the `drawString` method by specifying which object to call it on: in this case, the `Graphics` object designated by the variable `grph` inside the paint method and `g` inside the anotherMethod method.

Method Structure

Declaring methods requires us to follow Java's syntax structure for methods. We first specify the method header, which is the first line of the method before the squiggly braces:

```
accessModifer    returnType    methodName ( [parameter(s)] )
```

Example:

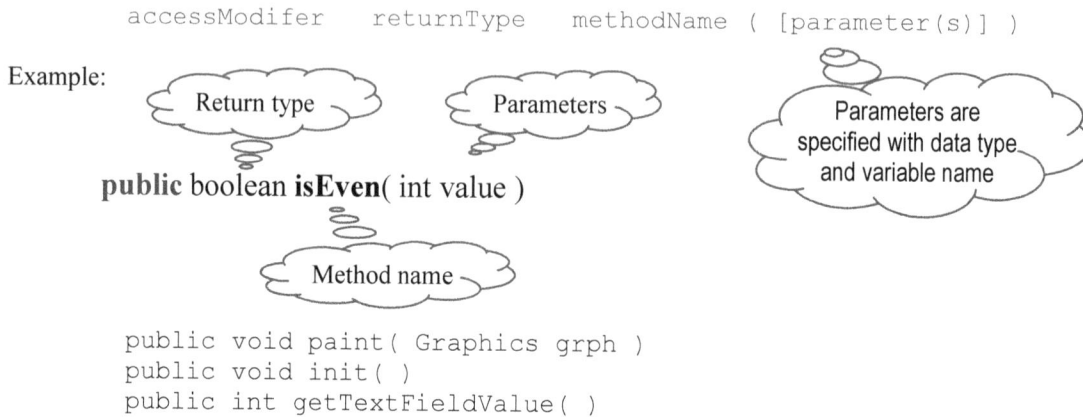

```
public void paint( Graphics grph )
public void init( )
public int getTextFieldValue( )
```

After the method header we add the open and close squiggly-brackets. The `public` is an access modifier which specifies that other classes can access this method. At this point, simply accept the fact that *most* methods should be declared public.

The `void` keyword specifies the *return type* for the method. A return type of `void` means the method isn't returning anything. Even though the method doesn't return a value, we still need a placeholder for the return type: which is why we use the word `void`. We could return a String, int, double, boolean, char, Graphics object, etc. However, we can only return *ONE* thing.

`paint` is an example name of a method. We can name our methods almost anything we like, following a few rules which also apply to variable names (see chapter 8). When we're drawing on our applet, we must name one method `paint` since this is the method that is automatically called by the browser when it needs to draw the applet.

The parameters inside parenthesis can contain any number of variable declarations. If we do not want any parameters, we still need to put the parenthesis but we can leave it empty inside the parenthesis. When we specify a parameter, we must *declare* the variable – define the data type and the variable name. If we need multiple parameters, separate each declaration with a comma. For example:

```
public void paintWindow( Graphics g, int x, int y)
```

We can put as many statements as we want within each method. Sometimes methods contain only one line of code – for example, to return the value of a variable. Sometimes we have 10 or 50 lines of code within a method. Although we can put an unlimited amount of statements within a method, the general guideline is to only put as many lines within a method that is viewable on the screen – without scrolling. This makes it easier to read our code and also look for errors, if we can see an entire method within the screen.

Example with methods with return types:

```java
import java.awt.*;
import javax.swing.*;

public class Calculate extends JApplet
{
    public void paint (Graphics g )
    {
        int addition = getAdd( 2, 7 );
        String added = "2 + 7 = " + addition;
        g.drawString ( added, 0, 12 );

        String subtracted = "2 - 7 = " + getSubtract( 2, 7 );
        g.drawString ( subtracted, 0, 24 );
    }
    public int getAdd( int num1, int num2 )
    {
        return num1 + num2;
    }
    public int getSubtract( int num1, int num2 )
    {
        return num1 - num2;
    }
}
```

Why have methods?

Using methods is essential when programming. Sometimes it's required, such as the methods we call on our Graphics object (drawString, fillOval) and when processing events. But we also want to make use of methods to help organize our code to make it easier to read as well as to enable us to reuse code we've already written. There are many reasons to use methods:

- Organize a program (easier to read)
- Modularize repeated code
- Make code accessible to other objects
- Handling events

Organize a program (easier to read)

As programs grow bigger, it gets harder to read through a program with lots of lines of code. By grouping related code segments into methods and naming the methods with something descriptive, the program becomes much easier to follow. The next example shows two ways to write a program to draw a house: one without methods and one with several methods. At a quick glance, the program on the left is more difficult to follow – we need to read through the code to figure out which code draws the tree, which draws the windows, etc. However, the code on the right is much clearer to read at glance by looking at the method names that segment the code.

```
import java.awt.*;
import javax.swing.*;
public class House extends JApplet
{
  public void paint (Graphics g )
  {
    g.setColor( Color.pink );
    g.fillRect ( 100,100,200,200 );
    g.setColor( Color.black );
    Polygon poly = new Polygon( );
    poly.addPoint(100,100);
    poly.addPoint(200,50);
    poly.addPoint(300,100);
    g.fillPolygon(poly);

    g.setColor( Color.blue );
    g.fillRect ( 200,230,40,70);
    g.fillRect ( 120, 150, 20, 30 );
    g.fillRect ( 150, 150, 20, 30 );
    g.fillRect ( 200, 150, 20, 30 );
    g.fillRect ( 230, 150, 20, 30 );
    g.setColor( Color.black );
    g.fillRect ( 400,130,30,170 );
    g.setColor( Color.green );
    g.fillOval( 370,80,100,100 );
    g.fillRect ( 0,295,500,5 );
  }
}
```

```
import java.awt.*;
import javax.swing.*;
public class HouseMethods extends JApplet
{
    int WINDOW_WIDTH = 20;
    int WINDOW_HEIGHT = 30;
    public void paint (Graphics g )
    {
        paintHouse( g );
        paintLandscape( g );
    }
    public void paintHouse( Graphics grph )
    {
        grph.setColor( Color.pink );
        grph.fillRect ( 100,100,200,200 );
        grph.setColor( Color.black );
        Polygon poly = new Polygon( );      // roof
        poly.addPoint(100,100);
        poly.addPoint(200,50);
        poly.addPoint(300,100);
        grph.fillPolygon(poly);
        grph.setColor( Color.blue );
        grph.fillRect ( 200,230,40,70);     // door
        paintWindow( grph, 120, 150 );      // windows
        paintWindow( grph, 150, 150 );
        paintWindow( grph, 200, 150 );
        paintWindow( grph, 230, 150 );
    }
    public void paintWindow( Graphics gp, int x, int y )
    {
        gp.setColor( Color.blue );
        gp.fillRect( x, y, WINDOW_WIDTH,WINDOW_HEIGHT);
    }
    public void paintLandscape( Graphics g )
    {
        g.setColor( Color.black );          // tree
        g.fillRect ( 400,130,30,170 );
        g.setColor( Color.green );
        g.fillOval( 370,80,100,100 );
        g.fillRect ( 0,295,500,5 );         // grass
    }
}
```

This example drawing a house makes it easy to work with the code if we have an error or want to add new features. For example, if the tree stump is off-center from the trees, we can easily find the few lines of code in the method `paintLandscape` that we need to modify.

Modularize Repeated Code

Sometimes a program has sections of code that are the same or nearly the same. These sections are ideal for placement inside a method. We can use the parameters to the method to customize the code fragment.

The following example creates a portion of a checkerboard of black and white squares. Which program will be easier and faster to modify to create a full-sized checkerboard? Which program will be easier and faster to modify the sizes to make the squares twice as big?

Example:

```
import javax.swing.*;
import java.awt.*;

public class Checkerboard
              extends JApplet
{
   public void paint ( Graphics g )
   {
      // row 1
      g.fillRect ( 20,20, 10,10 );
      g.fillRect ( 40,20, 10,10 );
      g.fillRect ( 60,20, 10,10 );
      g.fillRect ( 80,20, 10,10 );
      g.fillRect ( 100,20, 10,10 );

      // row 2
      g.fillRect ( 30,30, 10,10 );
      g.fillRect ( 50,30, 10,10 );
      g.fillRect ( 70,30, 10,10 );
      g.fillRect ( 90,30, 10,10 );
      g.fillRect ( 110,30, 10,10 );
   }
}
```

```
import javax.swing.*;
import java.awt.*;

public class Checkerboard2 extends JApplet
{
   public void paint ( Graphics g )
   {
      drawRows( g, 20, 20 );
      drawRows( g, 30, 30 );
   }
   public void drawRows( Graphics graphics, int x, int y )
   {
      graphics.fillRect ( x, y, 10,10 );
      graphics.fillRect ( x+20, y, 10,10 );
      graphics.fillRect ( x+40, y, 10,10 );
      graphics.fillRect ( x+60, y, 10,10 );
      graphics.fillRect ( x+80, y, 10,10 );
   }
}
```

Which program would be easier to use to create a full-size checkerboard? How would you do it?

For access by other objects

We've made use of many methods defined in another class: drawString, fillRect, setColor. All of these methods are defined in the `Graphics` class. When we call the drawString method, for example, the program will go inside the Graphics class and look for the method named drawString. It will run the statements listed within this method and ignore the code within the other methods. This is how the program distinguishes between statements to execute.

Example: The `Graphics` class defined some methods for us to use:

- drawString (...
- fillRect (...
- setColor(...

If these weren't methods, we wouldn't be able to draw anything!

When using methods defined in another class, we need to tell the compiler where to find these methods – which class are they in? This is important because you may have two classes that define the same method name. We can distinguish between them by calling the method on the class itself (e.g. Math.sqrt) or on an *instance* of the class (e.g. Graphics g where g is a declared variable of the data type Graphics). We use the period to separate the class name or class instance from the method name. For example, if we have a Graphics instance named grp:

- grph.drawString ("hi", 0,12);
- grph.setColor(Color.BLUE);
- int positiveVal = **Math.abs**(-55);   // returns the absolute value

There are also special types of methods called *constructors* which create an instance of an object. These methods are called when the **new** operator is used. Although we haven't used these methods yet, we will use them extensively throughout the rest of the book. For example, when we want to create a new instance of a button, we can call:

JButton myButton;
myButton = **new** JButton("text on button");

Notice that after the keyword new the method name matches the name of the data type. The new operator and the method name matching the data type is how we can recognize that we are calling a *constructor* method instead of a normal method.

Event handling

Events are triggered by events that occur and automatically call particular methods. Example events include: mouse click, mouse move, button click, list selection, etc. We need to write the required methods to handle the events, which are specified by the Java paradigm. We'll discuss events in more detail later.

Summary

- Variables are declared by specifying the data type and a name.
- boolean values are either true or false.
- Integers (positive, negative or zero) are stored in the data type int.
- Floating-point numbers in Java default to the data type double. Integer numbers in Java default to int.
- Declare variables at the top of the class under the class header so that the scope of reference for the variable is anywhere within the class. These are called *instance variables*.
- Local variables are those declared inside a method or as a parameter for a method. The scope of a local variable is only within the method.
- Method headers contain the access modifier (usually public), return data type, method name and parameters listed in parenthesis.
- Parameters in a method header require the data type and name for each variable, separating multiple parameters with a comma.
- Methods defined in the same class (or inherited class, e.g. JApplet) can be invoked by calling the method name and any paramters.
- Methods defined in other classes need to be called on an instance of that class, such as a Graphics object variable reference grp: grp.drawString(...
- Methods are useful for organizing a program to be easier to read, modularize repeated code, make code accessible to other objects and for handling events.

Exercises

1. Declare a character variable named **initial**. Declare a boolean variable named **done** and initialize it to **false**.

2. Declare variables for a birthday: the month, day and year. Assign each variable to your own birthdate.

3. In the following method header, what is the data type that is returned?
    public void getInteger(char value)

4. In the following method header, what is the data type that is returned?
    public double calcAvg(int x, int y, char value)

5. True or False: A method is a section of a program whose statements are only executed when the method is called.

6. True or False: Methods that do not return anything do not need a return data type in the method header.

7. True or False: If we have redundant code, we should try to put it into a method and have each code section call the method instead.

8. True or False: A method is a section of a program that causes the computer to take some action.

9. True or False: If no parameters are necessary for a method, leave off the parenthesis in the method header.

10. True or False: If there are multiple parameter that are all of type int, we could put the data type int once and list each variable name separated with commas.

11. What are the benefits of creating methods?

12. Write the method header for a method named **convertToKM** that takes an **int** as a parameter which is the number of miles and returns a **double** value for the converted value in kilometers.

13. Which of the following reasons are why we create methods? Choose all that apply.

    a. code is easier to read
    b. program is less likely to crash
    c. can group repeated code sections
    d. to order the code sequentially

Chapter 4

Swing Components

Adding components to an applet is like adding magnets to the fridge – easy to move around. Writing in the paint method is like finger painting your fridge – permanently placed.

Objectives:

- Swing
- Adding components to the applet
- JLabel
- JButton
- Text components
  - JTextField
  - JTextArea
  - JPasswordField
- JCheckBox
- JRadioButton
- JComboBox
- JList
- JScrollPane
- Components
- Examples with Methods

Swing

Swing is the name for a graphics library that has more enhanced graphics than the awt library. Swing components can be accessed by importing the **javax.swing** package at the top of our program:

```
import javax.swing.*;
```

Most components in the Swing package begin with the capital letter 'J', to distinguish them from their predecessors in the awt package. Swing components allow more flexibility over the look and feel of the components and extra functionality such as support for tooltips. We can also ensure our Swing components look the same on all platforms, whereas awt components will look different (e.g. checkbox may be a square or diamond depending on the operating system). The disadvantage of using Swing components is that the extra functionality also means more complexity.

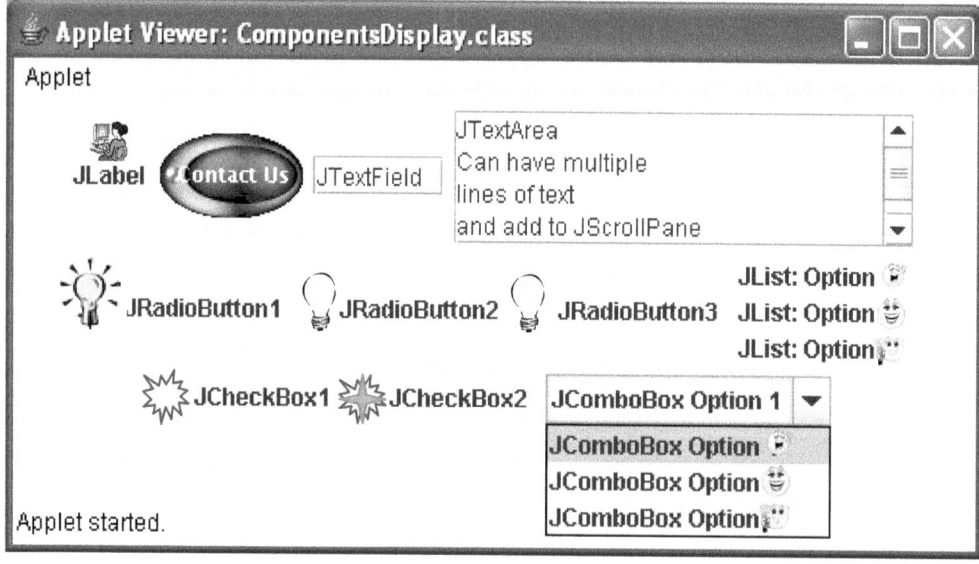

Adding components to the applet

JLabel is an example of a component we can place on our applets. When we used the `drawString` method in the `paint` method in Chapter 2, we were painting *directly* on the applet. With components, we *place* them on the applet and can modify their location based on a *layout manager*, which we'll discuss in more detail later. One way to look at it, is that with the `paint` method, it's like taking a marker and drawing on your fridge. With components, it's like having magnets that you place on the fridge, but they can be easily moved.

The general structure of an applet follows:

```
comments with you as author and purpose of the applet
import statements
public class name extends JApplet
{
        instance variables (declare components)
        public void init( )
        {
                create/modify components
                set layout manager for applet
                add components to the applet
        }
}
```

When we're working with components, we need to be careful of where we *declare* our components. We want to declare our components at the top of the class after the class header and first squiggly bracket so that we can access those components in any method we create. This has to do with the *scope* of a variable. This will be required when we get to events, but even now will be helpful to us when we use several methods to help divide up our tasks (example: see Chapter 3).

Component variable declarations include the *data type* and a *variable name*. Examples:

```
Image     image;
ImageIcon imgIcon;
JLabel    myName;
JTextArea message;
```

Our class then should appear as the following, declaring our variables at the top and initializing them (setting them equal to something) inside the `init` method.

```
import javax.swing.*;
public class Components extends JApplet
{
    // declare components here – declare means the data type and a variable name
    JLabel title;
    JTextField fullName;

    public void init( )
    {
        // initialize variables here
        title = new JLabel( "My Lovely Applet" );
        fullName = new JTextField( 20 );
    }
}
```

We haven't added the components to the applet yet, so if you run this program nothing is displayed

Now we need to figure out how to add them to the applet. We need to specify a particular layout for managing how the components are to appear on the applet. In the next chapter we'll learn about the different options for layout managers; right now we're going to use a basic one named **FlowLayout** which simply adds the components in order and places them centered at the top. When it runs out of room on a line, it goes to the next line. To set the layout, we need to make a call to the method **setLayout**.

```
setLayout( layoutManager );
```

Since we're going to use the `FlowLayout` manager for this chapter, we need:

```
setLayout( new FlowLayout( ) );
```

(further discussion on setLayout in chapter 6)

This line should be placed after the opening squiggly bracket of our init method:

```java
import javax.swing.*;
import java.awt.*;

public class Components extends JApplet
{
    // declare components here
    JLabel  title;
    JTextField  fullName;

    public void init( )
    {
        // set the layout manager
        setLayout( new FlowLayout( ) );

        // initialize variables here
        title = new JLabel( "My Lovely Applet" );
        fullName = new JTextField( 20 );

        // add components to applet
        add( title );
        add( fullName );
    }
}
```

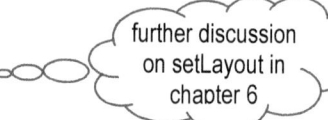

The order in which we call the `add` method is the order in which the components are displayed

Now let's take a look at the components we can add to our applet. We'll start off with the JLabel.

JLabel

JLabel is a component that we can put text and/or images in. It is simply a label, and a user cannot click on it or select/change the text from the label.

To create a label, we call the constructor method for JLabel with appropriate parameters.

```
JLabel variableName;

variableName = new JLabel( String );
variableName = new JLabel( ImageIcon );
variableName = new JLabel( String, ImageIcon, horizontalAlignment );
```

3 ways to create a JLabel: text, image, or both text and an image

where the *horizontalAlignment* can be one of the following:

```
JLabel.LEFT        JLabel.RIGHT        JLabel.CENTER
```

to determine where the text and/or image in the label should be positioned with respect to the layout manager. *NOTE: Until we use layout managers other than FlowLayout, these alignments will have no visible effect.*

Examples:

```
JLabel myName, mythought, meLabel;

myName = new JLabel( "Cookie Monster" );
mythought = new JLabel( "This label has a lot of text" );
meLabel = new JLabel( "Me, Myself and I" );
```

JLabels are not editable by the user; they are intended to simply be a label on the applet. In the example below we create two labels and add them to the applet. *If you resize the applet to be very wide, both labels will appear on the same line – this is based on our layout manager FlowLayout.*

```java
import javax.swing.*;
import java.awt.*;

public class JLabelEx1
            extends JApplet
{
   JLabel label1, label2;
   public void init ()
   {
        setLayout( new FlowLayout( ) );
        label1 = new JLabel("Java is fun to learn");
        label2 = new JLabel("But I like skiing too!");

        // add labels to applet
        add( label1 );
        add( label2 );
   }
}
```

```
Applet Vie... [_][□][X]
Applet

    Java is fun to learn
    But I like skiing too!



Applet started.
```

When working with the text in a JLabel, we can customize it using HTML tags. HTML is the language used to create web pages, and we can use some of the syntax inside our Swing components.

Basic HTML for JLabel:

- The text MUST start with the tag <HTML>
-
 - go to the next line
- <P> - create a blank line (works similar to <BR> tag)
- <B>the text</B> - put the text in bold: **the text**
- <I>the text</I> - put the text in italics: *the text*
- <CENTER>text</CENTER> - puts the text centered. Works best on multi-line HTML text
- <FONT COLOR=Red>the text</FONT> - change the text to the color red: the text
- <FONT SIZE=+1>the text</FONT> - change the text to one size bigger: the text
- <FONT SIZE=5>text</FONT> - change text size to 5 (sizes go from 1-7)

HTML tags are NOT case-sensitve!

Example:

+ with two strings appends them together (Chapter 9)

```
JLabel  fox, name;
   fox = new JLabel( "<HTML><FONT SIZE=+5>T</FONT>he "
      + " <FONT COLOR=RED>fox</FONT><BR> jumped <BR><B>over</B> da <I>moon.</I>" );
   name = new JLabel( "<HTML><B><I>GOOOOD MORNING!!!</B></I>");
```

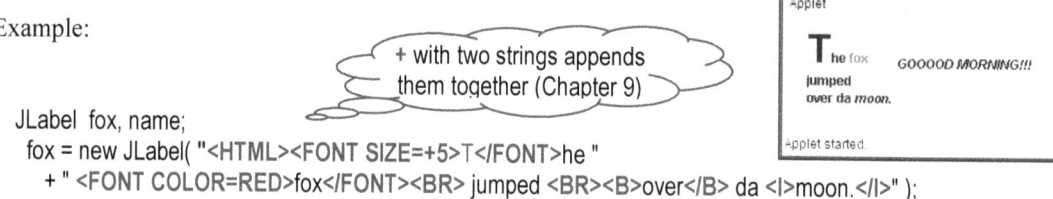

 *When creating String literals (text within double-quotes), we cannot have the double-quotes around the String on separate lines – because Java wouldn't know how much 'space' to put in to wrap it. However, we can add Strings together by having one String on the first line with the beginning and ending double-quotes, then a plus sign, and then the second String inside double-quotes on the next line.*

This next example shows the use of HTML tags to customize the text.

```
import java.awt.*;
import javax.swing.*;
public class JLabelEx extends JApplet
{
    JLabel  label1, label2;

  public void init( )
  {
     setLayout(new FlowLayout( )  );

     //Create the first label.
     label1 = new JLabel( "<HTML>Text<BR>on<BR>separate Lines", JLabel.CENTER );

     //Create the other labels.
     label2 = new JLabel( "<HTML><FONT COLOR=RED>Cookie</FONT>Monster" );

     //Add the labels.
     add( label1 );
     add( label2 );
  }
}
```

If we want the text to be centered within the label, JLabel.CENTER won't work (only centers the label as a whole within the placed location based on the layout manager). We use the HTML tag CENTER to center the text within the label

JLabel mylabel = new JLabel("<html><center>Text
on
separate Lines</center>");

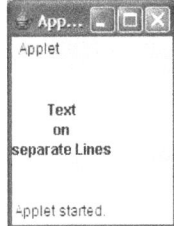

Images

We can also put images inside a JLabel. We can either have a JLabel with just an image, or with an image and text (or just text). To do so, we need to create an `ImageIcon` object. Then we can add the ImageIcon to the JLabel.

Therefore, there are four steps to adding an image to an applet:

1. Create an Image object with the name of the image file
2. Create an ImageIcon with the Image object we just created
3. Add the ImageIcon to the JLabel (or other component)
4. Add the JLabel (or other component) to the applet

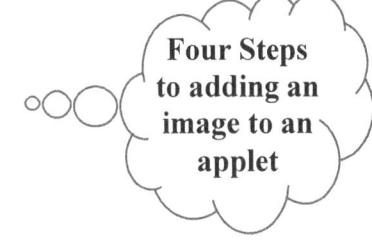

Step 1: Create an Image object with the name of the image file

First we *declare* a variable to hold our image in the instance variable section at the top of our code. In the example below, we have:

```
Image img;
```

Then inside the **init** method, we can grab the image by calling the **getImage** method. When we call this method, we need to specify where exactly the image is. For this book, we are going to store all our images in the same place as our source code. This is the easiest and also works when we transfer our final applets to the Internet. So to specify the location, we want to reference the fully specified location by calling the method **getCodeBase( )**.

The last part of this step is to reference the name of the image file. Be careful with upper-case and lower-case letters – running on Windows allows us to use either but running our applet on a Linux or UNIX system requires us have correct cases! Avoid using spaces in your filenames as this will mess things up later when we add our applets to the Internet as well.

```
img = getImage( getCodeBase( ), "oncomputer.png" );
```

*We cannot call the getImage method at the top of the program were we declare our instance variables. It won't work! We should **declare** our variables at the top only.*

Step 2: Create an ImageIcon with the Image object previously created

First we *declare* a variable to hold our ImageIcon object in the instance variable section at the top of our code. In the example below, we have:

```
ImageIcon imgIcon;
```

63

Then inside the **init** method, we can *instantiate* an ImageIcon object by calling the new operator and sending as a parameter our Image object:

    imgIcon = new ImageIcon(img);

Step 3: Add the ImageIcon to the JLabel

First we *declare* a variable to hold our JLabel in the instance variable section at the top of our code. In the example below, we have:

    JLabel label;

Then inside the init method, we can *instantiate* our JLabel object by calling the new operator and sending as a parameter our ImageIcon object:

    label = new JLabel(imgIcon);

We can also put images in JButton, JList, JRadioButton and other components following this same structure. See examples in their respective sections.

Step 4: Add the JLabel to the applet

To add the JLabel to the applet, we first need to make sure we've set our layout manager:

    setLayout(new FlowLayout( ));

Then we add our JLabel component using the **add** method:

    add(label);

 *We can<u>not</u> add an **Image** nor an **ImageIcon** object directly to the Applet or JPanel, We need to stash it into a component like a JLabel or JButton, etc.*

Example with just an image

```
import java.awt.*;
import javax.swing.*;
public class JLabelWithImage extends JApplet
{
    Image img;
    ImageIcon imgIcon;
    JLabel label;

  public void init( )
  {
        img = getImage( getCodeBase( ), "oncomputer.png" );
        imgIcon = new ImageIcon( img );
        label = new JLabel( imgIcon );
        setLayout( new FlowLayout( ) );
        add( label );
  }
}
```

Example with text and an image

```
import java.awt.*;
import javax.swing.*;
public class JLabelTextAndImage extends JApplet
{
    JLabel label;
    ImageIcon imgIcon;
    Image img;

    public void init()
    {
        img = getImage( getCodeBase( ), "oncomputer.png" );
        imgIcon = new ImageIcon( img );
        label = new JLabel( "Cookie Monster", imgIcon, JLabel.CENTER );
        setLayout( new FlowLayout( ) );
        add( label );
    }
}
```

By default, the image is to the left of the text.

JLabel.CENTER represents how to align the label with respect to the layout manager – which has no affect when we're using FlowLayout.

We can also adjust where the text is with respect to the image, using one of the following methods:

```
setHorizontalTextPosition( textPosition )
setVerticalTextPosition( textPosition )
```

For example, the table below shows the output based on the lines entered. Note that when creating the JLabel with the call to new JLabel, the position specified is for alignment of the text and image with respect to the layout manager and has no effect on the text or image when we're using the FlowLayout manager. The default for text alignment is right-aligned horizontally and centered vertically with respect to the image.

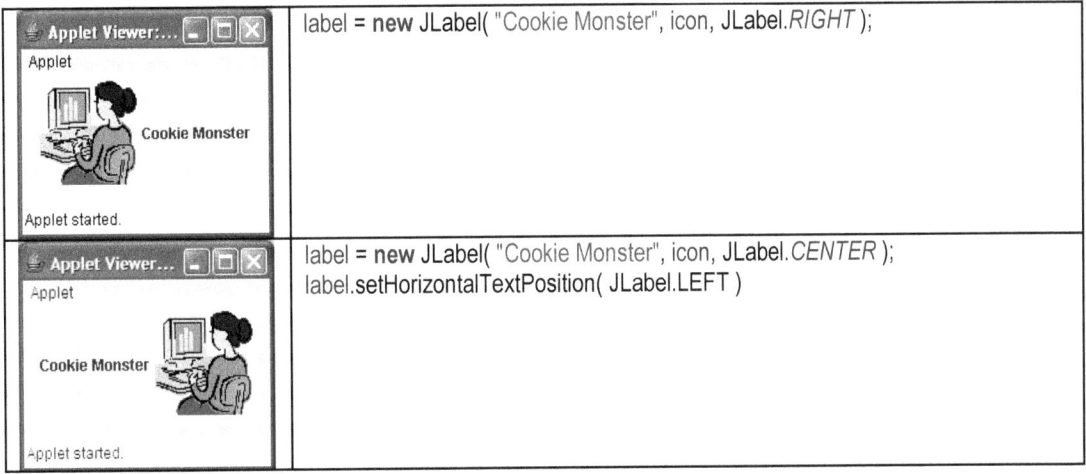

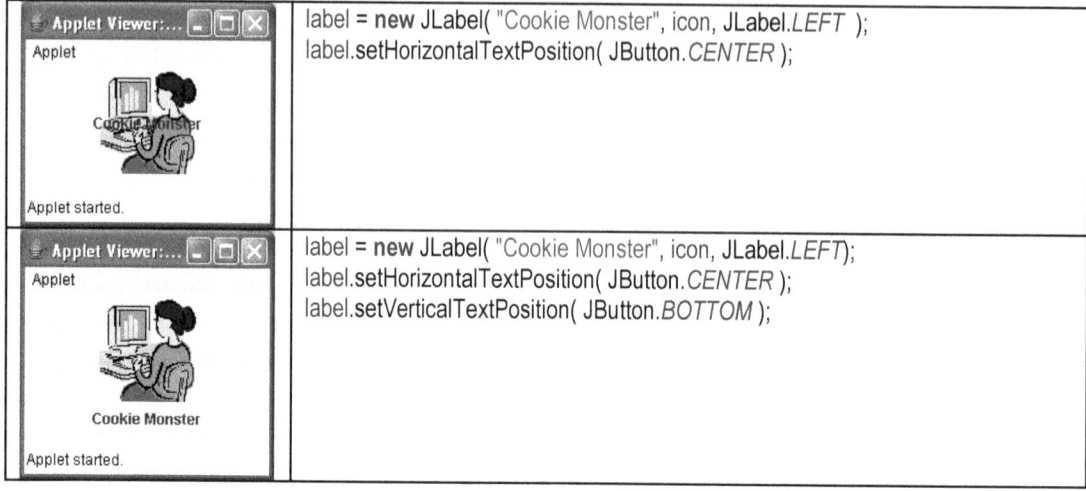

 *A shortcut for adding images is to combine the step of creating an ImageIcon and adding it to the button. For example:*
> *Image img;*
> *JLabel myLabel;*
> *img = getImage(getCodeBase( ), "img.gif");*
> *myLabel = new JLabel(new ImageIcon(img));*
> *and create objects inside our methods (e.g. inside the init method).*

JButton

We can add buttons to the applet by creating `JButton` objects. We specify a new button object in one of the following ways:

```
JButton btn;

btn = new JButton( String );              // creates button with text
btn = new JButton( ImageIcon );           // creates button with image
btn = new JButton( String, ImageIcon );   // creates button with text and image
```

where ImageIcon is created from the Image object.
Examples:

```
JButton btn
btn = new JButton( "Cookie Monster" );

Image img = getImage( getCodeBase( ), "happy.gif" );
ImageIcon ic = new ImageIcon( img );

btn = new JButton( ic );
btn = new JButton( "Coffee rules", ic );
```

The following example creates three JButtons and adds them to the applet using FlowLayout.

```
import javax.swing.*;
import java.awt.*;
public class JButtonEx extends JApplet
{
  JButton one;
  JButton two;
  JButton three;
  public void init( )
  {
        setLayout( new FlowLayout( ) );
        one = new JButton( "one" );
        two = new JButton( "two" );
        three = new JButton( "three" );
        add( one );
        add( two );
        add( three );
  }
}
```

Right now, our buttons don't do anything interesting – they just appear on our applet. We'll learn how to do things when the button is clicked later when we cover events.

We can extend this program to add images to the buttons. In the next example, we'll leave the first button as is with just text on it. On the second button we'll just add an image. The third button we'll show how to add both text and an image to the button.

```
import javax.swing.*;
import java.awt.*;
public class JButtonImg extends JApplet
{
  JButton one, two, three;
  Image img;
  ImageIcon icon;
  public void init( )
  {
        setLayout( new FlowLayout( ) );
        one = new JButton( "one" );
        img = getImage( getCodeBase( ), "idea.png" );
        icon = new ImageIcon( img );
        two = new JButton( icon  );
        img = getImage( getCodeBase( ), "oncomputer.png" );
        three = new JButton( "three", new ImageIcon( img ) );
        add( one );    add( two );    add( three );
  }
}
```

This next example is the same program as above but uses methods.

```java
import javax.swing.*;
import java.awt.*;
public class JButtonImg extends JApplet  {
   JButton one, two, three;
   Image img;
   ImageIcon icon;
   public void init( )
   {
        setLayout( new FlowLayout( ) );
        setupButtons( );
   }
   public void setupButtons( )
   {
        one = new JButton( "one" );
        img = getImage( getCodeBase( ), "idea.png" );
        icon = new ImageIcon( img );
        two = new JButton( icon  );
        img = getImage( getCodeBase( ), "oncomputer.png" );
        three = new JButton( "three", new ImageIcon( img ) );
        add( one );     add( two );     add( three );
   }
}
```

We can customize the layout of the text and image in our buttons in a similar way in which we did it for JLabels. We can adjust where the text is with respect to the image, using a method named

```
setHorizontalTextPosition( textPosition )
setVerticalTextPosition( textPosition )
```

For example, adding the following line to the code example above will put the text to the left of the image:

```
label.setHorizontalTextPosition( JLabel.LEFT )
```

To put the text below the image:

```
label.setHorizontalTextPosition( JLabel.CENTER )
label.setVerticalTextPosition( JLabel.BOTTOM )
```

Buttons also have additional customizations that we can apply. These include modifying the aesthetics of the button as well as which image is to be displayed depending on the state of the button. Each of the following examples assume we have created a button and an ImageIcon for the Image.

```
Image img;
ImageIcon imgIcon;
JButton myButton;

img = getImage( getCodeBase( ), "idea.png" );
imgIcon = new ImageIcon( img );
myButton = new JButton( imgIcon );
```

	[default]
	mybutton.setBorderPainted(false);
	mybutton.setContentAreaFilled(false);
	mybutton.setBorderPainted(false); mybutton.setContentAreaFilled(false);
	mybutton.setMargin(new Insets(0,0,0,0)); *where first 0 is top margin, second 0 is left, third 0 is bottom margin and last 0 is right*
	mybutton.setRolloverIcon(rolloverImageIcon); *changes the image displayed on the button when the mouse rolls over the button*

	mybutton.setEnabled(false);
	mybutton.setDisabledIcon(disabledImageIcon);
	
	user cannot select the button, and a different image is displayed

	mybutton.setFocusable(false); removes a border around text/image when focused/user selects it

Text Components

There are three types of text components where users can enter information:

- JTextField
- JPasswordField
- JTextArea

The JTextField only allows one line of text. JPasswordField also only allows one line of text; but when the user types in this box, the letters are displayed with the star echo character to ensure privacy. JTextArea allows the user to enter multiple lines of text (e.g., a comments field).

JTextField

We can create a JTextField component several ways:

Create a text field with no text, default width of zero characters

```
JTextField field1;
field1 = new JTextField( );
```

Default to zero characters-wide!

Create a text field with text inside the text field, the width will be the exact size of the text.

```
JTextField field2;
field2 = new JTextField( "Hello" );
```

Create a text field with text and specified width (# columns)

```
JTextField field3;
field3 = new JTextField( "Hello", 5 );
```

When determining the width, each column is approximately the size of the letter M in the current font. Therefore, when using a variable-width font, the columns will not match up to the number of characters in the text field.

```
import javax.swing.*;
import java.awt.*;
public class JTextFieldEx extends JApplet
{
  JTextField tf1, tf2, field1, field2, field3;
  public void init( )
  {
    setLayout( new FlowLayout( ) );
    tf1 = new JTextField( );
    tf2 = new JTextField( " ", 20 );
    field1 = new JTextField( );
    field2 = new JTextField( "Hello" );
    field3 = new JTextField( "Hello", 5 );
    add( tf1 );            add( tf2 );
    add( field1 );         add( field2 );
    add( field3 );
  }
}
```

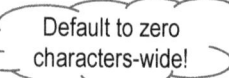

JPasswordField

The password field is identical to the JTextField, except that the characters typed into the field are replaced with the star * character to maintain some privacy for users entering sensitive information, such as passwords.

JTextArea

A text area allows users to enter multiple lines of information. This is useful when we want the user to enter comments or a description or such. When creating a text area, we need to specify the number of rows and columns.
We can create a text area either with default text or without it:

Create a text area with 3 rows and 20 columns, no text inside

```
JTextArea area;
area = new JTextArea( 3, 20 );
```

Create a text area with 5 rows and 10 columns, text inside

```
JTextArea area;
area = new JTextArea( "Enter message here", 5, 10 );
```

When adding JTextArea components to the applet, we need to display them inside a JScrollPane to ensure they display correctly. Then we add the JScrollPane to the applet.

```
JScrollPane scrollPane;
scrollPane = new JScrollPane( textareaComponent );
add( scrollPane );
```

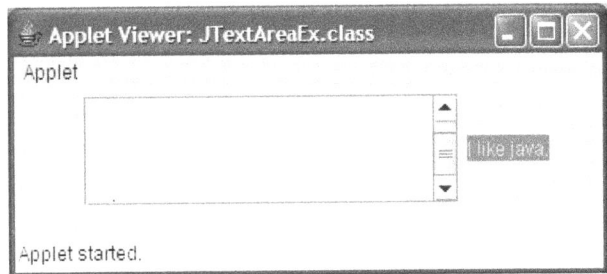

```
import javax.swing.*;
import java.awt.*;
public class JTextAreaEx extends JApplet
{
  JTextArea ta1, ta2, ta3;
  JScrollPane pane;
  public void init( )
  {
      setLayout( new FlowLayout( ) );
      ta1 = new JTextArea( );
      ta2 = new JTextArea( 4, 20 );
      ta3 = new JTextArea( "I like java." );
      add( ta1 );
       pane = new JScrollPane( ta2 );
      add( pane );
      ta3.setBackground( Color.RED );
      ta3.setForeground( Color.CYAN );
      add( ta3 );
  }
}
```

 *Put JTextArea components inside a JScrollPane and add the JScrollPane to the Applet to ensure the JTextArea displays properly.*

We can have the text area wrap within the columns set. To set wrapping enabled, call the `setLineWrap` method on a text area.

```
ta3.setLineWrap( true );
```

71

We can also specify to wrap only on word boundaries, by calling the `setWrapStyleWord` method:

```
ta3.setWrapStyleWord( true );
```

> *JTextArea components do NOT display HTML. We can still force it display text on multiple lines by using the newline character which is \n (backslash n). If we want to display HTML in a text area, we need to use JTextPane or JEditorPane.*

JCheckBox

JCheckBox is another component we can add to our applets. Essentially, a checkbox displays one of two states: checked or not. We usually use checkboxes for options that are not coupled, so that users can select independently from the options available.

We can create a checkbox several ways, depending on whether we want text and/or an image.

```
JCheckBox cb;
cb = new JCheckBox( String );
cb = new JCheckBox( ImageIcon );           // image instead of checkbox, no text with it
cb = new JCheckBox( String, ImageIcon );   // image with text on right
```

☐ happy

Examples:

```
JCheckBox cb;
Image img;
ImageIcon icon;

cb = new JCheckBox( "text" );
img = getImage( getCodeBase( ), "lightbulb.png" );
icon = new ImageIcon( img );
cb = new JCheckBox( "red", icon );
```

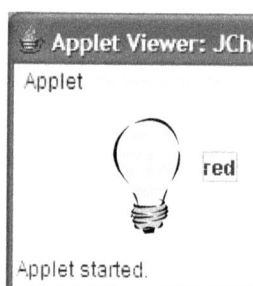

If we want to use images, the images replace the checkbox. So, we need an image for when the checkbox is selected and when it is not selected. When we call the constructor with an ImageIcon object, it designates the image for when it is not selected.

```
     JCheckBox cb;
     Image img;
     ImageIcon icon;


     img = getImage( getCodeBase( ), "gocart.png" );
     icon = new ImageIcon( img );

     cb = new JCheckBox( icon );
OR   cb = new JCheckBox( "text", icon);
```

To set the image for when the checkbox is selected, we need to call `setSelectionIcon`:

```
     cb1.setSelectedIcon( selectedIC );
```

```java
import javax.swing.*;
import java.awt.*;
public class JCheckBoxEx extends JApplet
{
   JCheckBox cb1, cb2, cb3;
   public void init( )
   {
        setLayout(new FlowLayout( )   );
        cb1 = new JCheckBox( "red" );
        cb2 = new JCheckBox( "blue" );
        cb3 = new JCheckBox( "pink" );
        add( cb1 );
        add( cb2 );
        add( cb3 );
   }
}
```

> To remove the border around the text when 'highlighted', call .setFocusable(false) on each radio button

```java
import javax.swing.*;
import java.awt.*;
public class JCheckBoxEx2 extends JApplet
{
   Image notsel, selected;
   ImageIcon notselIC, selectedIC;
   JCheckBox cb1, cb2, cb3;
   public void init( )
   {
        notsel = getImage( getCodeBase( ), "lightBulbOff.png" );
        notselIC = new ImageIcon( notsel );
        selected = getImage( getCodeBase( ), "lightBulbOn.png" );
        selectedIC = new ImageIcon( selected );

        cb1 = new JCheckBox( "red", notselIC );
        cb1.setSelectedIcon( selectedIC );

        cb2 = new JCheckBox( "blue" );
        cb3 = new JCheckBox( "pink" );

        setLayout(new FlowLayout());
        add( cb1 );
        add( cb2 );
        add( cb3 );
   }
}
```

Red is not selected

Red is selected

 *Call .setFocusable(false) on each checkbox to prevent a border drawn around the component when it has focus.*

JRadioButton

JRadioButton is another component that allows users to select or deselect. Essentially, a radio button displays a group of options with only one selected. Within a group the options are mutally exclusivel When a radio button is selected in a group, the button that is currently selected is automatically toggled to be unselected.

We can create radio buttons as follows:

```
JRadioButton rb;
rb = new JRadioButton( String );
```

Example:

```
JRadioButton rb1, rb2;
rb1 = new JRadioButton( "text" );
rb2 = new JRadioButton( "happy" );
```

Then we also have to associate the buttons to a particular group:

```
ButtonGroup grp;
grp = new ButtonGroup( );
grp.add( rb1 );
grp.add( rb2 );
```

```
import javax.swing.*;
import java.awt.*;
public class JRadioButtonEx extends JApplet
{
  JRadioButton jb1, jb2, jb3
  ButtonGroup group;
  public void init( )
  {
        setLayout( new FlowLayout( )  );
        jb1 = new JRadioButton( "red" );
        jb2 = new JRadioButton( "blue" );
        jb3 = new JRadioButton( "pink" );
        group = new ButtonGroup( );
        group.add( jb1 );
        group.add( jb2 );
        group.add( jb3 );
        add( jb1 );    add( jb2 );    add( jb3 );
  }
}
```

 Call .setFocusable(false) on each checkbox to prevent a border drawn around the component when it has focus.

JComboBox

JComboBox is another component we can add to our applets. A combo box is a drop-down list of items, where the user can select one (and only one) option. List items can be text, images, or text with an image. Scrollbars will automatically be added to the drop-down list if about 7 or more items are in the list (this number can be modified calling the `setPreferredSize` method.

To create a new combo box:

```
JComboBox comboBox;
comboBox = new JComboBox( );
```

To add things to the combobox, use the `addItem` method. We can add text or ImageIcon objects.

```
import javax.swing.*;
import java.awt.*;
public class JComboEx extends JApplet
{
  JComboBox majors;
   public void init( )
   {
        setLayout( new FlowLayout( ) );
        majors = new JComboBox( );
        majors.addItem( "CS" );
        majors.addItem( "Math" );
        majors.addItem( "History" );
        majors.addItem( "Leisure Studies" );
        majors.addItem( "Psych" );
        add( majors );
   }
}
```

Useful Methods

    void setEditable(boolean yesno)   allow users to enter text (true) or only select from list (false)
Example: `combolist.setEditable( false );`

    int getItemCount( )   returns the number of items in the list
Example: `int numItemsInList = combolist.getItemCount( );`

    int getSelectedIndex( )   returns the index of the selected item
Example: `int selectedIndex = combolist.getSelectedItem( );`

    void removeItem(Object obj)   removes the object from the list
    void removeItemAt(int index)   removes the object at the specified index

JList

JList is another component we can add to our applets. Essentially, a JList displays a bunch of items which the user can select one (or more) items. List items can be text, images, or buttons.

We're going to create lists with a simple list model.

```
DefaultListModel model;
JList list;
model = new DefaultListModel( );
list = new JList( model );
```

There are two ways to add text or images to the list:

- the `addElement( thing )` method to add the thing to the end of the list.
- the `add( index, thing )` method to add the thing to the list at a specified index.

Note: indices start at index 0.

We can set the type of selection allowed as either

- single-selection: only one item can be selected at a time (default)
  list.setSelectionMode(ListSelectionModel.SINGLE_SELECTION);
- multiple-selection: user can select one or more items at the same time
  list.setSelectionMode(ListSelectionModel.MULTIPLE_INTERVAL_SELECTION);

```java
import javax.swing.*;
import java.awt.*;
public class JListWithAddElement extends JApplet
{
  DefaultListModel model;
  JList majors;
  public void init( )
  {
        model = new DefaultListModel( );
        majors = new JList( model );
        model.addElement( "CS" );
        model.addElement( "Math" );
        model.addElement( "History" );
        model.addElement( "Leisure Studies" );
        model.addElement( "Psych" );
        setLayout( new FlowLayout( ) );
        add( majors );
  }
}
```

addElement adds each item to the end of the list

Example Program using `add` method

```java
import javax.swing.*;
import java.awt.*;
public class JListEx extends JApplet
{
  DefaultListModel model;
  JList majors;
  public void init( )
  {
        model = new DefaultListModel( );
        majors = new JList( model );

        model.add( 0, "CS" );
        model.add( 1, "Math" );
        model.add( 2, "History" );
        model.add( 3, "Leisure Studies" );
        model.add( 4, "Psych" );

        setLayout( new FlowLayout( ) );
        add( majors );
  }
}
```

lists start at index 0

add method requires us to specify the location of each element

Useful Methods
```
int getSelectedIndex( )
Object getSelectedValue( )
void setSelectionMode( int mode )
```
returns the index of the item that is selected
returns the object that is selected
single or multi-select items in list

where mode can be:
```
ListSelectionModel.SINGLE_SELECTION
ListSelectionModel.MULTIPLE_INTERVAL_SELECTION (default)
```

Scrollbars

In order to get scrollbars on the list, we need to put the list inside a `JScrollPane`.

Example:
```
JScrollPane pane;
pane = new JScrollPane( list );
```

Example program with JList inside a JScrollPane to show scrollbars.

```java
import javax.swing.*;
import java.awt.*;
public class JListExScrollPane extends JApplet
{
  DefaultListModel model = new DefaultListModel();
  JList majors = new JList( model );
  public void init( )
  {
          model = new DefaultListModel( );
          majors = new JList( model );
          model.addElement( "CS" );
          model.addElement( "Math" );
          model.addElement( "History" );
          model.addElement( "Leisure Studies" );
          model.addElement( "Psych" );

          setLayout( new FlowLayout( ) );

          majors.setVisibleRowCount( 3 );
          JScrollPane spane = new JScrollPane( majors );
          add( spane );
  }
}
```

Images

We can also add images into the list. To do this, create ImageIcon objects as we've done before (see JLabel examples). Then add the ImageIcon object into the list.

In the following example, we add both text and images into the same list.

```
import javax.swing.*;
import java.awt.*;
public class JListExImage extends JApplet
{
  DefaultListModel model;
  JList majors;
  Image img;
  ImageIcon icon;

  public void init( )
  {
    model = new DefaultListModel( );
    majors = new JList( model );
    img = getImage( getCodeBase( ), "gocart.png" );
    icon = new ImageIcon( img );
    model.add( 0, icon );

    model.add( 1, "Math" );

    img = getImage( getCodeBase( ), "idea.png" );
    icon = new ImageIcon( img );
    model.add( 2, icon );

    model.add( 3, "Leisure Studies" );

    img = getImage( getCodeBase( ), "oncomputer.png" );
    icon = new ImageIcon( img );
    model.add( 4, icon );

    setLayout( new FlowLayout( ) );

    majors.setVisibleRowCount( 3 );
    JScrollPane spane = new JScrollPane( majors );
    add( spane );
  }
}
```

Components

When we create components such as the JLabel, there are additional methods we can access through the hierarchy of inheritance. JLabel inherits from the `Component` class, which has other methods that we can use as well. This applies to many other components we'll be covering too, since they also inherit from the `Component` class.

The hierarchy looks similar to the following:

```
Component
    |
    |--JButton
    |--JComboBox
    |--JLabel
    |--JList
    |--JTextField
    |--JTextArea
```

Colors

We can change the coloring scheme of our components by using one of the following methods:

> setBackground(Color) - sets the background color of the component
> setForeground(Color) - sets the text color of the component
> setOpaque(false) – makes it "transparent" for background color to display through
> setOpaque(true) -- make it solid background, useful for setBackground method

Example:

```
JLabel name;
name = new JLabel( "Mr. Cookie Monster" );
name.setOpaque(true);      // necessary for background color
name.setBackground( Color.BLUE );
name.setForeground( Color.YELLOW );
```

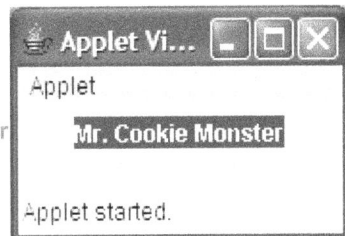

  setBackground will not work on the JApplet directly. Either fill in a rectangle the size of the applet inside the paint method, or create a JPanel and add all components to this JPanel and call setBackground on the JPanel .

  setBackground may require us to first call setOpaque(true) on the component - some components like JLabel default to transparent (opaque = false).

In the following example, we illustrate two ways to get the background colors of a component to work. We create a panel and set the background color (since we cannot setBackground directly on the applet). We then add three checkboxes. The first one is simply added to the panel. The second one sets the background color of the checkbox to match the color of the panel. The third checkbox just changes its opaqueness to false to allow a transparency, such that the panel's color shows through.

```
import java.awt.*;
import javax.swing.*;
public class OpaqueEx extends JApplet
{
    JCheckBox cb1, cb2, cb3;
    JPanel pane;
    public void init( )
    {
        setLayout( new FlowLayout( ) );
        pane = new JPanel( );
        pane.setBackground( Color.ORANGE );
        cb1 = new JCheckBox( "periwinkle" );
        cb2 = new JCheckBox( "snowflake" );
        cb2.setBackground( Color.ORANGE );
        cb3 = new JCheckBox( "magenta" );
        cb3.setOpaque(false);
        pane.add( cb1 );    pane.add( cb2 );    pane.add( cb3 );
        add( pane );
    }
}
```

Font

We can also change the font of the text in our component by calling:

```
setFont( Font )
```

Example:

```
JLabel name;
name = new JLabel( "Mr. Cookie Monster" );
Font bigFont = new Font( "Serif", Font.BOLD, 36 );
name.setFont( bigFont );
```

OR

```
name.setFont( new Font( "Serif", Font.BOLD, 36 ) );
```

OR

name = new JLabel("<HTML><FONT SIZE=16>Cookie Monster</FONT>"));

Enabled

Sometimes we want a component to be disabled, displaying it as grayed-out and for items such as buttons and lists - disallow users from clicking on them. To do this, we can call the following method on our component:

```
setEnabled( boolean )
```

Example:

```
JButton submit;

submit = new JButton( "Submit it!" );
submit.setEnabled( false );
```

```java
import javax.swing.*;
import java.awt.*;
public class setEnabledEx extends JApplet
{
  JButton one;
  JButton two;
  JButton three;
  public void init( )
  {
        setLayout( new FlowLayout( ) );
        one = new JButton( "one" );
        two = new JButton( "two" );
        three = new JButton( "three" );
        one.setEnabled( false );
        three.setEnabled( false );
        add( one );   add( two );   add( three );
  }
}
```

users can not select on disabled buttons

More Complicated Examples with Methods

Although we went through a bunch of simple examples to explore each component, it's time to see how we create a complicated applet with multiple components and ensure we make use of methods to keep the code more readable.

```java
import java.awt.*;
import javax.swing.*;
public class components extends JApplet
{
        JLabel l_address;
        JTextField  street, city, state, zip;
        JTextArea  ta_message;
        JButton  b_go;
        JCheckBox  cb_lucky, cb_happy;
        ButtonGroup  bg_mood = new ButtonGroup( );
        JRadioButton  rb_lucky2, rb_happy2;
        public void init( )
        {
                setLayout( new FlowLayout( ) );
                setupAddressInfo( );
                setupSelections( );
                ta_message = new JTextArea( "", 3, 50 );
                add( ta_message );
        }
        public void setupAddressInfo( )
        {
                l_address = new JLabel( "Address: " );
                street = new JTextField( );
                city = new JTextField(50);
                state = new JTextField( "CO", 2 );
                zip = new JTextField( "80521" );
                add( l_address );   add( street );
                add( city );   add( state );   add( zip );
        }
        public void setupSelections( )
        {
                b_go = new JButton( "Go!" );
                cb_lucky = new JCheckBox( "Lucky?" );
                cb_happy = new JCheckBox( "Happy?", true );
                bg_mood = new ButtonGroup( );
                rb_lucky2 = new JRadioButton( "Lucky2" );
                rb_happy2 = new JRadioButton( "Happy2", true );
                add( b_go );
                add( cb_lucky );     add( cb_happy );
                bg_mood.add( rb_lucky2 );
                bg_mood.add( rb_happy2 );
                add( rb_lucky2 );    add( rb_happy2 );
        }
}
```

Second Example with Methods

```java
import java.awt.*;
import javax.swing.*;
public class ComponentsWithMethods extends JApplet
{
   JLabel name, imageLabel1, imageLabel2, imageLabel3;      // instance data
   JTextField tfield;
   JButton button;
   Image img;
   ImageIcon ic;
   public void init( )
   {
      resize( 400,100 );
      setLayout( new FlowLayout( ) );
      setupName( );
      setupButton( );
      setupImage( imageLabel1,  "gocart.png" );
      setupImage( imageLabel2, "idea.png" );
      setupImage( imageLabel3, "oncomputer.png");
   }
   public void setupName( )
   {
      // sets up the Name label and textfield
      name = new JLabel( "Name: " );
      tfield = new JTextField( 5 );
      add( name );
      add( tfield );
   }
   public void setupButton( )
   {
     button = new JButton( "GO" );
     add( button );
   }
   public void setupImage( JLabel lab, String myimage)
   {
      img = getImage( getCodeBase( ),  myimage );
      ic = new ImageIcon( img );
      lab = new JLabel( ic );
      add( lab );
   }
}
```

each call to setupImage sends to the method which label should be set up and added to the applet

Summary

- Swing components are in the javax.swing package and usually begin with the letter 'J'.
- Declare components at the top of the class, after the class header and first squiggly bracket.
- Swing components are added to the applet by calling the add method.
- Most Swing components allow us to use HTML tags to customize the appearance.
- JLabel is simple text displayed on the applet. The user cannot click on it or change it.
- Image and ImageIcon objects cannot be added directly to the applet or JPanel. First put them into a JLabel or other component then add that to the applet/JPanel.
- The alignment on JLabel is used to align the component within the allocated space based on the layout manager. To center a multi-line text label, use the HTML <CENTER> tag.
- The alignment of text with respect to an image in a JLabel can be changed by calling setHorizontalTextPosition method.
- There are four steps to adding images; 1) create an Image object using getImage, 2) create an ImageIcon of the image, 3) add the ImageIcon to a Swing component and 4) add the component to the applet.
- Radio buttons are grouped together in a ButtonGroup. Multiple ButtonGroups can be used in an applet. The user can only select one item from each ButtonGroup.
- Checkboxes are used when users can select zero or more options. Radio buttons are used when users are to select only one from the group.
- JComboBox is a drop-down list that can be user-editable.
- Swing components can have their text color changed by calling .setForeground method on the component.
- Swing components can allow the background color to come through by making it transparent, by calling the .setOpaque method on the component and sending it the boolean value false.
- Call .setFocusable(false) on components to avoid a border painted around the component with focus.

Exercises

1. What package do we need to import to use Swing components?
2. Which component does a drop-down box?
3. Which letter do most Swing components begin with?
4. How many items can be true in a **ButtonGroup**?
5. What type of component should we use if we want a field where the user could enter a few lines of a text message?
6. True or False: We can have text on top of an image inside a **JButton**.
7. Write the **String** required to make a single **JLabel** with "Hello" on the first line and "World" on the next line.
8. What three types of image formats does Java support?
9. What are the four steps to add an image to an applet?
10. True or False. After a call to **getImage** to create the Image object from a file, we can add the **Image** object directly on to the Applet.
11. What method do we call on a **JButton** to set the image for when a mouse rolls over the button?
12. Given the following button, write a one-line code statement to change the color of the text to blue.
    JButton javaRocks = new JButton("I love Java");
13. How do we make a button with an image on it, not have any border around it?
14. True or False: The init method is called automatically by the browser whenever an applet is started.
15. How do we create radio buttons?
16. How do we get scrollbars on a **JTextArea**? on a **JList**?
17. How do we allow users to enter text into a **JComboBox**?
18. What method can we call to disable a **JList**? a **JTextField**? a **JButton**?
19. What method can we call to remove an element from a **JList**? a **JComboBox**?
20. What does the method getItemCount return?
21. True or False. Images can be displayed in a **JList**.
22. True or False. Images can be displayed in a **JComboBox**.
23. How do we set a **JList** to only allow a single selection?
24. What's the difference between a group of **JCheckBox** and a group of **JRadioButton**?
25. What's the difference between **JList** and **JComboBox**?
26. Which Java components can produce text on multiple lines? How? Are there multiple ways to achieve this, based on the type of components?
27. How does a **JLabel** differ from using the paint method? How are they similar?
28. Can a **JLabel** contain both text and images?
29. Create a **JLabel** with the text in both bold and italic.
30. Can a **JLabel** have HTML tags embedded?

31. How do we get the text to appear on multiple lines inside a **JLabel**?
32. If using HTML tags, what has to be the first thing inside the String?
33. Can we add an ImageIcon directly to the applet?
34. True or False: JLabel can contain text with multiple colors.
35. True orFalse: A ButtonGroup is necessary to group JCheckBox components together.
36. Put the following steps in order to add an image to the applet.
    - _____ create a JLabel
    - _____ create an ImageIcon
    - _____ call getImage

37. Create an applet that has 3 sets of radio button groups asking the user for their favorite color, movie and TV show.

38. Create an applet with 5 navigational buttons: Home, About Me, Resume, Portfolio and Friends. Make a button background image (use transparency as necessary) and display each button with your image and remove all decorations Java displays. Use the same image for all five buttons, centering the text of each button on top the image.

39. Create an applet that is a party invitation. Include a text field for them to enter their name, a checkbox to designate whether they are planning on attending or not, a drop-down list of what they will bring (appetizer, main dish, dessert), radio buttons for how many guests they will bring (0, 1, 2) and a text area for them to describe their costume.

40. Create an applet that displays a library of all your music. Include a list with each song listed, a drop-down list for different genres, and buttons to play/stop a song.

41. Create an applet of all your favorites: movies, bands, artists, people, quotes. Select appropriate components to display each.

Chapter 5

GUI Design

*I would love to change the world,
if only somebody would give me the source code!*

Objectives:

- Layout Managers
    - FlowLayout
    - BorderLayout
    - GridLayout
    - BoxLayout
- JPanels
- Warnings!
- Structuring with Methods
- Design
- Case Study

Layout Managers

Layout managers allow us to control where and how components are displayed. They divide the space of a container into regions and arrange the components in these regions. Different layout managers have different effects on the components – some layout managers will stretch components to fill the space allocated to it, and some layout managers allow the components to be whatever size they prefer.

We can add greater control by also using extra panels to nest components within layouts. A panel is a container that we can put components into, such as adding buttons and labels. The applet itself is a container which is how we added components in the previous chapter. We also want to make use of a panel, JPanel, as another container to hold components.

To create a JPanel, we can either specify the layout manager when we instantiate it or by calling the method **setLayout**, like we did with our applet:

```
        JPanel   pane;

        pane  =  new JPanel( new FlowLayout( ) );
OR
        pane  =  new JPanel( );
        pane.setLayout( new FlowLayout( ) );
```

Then we can add components to our JPanel, by specifying which JPanel and calling the **add** method:

```
        pane.add( myButton );
        pane.add( myLabel );
```

The last thing we need is to remember to add the panel to the applet. We do this in the same way we add other components like buttons and labels:

```
        add( pane );
```

When working with containers, be it the applet or JPanels, we can add as many components or other containers as we wish – there are no limits (until we run out of memory!).

FlowLayout

FlowLayout is the easiest layout manager to work with, but it is not very ideal. We've been using FlowLayout in our previous examples to keep it simple. Let's now analyze this layout scheme in more detail.

The way our components are laid out on the screen in FlowLayout is by placing them centered at the top of our applet. As we add more components, we run out of room in that "row" and therefore the remaining components are added beneath the first row, starting out centered again.

The following example is shown three times in different applet sizes. Notice how the components wrap depending on the size of the applet.

width=150 height=200

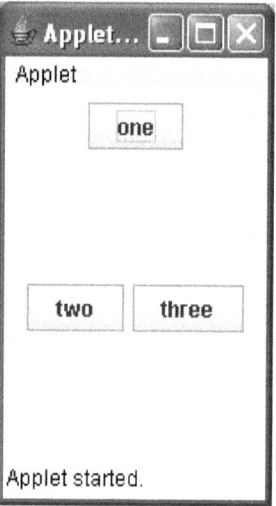

width=400 height=100

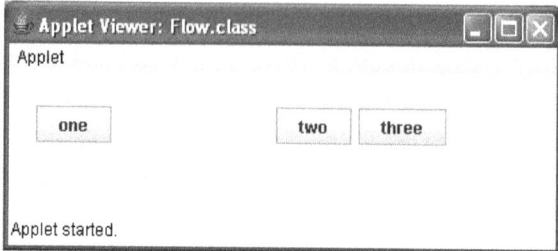

width=300 height=150

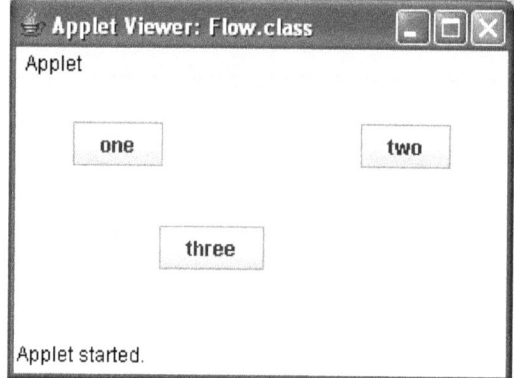

Code for the 3 examples above (Change dimensions to see above):

```java
import javax.swing.*;
import java.awt.*;
public class FlowEx extends JApplet
{
   JButton one, two, three;
   JTextArea ta1, ta2;
   public void init( )
   {
         setLayout( new FlowLayout( ) );
          one = new JButton( "one" );
          two = new JButton( "two" );
          three = new JButton( "three" );
          ta1 = new JTextArea( 4,10 );
          ta2 = new JTextArea( 3,5 );
         add( one );
         add( ta1 );
         add( two );
         add( three );
         add( ta2 );
   }
}
```

We can customize this layout a little by specifying that we want our components aligned to either the left or right. We can do this when we declare the FlowLayout manager by specifying

- FlowLayout.LEFT
- FlowLayout.RIGHT
- FlowLayout.CENTER (default)

Example:

```
setLayout( new FlowLayout( FlowLayout.RIGHT ) );
```

By changing this line in the program provided above, we can see the following output based on a 300x200 applet:

Advanced Concept

FlowLayout does not support an easy method for vertical alignment of components. If, for example, we wanted to center 3 buttons vertically on a JPanel (see next section) in BorderLayout.CENTER (see next section), we would need to calculate the dimensions of the JPanel and set the vertical gap on the JPanel. However, we cannot calculate the dimensions of a component until after all the components are on the applet and displayed. This means we need to put our code to calculate the dimension and change the vertical gap in a different method, the start method, which is called when everything is ready to go in the applet. The example below demonstrates how to get three buttons to show up centered vertically:

```
import javax.swing.*;
import java.awt.*;
public class FlowVertEx extends JApplet
{
    JButton one, two, three;
    FlowLayout flow = new FlowLayout( );
    JPanel pane = new JPanel( );
    public void init( )
    {
            one = new JButton( "one" );
            two = new JButton( "two" );
            three = new JButton( "three" );
            pane.add( one );
            pane.add( two );
            pane.add( three );
            add( pane );
    }
    public void start( )
    {
            flow.setVgap( (int )(pane.getSize( ).getHeight( )/2) – (int )(one.getHeight( )/2) );
            pane.setLayout( flow );
    }
}
```

setVgap method takes integers; getHeight returns a double, so we must cast final value to int

BorderLayout

BorderLayout allows us to align components within 5 areas:

- NORTH
- SOUTH
- EAST
- WEST
- CENTER

The layout scheme appears to the right:

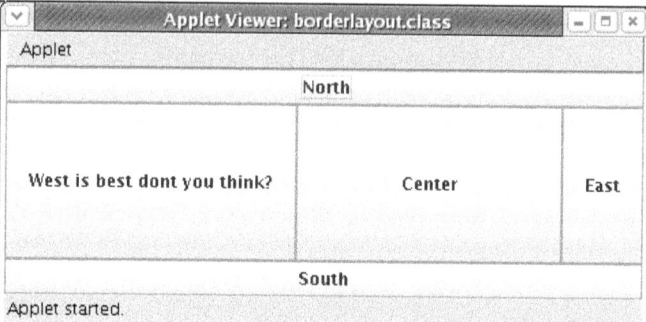

This was based on the following code:

```
import java.awt.*;
import javax.swing.*;
public class BorderLayoutEx extends JApplet
{
        JButton b1 , b2, b3, b4, b5;
   public void init( )
   {
        setLayout( new BorderLayout( ) );
        b1 = new JButton( "North" );
        b2 = new JButton( "South" );
        b3 = new JButton( "West is best dont you think?" );
        b4 = new JButton( "East" );
        b5 = new JButton( "Center" );

        add( b1, BorderLayout.NORTH );
        add( b2, BorderLayout.SOUTH );
        add( b3, BorderLayout.WEST );
        add( b4, BorderLayout.EAST );
        add( b5, BorderLayout.CENTER );
   }
}
```

When using the BorderLayout, we first need to specify that we want to use this layout manager. We can do so by calling the method `setLayout`, as follows:

```
setLayout( new BorderLayout( ) );
```

Once we set the layout for our applet to BorderLayout, we now have to specify where to add the components. When we call the `add` method, we specify which component we want to add to the applet, and also the location.
The format for the `add` method:

```
add( component, location );
```

The locations we can specify for BorderLayout are:

- BorderLayout.NORTH
- BorderLayout.SOUTH
- BorderLayout.EAST
- BorderLayout.WEST
- BorderLayout.CENTER

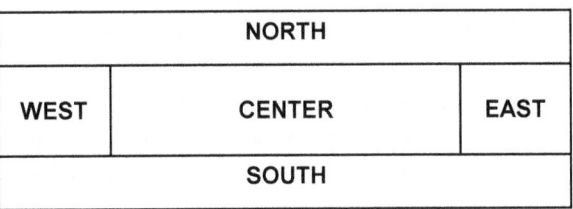

There are some peculiarities that we need to look at: how components are stretched to fill the space and limitations and rules for adding components to each space. When we add components to a container using BorderLayout, they stretch in different ways...

- Components added to the NORTH and SOUTH stretch the entire horizontal width, but only take up as much space vertically as necessary.
  (Example above, only enough space for the text on the buttons)
- Components added to the WEST and EAST stretch the vertical height between the components in the north and south, but only take up as much space horizontally as necessary.
  (Example above, only enough space for the text on the buttons)
- Components added to the center will stretch to fill in whatever remaining space is available.
  NOTE: if there is nothing added to the center, we may have a "hole" in our applet!

If we modify the previous example and comment out the line:

```
add( b5, BorderLayout.CENTER );
```

from the program above, the applet displays as shown on the right. Notice the 'hole' in the center region. Only the center region will stretch in both directions to fill any empty space. Therefore we'll probably always want to put at least *something* in the center region.

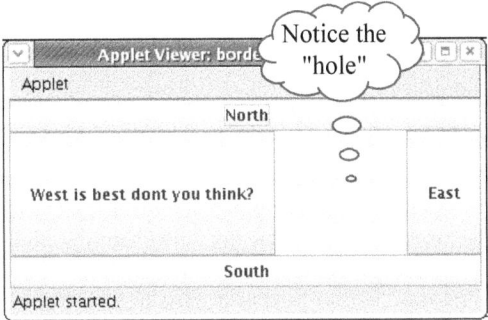

The second peculiarity concerns how many components we can add to each area. We can only add **ONE** component into each area: North, South, West, East, and Center! This is where things become complex. If we wanted to have a label and a button in the West side of our applet, we can do this by placing those two components into a JPanel and then add the JPanel to the applet to the West side.

What is a JPanel? A JPanel is component which is a surface pane where we can add components to. Since we can only put one component into each area of BorderLayout, we can work around this by placing multiple components on to a JPanel then add the JPanel into the area in the BorderLayout.

Below is a diagram depicting this nesting of components.

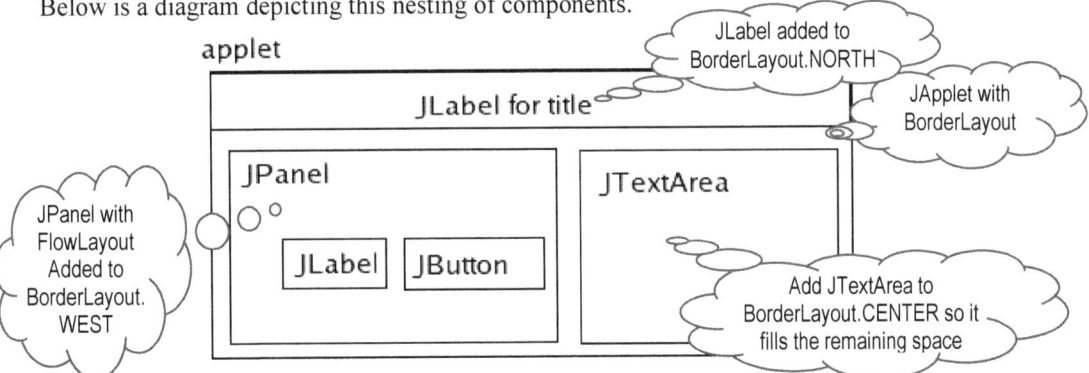

An example program using a JPanel for nesting components follows:

```java
import java.awt.*;
import javax.swing.*;
public class Nesting extends JApplet
{
    JLabel title, agree;
    JButton yes;
    JTextArea msg;
    public void init( )
    {
        setLayout( new BorderLayout( ) );   // set layout
                // create components
        title = new JLabel( "I'm a Star!", JLabel.CENTER);
        agree = new JLabel( "Agree? " );
        yes = new JButton( "Yes!" );
        msg = new JTextArea( 2, 10 );
        JPanel pane = new JPanel( new FlowLayout( ) );   // create nested panel
        pane.add( agree );
        pane.add( yes );
        add( pane, BorderLayout.WEST );     // add panel to West side
        add( title, BorderLayout.NORTH );   // add title to North
        add( msg, BorderLayout.EAST );      // add text area to East side
    }
}
```

Notice that we cannot see the JPanel, it is mostly there to help us organize our components on the applet. However, we could make the JPanel more obvious by changing it's color. If we add the line below to the example above, we'll see exactly where the JPanel is:

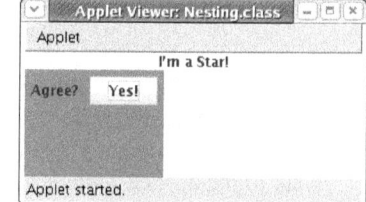

```
pane.setBackground( Color.RED );
```

Nesting JPanel components is the secret for customizing the appearance of our applet. But how are components arranged inside JPanel? By default, JPanel is set to use the FlowLayout manager. If we want to change the layout manager for a JPanel, we can do so in two different ways:

- When creating the JPanel:

```
JPanel pane;
pane = new JPanel( new BorderLayout( ) );
```

- By calling the setLayout method:

```
pane.setLayout( new BorderLayout( ) );
```

We can use any of the layout managers either on our applet or in a JPanel (including the ones we have yet to learn!).

 *We can only put ONE component in each of the five regions of BorderLayout! Hint: use JPanels to nest components and add the single JPanel to the region.*

BorderLayout and JLabel

Let's go back again and take a look at our JLabel. Remember there were options for alignment on a JLabel? When using FlowLayout, the size of the label is the exact size to encompass the text, so the alignment is irrelevant. However, with BorderLayout, the size of the label stretches to fill the region. Now we can make use of our alignment in JLabel. The default alignment for JLabel is left-justified if there is only text. The default for JLabel if there is only an image is to be center-justified. JLabels with both text and an image require us to specify the alignment when we create the JLabel.

In the following example, we can see JLabels in the NORTH and SOUTH as left-aligned. WEST and EAST alignment are irrelevant since the width is the same size as the label's text.

```java
import java.awt.*;
import javax.swing.*;

public class BorderLayoutJLabel extends JApplet
{
    JLabel n1, n2, n3, n4, n5;
    public void init( )
    {
        setLayout( new BorderLayout( ) );
        n1 = new JLabel( "North" );
        n1.setOpaque(true);
        n1.setBackground( Color.GREEN );
        n2 = new JLabel( "South" );
        n3 = new JLabel( "West is best dont you think?" );
        n4 = new JLabel( "East" );
        n5 = new JLabel( "Center" );
        add( n1, BorderLayout.NORTH );
        add( n2, BorderLayout.SOUTH );
        add( n3, BorderLayout.WEST );
        add( n4, BorderLayout.EAST );
        add( n5, BorderLayout.CENTER );
    }
}
```

GridLayout

GridLayout sets up a spread-sheet like grid of cells, where each cell has the same width and same height. (Width may not be the same as the height).
When using the GridLayout, we first need to specify that we want to use this layout manager. We can do so by calling the method setLayout, and specify the number of rows and columns, as follows:

```
setLayout( new GridLayout( numRows, numColumns ) );
```

Once we set the layout for our applet to GridLayout, we now have to add the components. When we call the add method, we specify which component we want to add to the applet. The format for the add method:

```
add( component );
```
GridLayout adds each component in order to the cells from the top in left-to-right order.
It also stretches out each component to fill the entire space of the cell.

93

```
import java.awt.*;
import javax.swing.*;
public class GridLayoutEx extends JApplet
{
    JButton b1, b2, b3, b4, b5, a, b;
    JPanel pane;

    public void init( )
    {
        setLayout( new GridLayout(3,2) );
        b1 = new JButton( "First" );
        b2 = new JButton( "Two" );
        b3 = new JButton( "Three" );
        b4 = new JButton( "Four" );
        b5 = new JButton( "Five" );
        add( b1 );
        add( b2 );
        add( b3 );
        add( b4 );
        add( b5 );
        pane.setLayout( new BorderLayout( ) );
        a = new JButton( "go" );
        b = new JButton( "there" );
        pane.add( a, BorderLayout.NORTH );
        pane.add( b, BorderLayout.CENTER );
        add( pane );
    }
}
```

The JPanel *pane* has two buttons: go and there

We can add spacing between each of the components by adding the horizontal and vertical spacing when we create the GridLayout.
In the example above, change the setLayout method call to be the following:

```
setLayout( new GridLayout( 3, 2, 15, 5 ) );
```

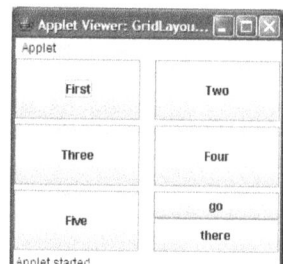

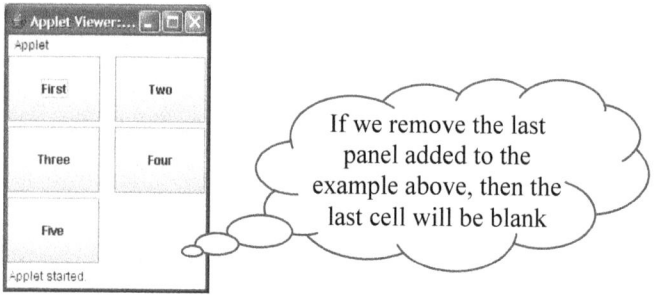

If we remove the last panel added to the example above, then the last cell will be blank

BoxLayout

BoxLayout sets up a grid-like structure in either a row or a column. BoxLayout differs from GridLayout in that it is only one row or column, and the components added to the cells are not stretched to fill in the space. BoxLayout is good for creating toolbars.

When using the BoxLayout, we first need to specify that we want to use this layout manager. We can do so by calling the method **setLayout**, and specify whether to create a row or column, as follows:

ROW

```
setLayout( new BoxLayout( getContentPane( ), BoxLayout.X_AXIS ) );
```

COLUMN

```
setLayout( new BoxLayout( getContentPane( ), BoxLayout.Y_AXIS ) );
```

Once we set the layout for our applet to BoxLayout, we now have to add the components. When we call the add method, we specify which component we want to add to the applet. The format for the add method:

```
add( component );
```

BoxLayout adds each component in order to the cells in order either from top to bottom if set to Y_AXIS or in left-to-right order if set to X_AXIS.

An example is shown below:

```
import javax.swing.*;
public class BoxLayoutEx extends JApplet
{
    JButton one, two, three;

    public void init( )
    {
        one = new JButton( "one" );
        two = new JButton( "two" );
        three = new JButton( "buckle my shoe" );

        setLayout( new BoxLayout( getContentPane( ), BoxLayout.Y_AXIS ) );
        add( one );
        add( two );
        add( three );
    }
}
```

BoxLayout in JPanel

Using BoxLayout in a JPanel is a little tricky. First we need to declare the JPanel. Then we can call the method **setLayout** on the JPanel and instantiate a new BoxLayout. When we do this, we need to specify the JPanel again as well as the axis. For example:

```
JPanel verticalPanel = new JPanel( );
verticalPanel.setLayout( new BoxLayout( verticalPanel, BoxLayout.Y_AXIS ) );
```

```java
import javax.swing.*;
public class BoxLayoutExInJPanel extends JApplet
{
  JButton one, two, three;
  JPanel verticalPanel;

  public void init( )
  {
    setLayout( new BoxLayout( getContentPane( ), BoxLayout.X_AXIS ) );
    one = new JButton( "one" );
    two = new JButton( "two" );
    three = new JButton( "buckle my shoe" );

    verticalPanel = new JPanel( );
    verticalPanel.setLayout( new BoxLayout( verticalPanel, BoxLayout.Y_AXIS ) );
    verticalPanel.add( new JButton ( "abc" ) ) ;
    verticalPanel.add( new JButton( "def" ) );
    verticalPanel.add( new JButton( "ghi" ) );
    add( verticalPanel );

    add( one );
    add( two );
    add( three );
  }
}
```

Warnings!

We have to be careful about adding components. If we attempt to add a component that is already contained elsewhere, it will be <u>removed and reinserted!</u> For example, in the following code, button1 will only be displayed in the EAST section!

```
import java.awt.*;
import javax.swing.*;
public class Warning2 extends JApplet
{
   JButton button1, button2;
   public void init( )
   {
      button1 = new JButton( "one" );
      button2 = new JButton( "two" );
      JPanel panel = new JPanel( );
      panel.setLayout( new BorderLayout( ) );
      panel.add( button1, BorderLayout.NORTH );
      panel.add( button2, BorderLayout.WEST );
      panel.add( button1, BorderLayout.EAST );
      add( panel );
   }
}
```

Another warning is that we can only put one component into a region with some of the layout managers. For example, if we try to add two components to the NORTH of BorderLayout, only the <u>last component added will be displayed</u>!

```
import java.awt.*;
import javax.swing.*;
public class Warning1 extends JApplet
{
   JButton button1, button2;
   public void init( )
   {
      button1 = new JButton( "one" );
      button2 = new JButton( "two" );
      JPanel panel = new JPanel( );
      panel.setLayout( new BorderLayout( ) );
      panel.add( button1, BorderLayout.NORTH );
      panel.add( button2, BorderLayout.NORTH );
      add( panel );
   }
}
```

 *To change the background color of the applet, create a JPanel and call .setBackground on the JPanel, add the JPanel to the BorderLayout.CENTER of the applet and add all components to the JPanel.*

Structuring with Methods

Now is a good time to see a structured approach to using methods for layouts. Based on a BorderLayout type of structure, we can divide up the applet into the 5 regions, and create methods to set up each region.

```java
import javax.swing.*;
import java.awt.*;
public class Structure extends JApplet
{
        // Declare all your variables HERE!
        // this includes all your components!
    JPanel title, leftside, rightside, center, bottom;
    public void init( )
    {
        // set up a layout manager for the applet here
        setupTitle( );
        setupLeftSide( );
        setupRightSide( );
        setupCenter( );
        setupBottom( );
    }
    public void setupTitle( )
    {
        // add title at the top of applet
    }
    public void setupLeftSide( )
    {
        // set the layout manager for the left side
        // set background color on this panel
        // add components on this panel
        // add this panel to the applet
    }
    public void setupRightSide( )
    {
        // set the layout manager for the right side
        // set background color on this panel
        // add components on this panel
        // add this panel to the applet
    }
    public void setupCenter( )
    {
        // set background color on this panel
        // add components on this panel
        // add this panel to the applet
    }
    public void setupBottom( )
    {
        // set the layout manager for the bottom panel
        // set background color on this panel
        // add components on this panel
        // add this panel to the applet
    }
}
```

Design

When we work with applets, we need to first design how the GUI should look (GUI = Graphical User Interface). The first step is to determine the purpose of the applet – is it for your company, your personal resume, your list of favorite recipes, your favorite football team statistics, etc.? Once we figure out what we want to do, the next step is to lay it out on paper (you can also use various computer programs to do this, but it can take a lot more time than simply sketching it on paper). Sometimes it helps to look at other programs to get ideas of what to do. Fortunately, the Internet is an excellent source for design – with tons of good and bad examples. We can use these as templates for our own design ideas.

A drawing example is listed below. Notice how each of the components is labeled as the type of component, and all JPanels are specified with their layout managers. It is much easier to figure this out on paper before attempting to program it – even for the programmer experts!

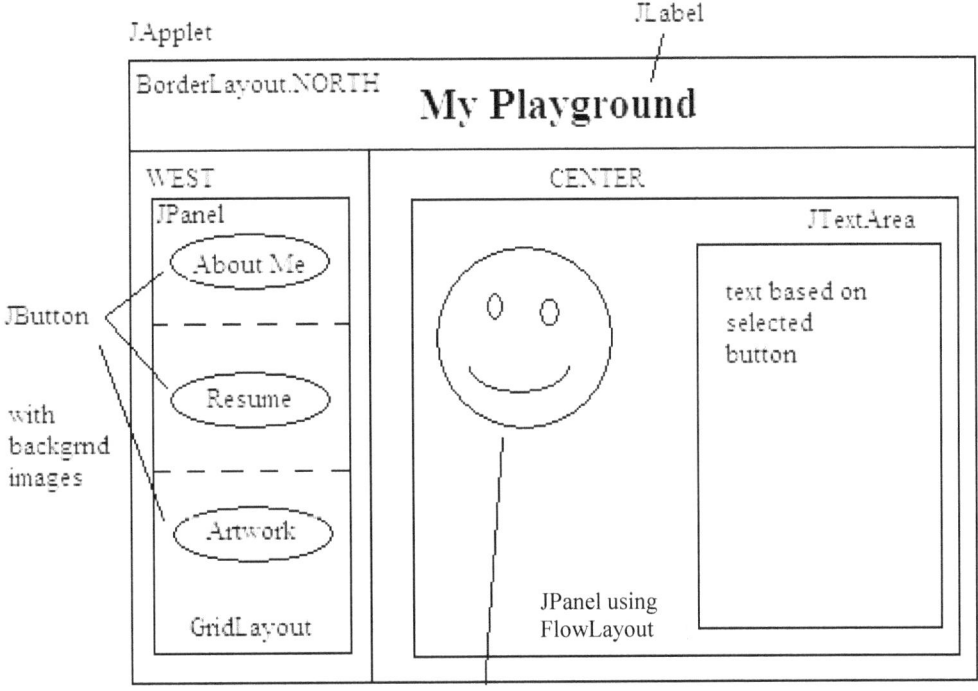

Image in a JLabel

Let's take a look at another example. The diagram below depicts how would achieve the end result. For practice, try programming this GUI.

This example shows different colors for different panels to make it easier to see how we could divide up the layout. We can see how the overall aspects of the applet is based on BorderLayout, with a title in the NORTH and checkboxes in the SOUTH. The left side then appears to have a GridLayout with two rows of the same size. In the bottom one, it looks like we can use GridLayout again for the three labels and drop-down boxes.

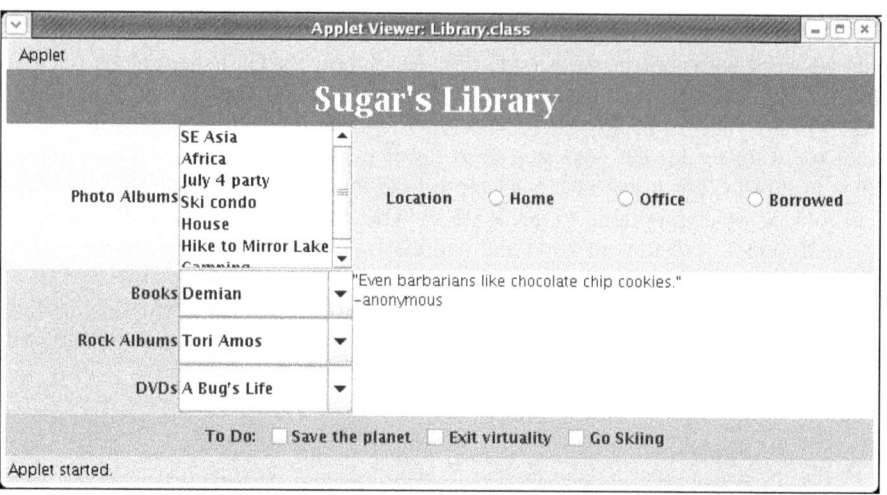

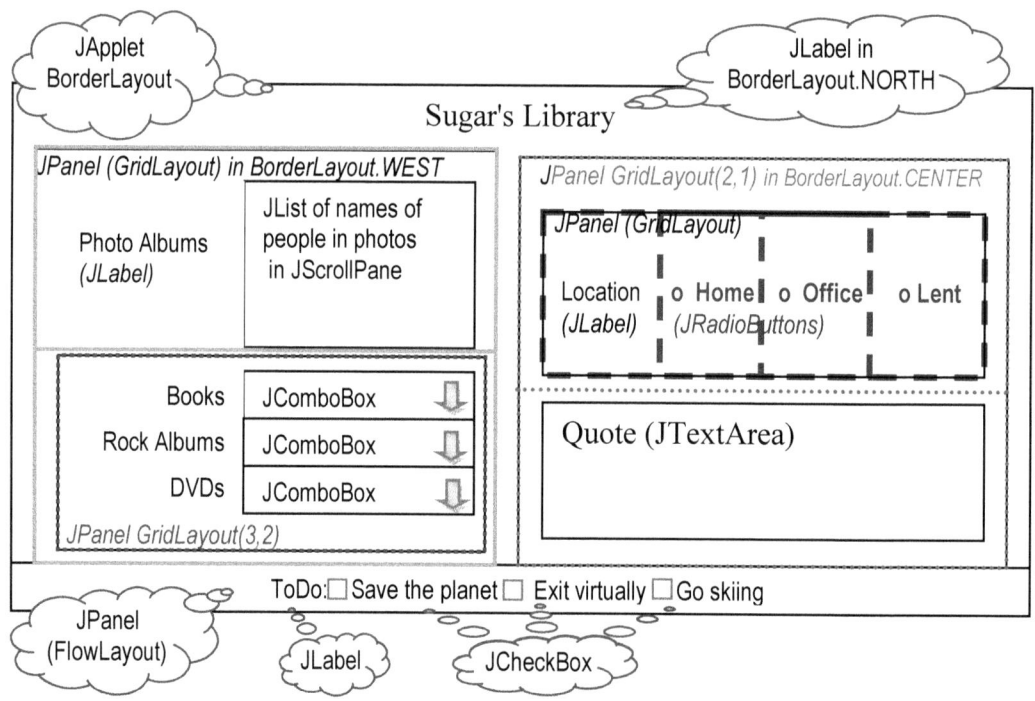

Design Guidelines

Although designing may seem easy, it's actually very complex if we want good design. There are many theories on good design, and we're going to look at a few of them related to web site design.

One Page: Web sites (and applets that run on them) are best if the user does not have to scroll on the page. Unfortunately this is difficult as everyone has different sized monitors and use different resolutions. However, we can keep this in mind when we choose how much to display and the size of our images.

Navigation: Users should be able to navigate easily to different areas. With applets, we can use JTabbedPane to allow users to access different screens easily.

Recognition vs. Recall: It is easier for a user to recall something by selecting it in a list as opposed to having to type it in (which also leads to errors). Use drop-down lists for selections with many standard items (e.g., state code) or radio buttons for smaller set of selections.

Consistency: Keep buttons in consistent locations (e.g., OK and Cancel), use same color scheme (otherwise the user's eyes go nuts focusing), etc.

Progress Indicators: Update the user of what's going on when processing something big – such as loading a lot of images. Use a status notice or a progress bar.

Who are you?: Users that surf the net and especially those who buy from a website like to see some humanity associated with the site. Adding an "About Us" info page on who's behind the company and/or design of the website helps users feel more comfortable and secure with your website. It is also very important to provide contact information – such as an e-mail address and/or phone number (well, unless it's your personal homepage – you may not want random people calling you up!).

Not too much!: Some developers get carried away with nifty things they can do – one of the worst examples is the use of too many animated graphics. Anything that moves/animated catches the user's eyes and draws them up there. If they are trying to read an article on your site, it is difficult when their eyes are constantly drawn to different areas on the screen.

Readable text: Substantial text that is either too small or too big is hard to read, as well as text beyond 80 characters in width. Beyond 80 characters, users have a hard time finding their place as they go to the next line.

Case Study

In the remaining chapters, we're going to develop a program for a coffee club. We'll follow the Software Engineering methodology of the Software Development Life Cycle (SDLC). The SDLC consists of four main phases: Requirements, Design, Implementation and Testing. The Requirements phase is when we discuss with the client their wants and needs. Usually a requirements document is written up to document the client's specification. The second phase is Design, where the programmers develop solution ideas to meet the client's needs. It is important to note that no programming is involved in this phase! Instead, the GUI (graphical user interface) will be drawn out and potential solutions sketched out designating layout managers, extra JPanels and all the components necessary. The Design phase may also include descriptions on how to implement the solution, without actually writing any programming code. Once a solution is designed, we proceed to the Implementation phase where the program is written in a programming language. The Testing phase is partially accomplished by the programmers as they write the code and test to ensure that their piece works. Once the system is complete, a full testing cycle is run as if the client were using the system. This is necessary as sometimes programs will break after a particular sequence of instructions or after running for a period of time. All of these phases are iterative; as we start at the Requirements and proceed into the design phase, we may need to go back to the client for clarification and modify the requirements before working again through the Design phase. Sometimes projects will go through all four phases and be in the Testing phase when something comes up that necessitates modifying the Requirements again, work through a modified design, implement the modification and repeat the testing.

First we begin with a client's request. For our examples, our clients are providing us a sketch up of what they want their program to look like and some simple directives of how it should work. This is similar to the homework assignments you get! In industry, we would fully document every single feature and how it should work to use for legal purposes in determining whether the final software product actually delivers what the company promised for the pay.

Our first example is from a coffee club company. They want to sell a monthly membership where their customers will get a gourmet coffee, regional gift and information sheets each month. They have four main views of the applet: Home, Join the Club, FAQ and Contact Us. Below are two screenshots of how the client wants the overall look-and-feel to be for the applet.

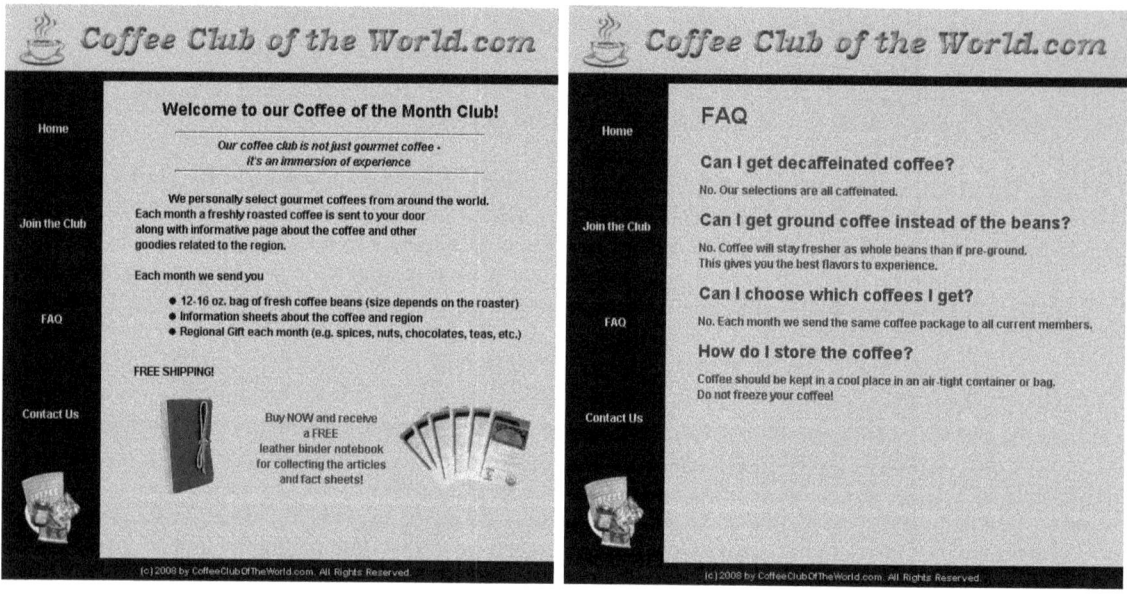

The client isn't providing screen shots for the "Join the Club" and "Contact Us" buttons, but wants you to come up with something that looks professional. For our purposes, we're going to leave that as an exercise for you! We're going to walk through the design phase for setting up these two screen shots, and in later chapters we'll look at various ways to implement it.

Our first step is to sketch out how we can design a layout for each of these screens. We're going to work through the main screen. Since we have a screen shot, we'll use that as our basis for sketching our design and draw our design on top. Overall our applet can make use of BorderLayout, since the logo would work well in BorderLayout.NORTH, the buttons with the image in a GridLayout in BorderLayout.WEST, and the copyright information listed in BorderLayout.SOUTH. The inside of the main center section takes a little work. At first glance, it appears there are many JLabels necessary to get this to work. But in actuality, we can create lists and the lines using HTML codes inside our JLabel so we can put the top half of the screen all into one JLabel. The HTML code for the horizontal lines is the <HR> tag, and for lists we use <UL> to start an unordered list, and the <LI> tag for each list item.

The bottom section then has an image, text and another image. We could design this with three JLabels inside a separate JPanel using GridLayout. The following sketchup shows our design idea.

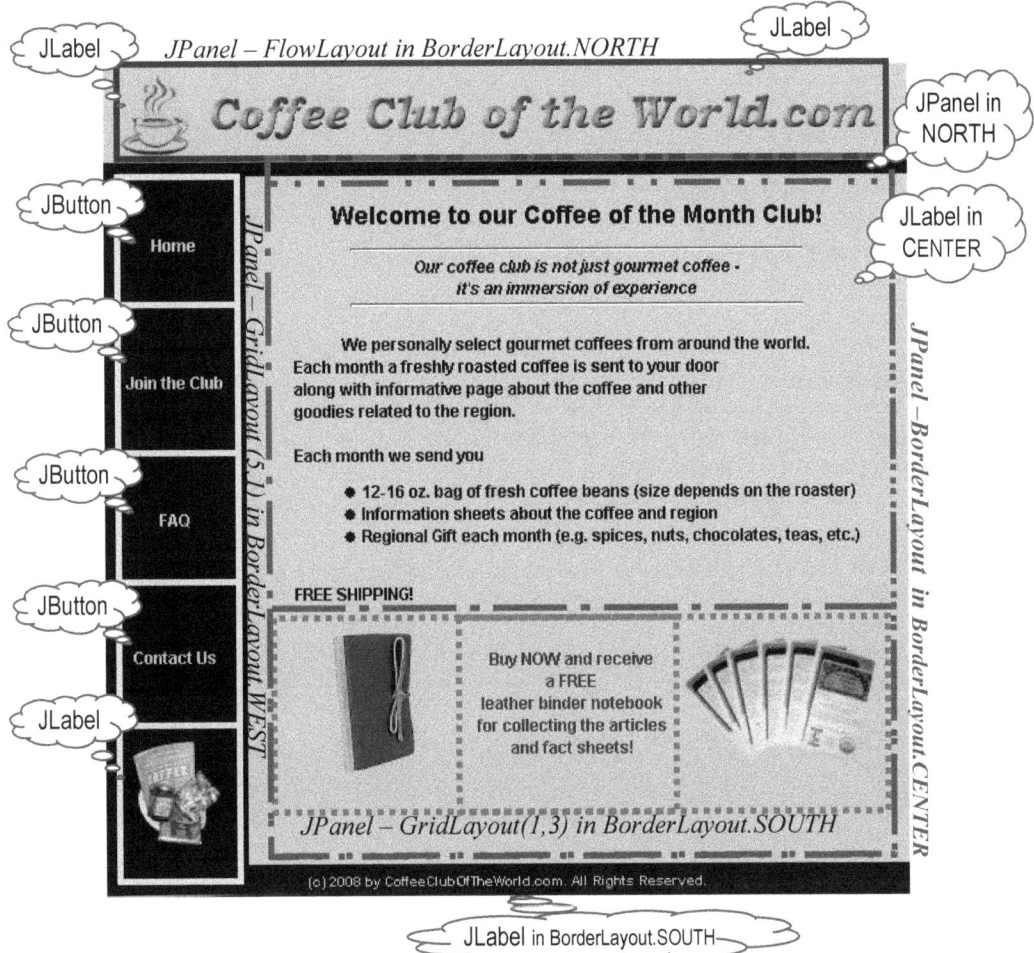

Now that we have a design to work from, we can start to implement the GUI. The first step is to copy the Structure class to set us up for using BorderLayout. We can remove the code for the right side since we're not using it. The code is developed below.

```java
import java.awt.*;
import javax.swing.*;
public class CoffeeClubDesign extends JApplet
{
    JButton home, join, faq, contact;
    Image img;
    JLabel title, logo, copyright, ntbkImg, ntbkDesc, infoSheets, welcomeMsg;
    Color tanColor = new Color( 204, 153, 51 );
    Color darkColor = new Color( 51, 17, 0 );
    Color bkgrdColor = new Color ( 17, 8, 0 );
    JPanel leftside, top, center, welcomePanel, separator, freeNotebook;
    public void init( )
    {
```

```java
        setLayout( new BorderLayout( ) );
        doTitle( );
        doLeftSide( );
        doBottom( );
        doCenter( );
    }
    public void setupButton( JButton b )   // method makes it easier to do all method calls for each button
    {
        b.setContentAreaFilled( false );
        b.setBorderPainted( false );
        b.setFocusable( false );
        b.setForeground( tanColor );
        leftside.add( b );
    }
    public void doTitle( )
    {
      img = getImage( getCodeBase( ), "coffeeLogoMetal.png" );
      logo = new JLabel( new ImageIcon(img) );
      img = getImage( getCodeBase( ), "logoName.png" );
      title = new JLabel( new ImageIcon(img) );
      top = new JPanel( new FlowLayout( ) );
      top.add( logo );
      top.add( title );
      top.setBackground ( tanColor );
      add( top, BorderLayout.NORTH );
    }
    public void doLeftSide( )
    {
      // left side menu
      leftside = new JPanel( new GridLayout(5,1 ) );
      leftside.setBackground ( darkColor );
      home = new JButton( "Home" );
      join = new JButton( "Join the Club" );
      faq = new JButton( "FAQ" );
      contact = new JButton( "Contact Us" );
      setupButton( home );
      setupButton( join );
      setupButton( faq );
      setupButton( contact );
      JLabel basket = new JLabel( new ImageIcon( getImage( getCodeBase( ), "coffeeBasket.png" ) ) );
      leftside.add( basket );
      add( leftside, BorderLayout.WEST );
    }
    public void doBottom( )
    {
      copyright = new JLabel( "<HTML><SMALL>(c) 2008 by CoffeeClubOfTheWorld.com."
          + "  All Rights Reserved.", JLabel.CENTER );   // String can go across multiple lines using + to append
      copyright.setForeground( tanColor );
      copyright.setOpaque(true);
      copyright.setBackground( darkColor );
      add( copyright, BorderLayout.SOUTH );
    }
```

```java
public void doCenter( )
{
    center = new JPanel ( new BorderLayout( ) );
    center.setBackground( tanColor );
    // add the dark separator as a blank colored panel in the NORTH of the center panel
    separator = new JPanel( );
    separator.setBackground ( darkColor );
    separator.setPreferredSize( new Dimension( 10, 20 ) );
    center.add( separator, BorderLayout.NORTH );

    welcomePanel = new JPanel( new FlowLayout( ) );
    welcomePanel.setOpaque( false );
    welcomeMsg = new JLabel( "<html><center><H2>Welcome to our Coffee of the Month Club!"
        + "</h2><HR WIDTH=80%><I>Our coffee club is not just gourmet coffee – "
        + "<BR>it's an immersion of experience"
        + "<HR WIDTH=80%><BR>We personally select gourmet coffees from around the world. "
        + "<BR></CENTER>Each month a freshly roasted coffee is sent to your door "
        + "<BR>along with informative page about the coffee and other <BR>goodies related to the region."
        + "<BR><BR>Each month we send you"
        + "<UL><LI>12-16 oz. bag of fresh coffee beans (size depends on the roaster)"
        + "<LI>Information sheets about the coffee and region "
        + "<LI> Regional Gift each month (e.g. spices, nuts, chocolates, teas, etc.)"
        + "</UL><BR><B>FREE SHIPPING!</B><BR> <BR> ");
    welcomeMsg.setForeground( darkColor );
    welcomePanel.add( welcomeMsg );
    // create the bottom free notebook offer
    freeNotebook = new JPanel( new GridLayout( 1, 3 ) );
    freeNotebook.setOpaque(false);
    ntbkImg = new JLabel( new ImageIcon( getImage(getCodeBase( ), "ntbk.png")));
    ntbkDesc = new JLabel( "<HTML><CENTER>Buy NOW and receive<BR> a FREE<BR>"
        + " leather binder notebook <BR>for collecting the articles<BR>and fact sheets!" );
    infoSheets = new JLabel( new ImageIcon( getImage(getCodeBase( ), "IntoSheets.png")));
    freeNotebook.add( ntbkImg );
    freeNotebook.add( ntbkDesc );
    freeNotebook.add( infoSheets );
    welcomePanel.add( freeNotebook, BorderLayout.SOUTH );
    center.add( welcomePanel, BorderLayout.CENTER );
    add( center, BorderLayout.CENTER );
}
}
```

Summary

- Layout managers determine how and where components are to be displayed.
- Some layout managers will stretch components to fill the space.
- Call setLayout method to change the layout of a container.
- JPanels can be nested inside other JPanels and the applet.
- The default layout for the JApplet is BorderLayout. The default layout for JPanel is FlowLayout.
- GridLayout makes each cell of equal size: same widths, same heights. The width is not necessarily the same as the height.
- The number of rows and columns must be specified when creating a GridLayout (e.g. setLayout(new GridLayout(numRows, numCols));   ).
- BorderLayout has only 5 regions: North, South, West, East and Center. Each region follows specific rules on how it stretches its components.
- If nothing is added to the center in BorderLayout, a gap *may* appear in the applet.
- When adding components to a container with BorderLayout, the location must be specified with the component in the add method (e.g. add(component, BorderLayout.EAST);).
- The default alignment for JLabel if there is only text is to be left-justified. The default for JLabel if there is only an image is to be center-justified. JLabels with both text and an image require us to specify the alignment when we create the JLabel.
- Attempting to add a component that is already contained elsewhere will be removed and reinserted.
- Only one component can be added to each region in BorderLayout and GridLayout. To fit multiple components in a particular region, add them to a separate JPanel and then add this JPanel to the region.
- Structuring code can be done based on regions of the applet based on the layout manager in use.
- Design is an important step *before* starting to program.
- Design of the GUI should be sketched out, fully specifying all JPanels with their layout managers.
- All components should also be displayed with the appropriate text and Java component type.
- Good design includes following standard practices and be consistent.
- Designs should not have too much in a single view.

Exercises

1. True or False. The default layout for a JPanel is NullLayout.
2. Which layout manager(s) position everything based on equal-sized rows and columns?
1. Which layout manager positions everything based on a north, south, east, west, and center positioning?
2. True or False: FlowLayout defaults to laying out components centered both horizontally and vertically.
3. True or False: FlowLayout, GridLayout and BorderLayout resize objects to stretch either horizontally or vertically (or both).
4. Given the following code, draw out how it should look when I run it: **Be SURE to draw out the SIZE and location of each item.**

```
import java.awt.*;
import javax.swing.*;
public class layoutsEx extends JApplet
{
  JLabel l_cat ;
  JTextField tf_age;
  JButton b_go;
  JCheckBox cb_fun;
  public void init( )
  {
        setLayout( new BorderLayout( ) );
         l_cat = new JLabel( "Cat:", JLabel.RIGHT );
         tf_age = new JTextField( 2 );
         b_go = new JButton( "Go" );
         cb_fun = new JCheckBox( "Fun?" );
        add( l_cat, BorderLayout.NORTH );
        add( tf_age, BorderLayout.CENTER );
        JPanel p2 – new JPanel( );
        p2.add( b_go );
        add( p2, BorderLayout.EAST );
        JPanel p3 = new JPanel( );
        p3.add( cb_fun );
        add( p3, BorderLayout.SOUTH );
  }
}
```

5. True or False: We can nest JPanels inside another JPanel.
6. True or False: A layout manager is an object that determines the way that components are arranged in a container.
7. True or False: When using BorderLayout, we can only add one thing to each of the five sections.
8. What is the code to set the layout for the applet to 2 rows and 3 columns?
9. True/False: If we add a component that is already contained elsewhere, it will be displayed in two locations.

10. Develop a program using various layout managers and JPanels for the following:

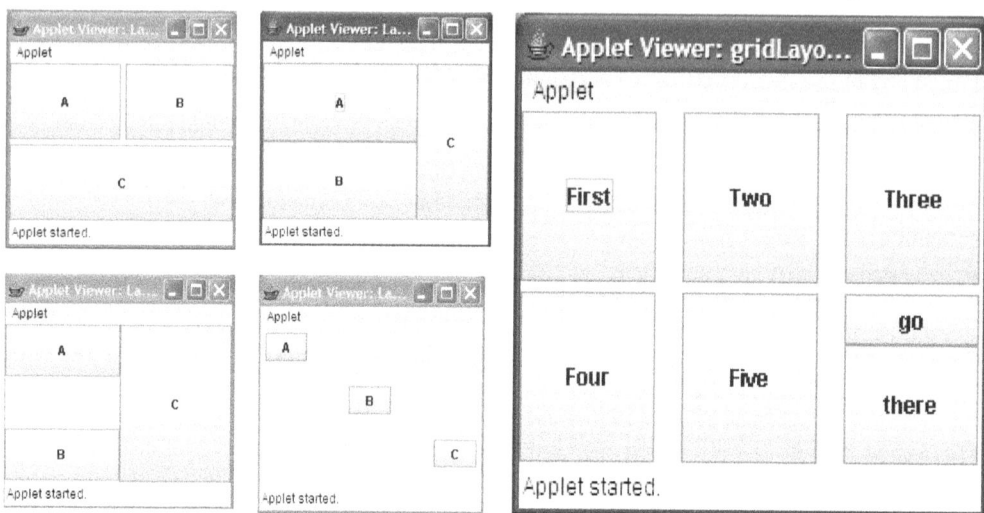

11. Create an applet that has 3 sets of radio button groups asking the user for their favorite color, movie and TV show. Add a title at the top: "What's your favorite?". Display appropriately.

12. Create an applet that is a party invitation. Include a text field for them to enter their name, a checkbox to designate whether they are planning on attending or not, a drop-down list of what they will bring (appetizer, main dish, dessert), radio buttons for how many guests they will bring (0, 1, 2) and a text area for them to describe their costume. Display appropriately with labels associated with each component and a title at the top of the applet.

13. Create an applet that displays a library of all your music. Include a list with each song listed, a drop-down list for different genres, and buttons to play/stop a song.

14. Create an applet of all your favorites: movies, bands, artists, people, quotes. Select appropriate components to display each.

15. For the first drawing example in this chapter, create sketches for when the other two buttons get selected: Resume and Artwork. What should be displayed? How should it be layed out? How many art pieces should be displayed at a time? How will the user get to see the rest of them?

16. Layout a full design for any corporate web page on the Internet.

17. Layout a full design for your mail program.

18. What are some good practices in design of web pages?

19. What's the problem if the text is more than 80 characters across?

20. Sketch out a design for a company website. Find one on the Internet and draw out how you would implement it in Java.

21. Sketch out a design for your own personal website. Include your resume, portfolio or information about your friends.

22. Sketch out a design for your school's main website.

Chapter 6

Data Types and Operators

*They aren't all just objects to me,
some of them are primitive.*

Objectives:

- Variables
    - Rules
    - Reserved Words
    - Data Types
    - Instance Variables
- Math Operators
    - Math class
    - Arithmetic
    - Relational
    - Conditional
- Order of Operations
- Instanceof Operator
- Conversions
    - int to String
    - String to int or double
    - Object to specific type

Variables

What is a *variable*? Remember from chapter 3 that a variable is data that is referenced by a named identifier. What's an *identifier*? It's anything we name, such as the name of a class, the name of a method we create, or the name of a variable!

The first thing we do with variables is *declare* them. We do this by specifying the data type (e.g. JButton, Graphics, JLabel) and then specify a name for us to reference it.

Examples:

```
JButton submit;
JTextField tf_street;
Graphics grp;
```

We can name our variables almost anything we want, as there is no real limit to the length of the variable name. However, we do have to conform to a few rules concerning our variable names.

Rules:

1. Can contain any letter, number, the underscore _ or dollar sign $
2. Can not begin with a number
3. Must not be a Java *reserved word (Java keyword)* see table below (e.g. public, class, void, etc.)

No spaces in names!

Some conventions that most programmers follow include:

1. Constants are in all uppercase letters (e.g., MAX_SCORE) declared with keyword `final`
2. Classes are named in mixed case, with the first letter a capital letter (e.g. MyFirstApplet)
3. Methods are named in mixed case as well, but the first letter is usually lower-case letter (e.g., paintComponent, setupButtons)
4. Variables are named in mixed case with the first letter a lower-case letter. These should be meaningful, such that a person reading the variable name can decipher what data is stored in the variable. The alphabet is not acceptable: a, b, c, d, ... Good examples are:
   firstName, lastName, midtermGrade, labGrade, qtyShirts, qtyShorts
5. Be consistent: e.g. Frequency as freq or fqy or fq: temp**Fqy**, hit**Fqy**, cnt**Fqy**

Java Reserved Words

There are many reserved words in Java, meaning that we cannot use them as identifiers because they already have special meaning as part of the Java syntax.
The following is a list of Java reserved words:

abstract	continue	for	new	switch
assert	default	goto	package	synchronized
boolean	do	if	private	this
break	double	implements	protected	throw
byte	else	import	public	throws
case	enum	instanceof	return	transient
catch	extends	int	short	try
char	final	interface	static	void
class	finally	long	strictfp	volatile
const	float	native	super	while

Data Types

Java is an *object-oriented* language, meaning that all of the data types we work with are *Objects* - except for the eight primitive data types. The difference is that a primitive data type can only keep track of one value, whereas objects may keep track of multiple data of various data types and also have methods that we can call on it.

For the most part, we're only going to be concerned with four primitive data types that are used most frequently:

int – for whole numbers (negative and positive)
double – real numbers (negative and positive)
char – single characters
boolean – holds either the Java reserved word `true` or `false`

The 8 primitive data types are as follows:

	data type	description	number of bits used to represent the number
integers	byte	Byte-length integer	8-bit
integers	short	Short integer	16-bit
integers	int	Integer	32-bit
integers	long	Long integer	64-bit
reals	float	Single-precision floating point	32-bit
reals	double	Double-precision floating point	64-bit
	char	A single character	16-bit Unicode character
	boolean	holds either the value true or false	1-bit

Examples of usage:

```
int    age = 13;
double gpa = 3.76
char   firstInitial = 'E';
boolean isHappy = true;
```

Primitive data types can only store ONE value, and have no methods we can call on them

Examples of objects:

```
String name = "Cookie Monster";
JLabel title = new JLabel( name );
JButton submit ;
```

Object data types can store multiple values, and have methods associated with them.

With objects, we can call methods on them:

```
String value = nameTextField.getText( );
```

Instance Variables

Instance variables are those that are declared at the top of the class, just inside the squiggly brackets after our class header. This is where we want to <u>declare</u> our variables, not necessarily <u>initialize</u> them. Remember, declaring a variable means we specify the data type and the variable – we do not set it equal to anything! This will become very important that we follow this methodology as we begin working with images and events.

Instance variables are accessible throughout our entire class. This way, we can reference variables inside any methods that we create. If we declare a variable inside a method, then we only have access to that variable inside that method only! So usually we want most of our variables to be instance variables, so we need not worry about whether we can access them or not.

```java
import java.awt.*;
import javax.swing.*;
public class int2String extends JApplet
{
   JLabel name;                    // Instance variables are declared here
   JButton go;
   public void init( )
   {
       setLayout( new FlowLayout( ) );
       name = new JLabel( "Cookie Monster" );
       go = new JButton( "GO!" );      // We can reference instance
       add( name );                    // variables throughout our
       add( go );                      // program
   }
}
```

A problematic example follows: What's wrong and what happens?

```java
import javax.swing.*;
import java.awt.*;
public class Fun extends JApplet
{
        public void init( )
        {
               JButton  b_submit = new JButton( "Submit" );
               JTextField  tf_state = new JTextField( "great", 10 );
               doLeftSide( );
        }
        public void doLeftSide( )
        {
               JPanel p = new JPanel( new FlowLayout( ) );
               p.add( b_submit );
               p.add( tf_state );
        }
}
```

This is a common mistake new programmers make. The problem is that the variables **b_submit** and **tf_state** are declared inside the **init** method, and therefore only accessible inside the init method. When we try to reference these variables inside the **doLeftSide** method, it doesn't know anything about these variables!

To fix this code, we need to declare these variables at the top of the class.

Math

Mathematical expressions are essential in programming. To express mathematical equations in Java, we can make use of methods in the Math class and many provided operators. Java operators include arithmetic, relational and conditional operators.

Math Class Methods

The Math class contains some methods that can be useful to us in our programs. This way we don't have to reinvent the wheel on performing common functions such as determining the absolute value of a number or finding trigonometric values. Below is a table of some common math functions that are available in the Math class.

Math class method	Example	Description
number abs(number)	double posX = Math.abs(x);	Returns the absolue value of the number, where the data type will match int or double
double ceil(double)	double x = Math.ceil(y) ;	Returns the number rounded to the next higher nteger value
double exp(double)	double x = Math.exp(double)	Returns Euler's number e raised to the power of a double value
double floor(double)	double x = Math.floor(y);	Returns the number rounded down to the next lower integer value
double log(double)	double x = Math.log(y) ;	Returns the natural logarithm (base e) of a double
double pow(double1, double2)	double x = Math.pow(x, y) ;	Returns the value of x^y
double sqrt(double)	Double x = Math.sqrt(y) ;	Returns the square root of a double

Advanced Concept

The methods we reference in the Math class are declared *static*, which allows us to call the methods without instantiating an instance of the Math class. For example, usually we would need to write code such as

```
Math m = new Math( );
m.sqrt( 43.2 );
```

We do not do this for the methods in the Math class because they are declared with the keyword *static*. The static keyword designates that the method can be accessed simply by calling the method on the class, such as `Math.sqrt( 25 )`.

If we wanted to make our own methods static in our classes, we can do so by adding the static keyword in the method header. Methods can only be declared static when they are either fully encompassed modular methods or methods to access shared class variables which are declared static. In other words, they cannot access instance variables. The example below demonstrates how to declare a method static:

```
public static double sqrt( double x )
```

Arithmetic Operators

Mathematical operations is important in many programs. The standard mathematical operations are available, but some may be a twist from what you know. For example, the plus sign is used for adding numbers as well as concatenating Strings together. In fact, anytime a String and a number is added with the plus sign, it forces the number to concatenate to the String.

Another twist is Java division. When we divide two integer numbers, we end up with an integer result – the remainder is dropped! However, if we use division on two double values, the result is what you would think.

The modulus operator is sometimes a new concept to students. The percent sign % represents the modulus operator. It computes the remainder of dividing the two operands. Essentially, it returns the value thrown away during integer division.

Operator	Java code	Description
+	op1 + op2	Adds op1 and op2; also used to concatenate strings
-	op1 - op2	Subtracts op2 from op1
*	op1 * op2	Multiplies op1 by op2
/	op1 / op2	Divides op1 by op2
%	op1 % op2	Computes the remainder of dividing op1 by op2

Examples:

```
int x = 7 + 2 * 3;              // equals 13
int y = 14 / 5;                 // equals 2
int z = 14 % 5                  // equals 4
double yy = 14.0 / 5;           // equals 2.8
String a = "Hello" + "World";   // equals "HelloWorld"
String result = "x is " + x;    // equals "x is 13"
```

When would the use of the modulus function be useful? When do you use this technique in your daily life?

Shortcuts

Our assignment statements can include the variable on both sides of the equal sign:

```
int x = 5;
x = x * 2;       // x gets the value 10
```

A shortcut way to express this is to apply the operator before the equal sign and leave off the variable on the right side:

```
int x = 5;
x *= 2;          // x gets the value 10
```

There are shortcuts for each of the operators:

Operator	Java code	Expansion
+=	x += 3;	x = x + 3;
-=	x -= 3;	x = x – 3;
*=	x *= 3;	x = x * 3;
/=	x /= 3;	x = x / 3;
%=	x %= 3;	x = x % 3;

Relational Operators

Relational operators are used to compare two operands. Although you may be familiar with some of these, take notice of the Java syntax. For example, to see if two operands are the same, Java uses two equal signs together. We cannot use a single equals statement because that is for assignment of a value to a variable.

All of the relational operators return a boolean value, either true or false. This will be very useful to us when we start using conditionals and loops.

Operator	Use	Description
>	op1 > op2	Returns true if op1 is greater than op2
>=	op1 >= op2	Returns true if op1 is greater than or equal to op2
<	op1 < op2	Returns true if op1 is less than op2
<=	op1 <= op2	Returns true if op1 is less than or equal to op2
==	op1 == op2	Returns true if op1 and op2 are equal
!=	op1 != op2	Returns true if op1 and op2 are not equal

Examples:

```
int x = 3;
boolean g = (x >= 10);      // equals false
boolean h = ( x != 3 );     // equals false
boolean j = ( x == 3 );     // equals true
```

The symbols ≤ and ≥ are NOT in Java! (Remember – they're not on our keyboards!)

Let's practice the math operators so far and create a method that determines whether an integer value is even or odd. If we name our method **isEven**, then we should return true if is is even and return false if it is an odd number. Remember that true and false are boolean values. So our method header should be the following

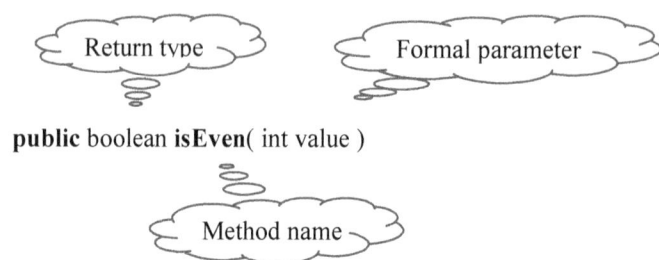

public boolean **isEven**(int value)

To fill in the method body, we need to figure out a way to determine whether an int is even or odd. This can be tricky, but once you see some examples like this one you'll start thinking inline with a computer. Remember how the % operator works? The modulus operator % gives us the remainder after dividing two numbers. What are all even numbers divisible by? 2! So if we divide by 2 and get a zero for a remainder, then the number is an even number.

So how to we implement this in code?

    return value % 2 == 0;

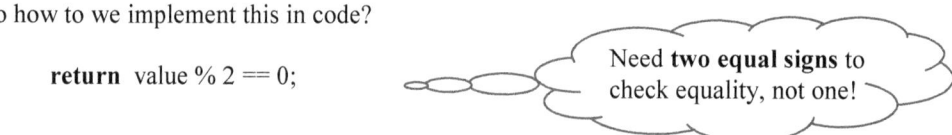

Warning!

When we check for equality on numbers, we cannot use the == operator on floating point data types. The problem is that some floating point numbers cannot be accuaratly stores in memory, so an approximation occurs. The following simple example shows this problem:

```
import java.awt.*;
import javax.swing.*;
public class ProbDblPrecision extends JApplet
{
    JLabel value;
    public void init( )
    {
        double val = 1.0/5 + 1.0/5 + 1.0/5 - 0.6;
        value = new JLabel( "val should be zero but is = " + val );
        add( value );
    }
}
```

Applet Viewer: ProbDblPrecision.class
Applet
val should be zero but is = 1.1102230246251565E-16
Applet started.

So we need a different solution to checking whether a floating point value is *nearly equivalent* to a particular value. We can do this by checking to see if the difference between the two values are within a specified tolerance of error. In our solution we can make use of the absolute value function in the Math class to find the absolute value of the difference and determine if this value is less than the tolerance. The example below shows a solution:

```
Math.abs(  val1 - val2 ) < 0.0001
```

Object data types such as Strings are also problematic for a different reason. Variables that are object data types are actually reference pointers to somewhere in memory where the object itself is stored. Since two objects (e.g. Strings) may have the same value but stored in two different places in memory, the == will return false even though the values each object contains are the same. Therefore we need to use the .equals method on the two strings. Below is an example of how memory may look and why the == may fail even though the two strings have the same value.

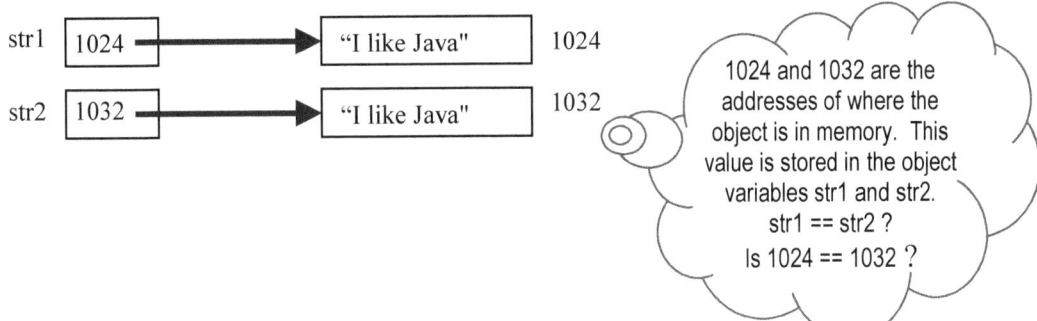

> We cannot compare Strings or other objects using the relational operators. If we want to determine whether two objects are equal, we need to use the .equals method.
> Example:
>   String name = "Elizabeth";
>   boolean isEqual = name.equals("elizabeth");
> In this example, isEqual would be false because 'E' is differeent than 'e'.
> If it was   name.equals("Elizabeth") it would then be true.

Conditional Operators

Operator	Use	Description
&&	op1 && op2	Returns true if op1 and op2 are both true
||	op1 || op2	Returns true if either op1 or op2 is true
!	!op	Returns true if op is false

Examples:

```
int x = 5;
int y = 10;
boolean a = ( x == 5 && y < 10 );      // equals false
boolean b = ( x == 5 || y < 10 );      // equals true
boolean c = ( a && b );                // equals false
boolean d = !c;                        // equals true
boolean e = ( 0 < x && x <= 10 );      // equals true
```

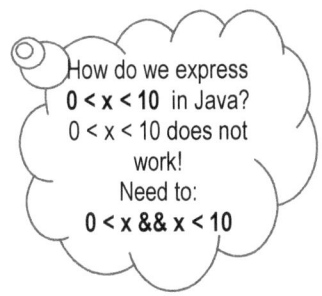

In the examples above, a is false because y is not less than 10, and since it is an AND operation (&&) both x==5 and y<10 have to be true for it to be true. b is true because only one of the operands need to be true, and x==5 is true.

To evaluate conditional operators, we sometimes set up truth tables to define all the possibilities that could occur. Each row represents a possible state in the program based on each of the variables. The variables used evaluate to either true or false. The number of rows is based n the number of variables involved: if there are two variables (e.g., A and B) then there are four possible permutations: A is false

117

and B is false, or A is false and B is true, or A is true and B is false, or A is true and B is true. Then we create a column for different conditional operator combinations.

To make it easier to fill out, we sometimes represent true as 'T' and false as 'F'.

VARIABLES

A	B	!A	!B	A && B	A || B	A && !B	!(A || !B)
F	F	T	T	F	F	F	F
F	T	T	F	F	T	F	T
T	F	F	T	F	T	T	F
T	T	F	F	T	T	F	F

Order of Operations

Determining the order of operations in a combination expression is based on the following:

1. ( ) parenthesis first
2. unary operators (positive/negative !)
3. *, /, %
4. +, -
5. < <= > >= instanceof
6. == !=
7. &&
8. ||
9. =

Examples:
$$3 * (2 + (3 - 4 * 2 + (5-1))) =$$
$$3 * (2 + (3 - 4 * 2 + 4)) =$$
$$3 * (2 + (3 - 8 + 4)) =$$
$$3 * (2 + (-1)) =$$
$$3 * 1 = 3$$

```
5 + 2 >= 7 && 5 - 2 != 0
     7 >= 7 && 3 != 0
       true && true
           true
```

boolean isGood = 5 + 2 >= 7 && 5 - 2 != 0;
isGood is equal to true

instanceof Operator

The **instanceof** operator tests whether a variable is a particular class type, such as JButton or JCheckBox.
Examples:

  obj **instanceof** JButton
  obj **instanceof** JCheckBox
  obj **instanceof** JFrame

Can not check if something is an instance of a primitive data type (e.g. int, boolean).
We will make use of this instanceof operator when we get to events.

Converting Types

Sometimes we want to convert one type to another type: for example, if we want to append an int to a JTextArea, we need it to be a String before we can do so. This chapter covers some of the common conversions we need to know.

Converting int to String

Call the method `valueOf` from the `String` class:

```
int value = 5;
String strValue = String.valueOf( value );
```

```
import java.awt.*;
import javax.swing.*;
public class int2String extends JApplet
{
   JComboBox list;
   int num1, num2, num3;

   public void init( )
   {
      setLayout( new FlowLayout( ) );
      num1 = 10;
      num2 = 20;
      num3 = 30;
      setupList( );
   }
   public void setupList( )
   {
      list = new JComboBox( );
      list.addItem( String.valueOf(num1) );
      list.addItem( String.valueOf(num2) );
      list.addItem( String.valueOf(num3) );
      add( list );
   }
}
```

Converting String to int or double

To convert a String to an int, we use the method `parseInt` from the `Integer` class:

```
int value = Integer.parseInt( String );
double dval = Double.parseDouble( String );
```

Examples:

```
String text = "52";
int num = Integer.parseInt( text );
double cost = Double.parseDouble( textFieldCost.getText( ) );
```

Converting from a String to a number is important for tasks where we need to read a value from a JTextField or JComboBox where the user entered a value that we need to convert to a number so we can perform mathematical operations on it.

Converting Object to String or component

Sometimes when we call particular methods, they return `Object` types instead of the actual type like `String` or `ImageIcon`. What we need to do is called **casting**: to cast the Object type to a specific type like String or ImageIcon.

The way we cast is specify before the Object the data type in parenthesis:

```
String str = (String )obj;
ImageIcon str = (ImageIcon )obj;
JButton button = (JButton )obj;
```

This can be useful when grabbing elements out of a JList or JComboBox:

```
ImageIcon icon = (ImageIcon ) list.getSelectedValue( );
String txt = (String ) combobox.getSelectedItem( );
```

This is also useful inside our event listener methods, after we pull out the object type:

```
Object src = event.getSource( );
JButton button = (JButton )src;
```

Since we haven't covered events yet, hold on to this example and reference back to it later.

Fun Interlude - Java Reserved Words

Circle the 20 Java reserved words hidden in the following puzzle.

```
v a e s l w h i w e t u r n e x t e n e d i o
v o l s e f a i s t h i e t r x n u o p s r l
r u i t r t u r x e f r w e p o t r r u e s p
o u p d f a l u s i c h e n w l i p l s s r w
w p e r l c l p u b l i s d x t e m t r c u e
s r p u b l i c s o a h l f w h i l e r h i p
s o t h w a x m e l s u p n f r t c t a u p o
u t f a l s i n p r i v a t e o t p u p a w v
p e c l a s u p e l s n e s n w r e r r e x d
e c l e f t i p i i e o x e l s e i s a d v e
t r u x t a t i e x s m t s k i t e o x w r r
a s t e f t l s a r u r e s k i u r l s e u o
x v d x s i s s s s p i n n e x r e a e p b t
p r o t e c t e d i r g d x t u n u s u e l e
f a m e r s s s b f a l s e h s e e s m r i c
p l c n l u a f o x t l w x i d n e t x s c t
a s m f t r e r o n o h r t s u p e p m o i d
a p c o o k i e m o n s t e s t a t t r u x l
x w v n w e l i b x u b l u a e a l r e o a k
i l o v e t o s k i p l p t l e c h d p x t f
t x e x t h r w s s l n e t x e s t m a l s e
```

Summary

- Variable names can contain any combination of letters and numbers, the _ and $ as long as the first does not begin with a number.
- Idenitifers include any variable name, class name, method name that the programmer defines.
- Identifiers cannot be a Java reserved word.
- Java reserved words have special meaning in the Java programming language.
- The Math class contains many useful methods.
- There are 8 primitive data types in Java. The most commonly used ones are: int for integers, double for floating point values, char for characters and boolean for true or false values.
- Division of two integers results in an integer; any fractional part is disguarded.
- % operator gets the remainder from integer division.
- When comparing Strings, the == operator may not work; instead use the .equals method.
- Order of operations for expressions follow similar to math. The = is evaluated last.
- The instanceof operator checks to see if a variable instance is of a particular type of object. It cannot be used on primitive data types.
- Truth tables show all states of a program based on the variable values.
- Numbers can be converted to Strings by calling String.valueOf(number).
- Strings can be converted to a number by calling Integer.parseInt(String) to get an integer or Double.parseDouble(String) for a double.
- Data types of type Object need to be cast to a specific data type such as String or JButton. This is necessary when getting items out of a JList or JComboBox.

Exercises

1. Which operator would you use to determine whether a number is even?
2. Which operator would you use to determine if a number is divisible by three?
3. What is the result when you add a number to a String? e.g., 25 + "1010"
4. What can you not use for a variable name?
5. Is it required that you name your variables beginning with a lower case letter?
6. What is the line of code to calculate the square root of 99?
7. What is the code to determine the absolute value of an integer named amt?
8. What is the main integer type used?
9. True or False: Java reserved words can be used for class names but not variable names.
10. What two values can a boolean be equal to? Do you put quotes around the values?
11. Why declare variables at the top of the class and not inside the methods?
12. What's a good example in real life for using the modulus function?
13. What's the difference between relational and conditional operators?
14. True or False. The expression p && q will be true if either or both is true.
15. True or False. Variables declared inside a method can be referenced anywhere in the class.
16. What is the final value of xVal in the following Java code? xVal = 12 / 7;
17. What is the final value of xVal in the following Java code? xVal = 12 % 7;
18. How do you convert a String to an int? From an int to a String?
19. Can you use the instanceof operator on a char?
20. How would you represent "not equal" in Java?
21. Fill in the following truth table

A	B	A || !B	!(A && ! B)
F	F		
F	T		
T	F		
T	T		

Chapter 7

Conditionals

What if?

Objectives:

- Conditionals
- If Structure
- If-else Structure
- Comparing data types
- Nesting if Statements
- Switch Statements
- Comparing if-else and switch
- Example: Seasons

Conditionals

Conditional statements allow us to choose which statements we would like to execute. Usually the *flow of control* of a program follows line-by-line through the code. Conditional statements allow us to skip a statement or statements based on some condition. A condition must evaluate to either `true` or `false` – boolean values. The conditional structures in Java are: if, if-else and the switch structure.

If Structure

The `if` statement allows us to select which statements we would like to execute. This allows us to have some statements that may or may not execute. The format of the `if` statement is shown below:

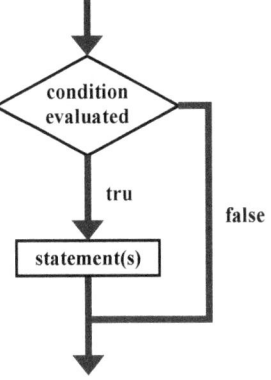

```
if   ( booleanExpression )
{
      statements;
}
```

where *booleanExpression* is any expression that evaluates to either `true` or `false` and the statements are any number of Java statements. If the booleanExpression evaluates to true, then the statements are executed. If the booleanExpression evaluates to false, then the statements are skipped.

Note: the squiggly braces are optional if there is only one statement under the if, but required if we want more than one statement for the if.

An example of an `if` structure:

```
if (   value > maxAllowed )
   warning.setText( "Warning! Value exceeds the maximum allowed." );
```

Commonly we have boolean expressions that make use of relational or logical operators. We can use these operators discussed in the previous chapter. For example:

```
if ( value <= 0 || value > 10 )
   warn.setText( "Value out of range. Enter a # between 1 & 10." );

if ( total != 100 )
   status.setText( "Total does not add up to 100." );
if ( ! hasPermission )
   status.setText( "You don't have permission to access." );
```

hasPermission is a variable of type boolean

In the examples above we can decipher the data types that would work for the variables involved in each boolean expression. Value and total could be any integer or floating point data type and hasPermission has to be a boolean since the not operator ! only works on boolean values.

We can also utilize some of the methods provided from our components. For example, we can check to see if our radio buttons and checkboxes are selected or not with a call to the isSelected method on the components.

```
if ( ! chkboxIsAttending.isSelected( ) )
   msg.setText( "You aren't coming?" );
```

Some of our components have multiple states. For example, a JList may have 3 options that can be selected. To figure out which one was selected, we first determine which option is selected then check to see if it is equal to one of the three options. If we have a JList named myList with the options "red", "blue" and "green", we can customize a message to the user based on the selection with the following code:

```
String selection = (String )myList.getSelectedValue( );
if ( selection.equals( "red" ) )
   msg.setText( "Red is HOT!" );
if ( selection.equals( "blue" ) )
   msg.setText( "Blue is cool" );
if ( selection.equals( "green" ) )
   msg.setText( "Green's my favorite color too!" );
```

Notice that when we compare strings to other strings we need to use the .equals method instead of the == operator. Although the == works most of the time, it is inconsistent based on how memory is allocated. The .equals method verifies character by character to see whether the two strings are identical or not (and is case-sensitive).

This last example leads us to another conditional structure we can use, called the if-else structure. Assuming our JList allowed only one option to be selected at a time, a more proper structure would check each option until it finds one that matches and then quit checking for other matches. This is what the if-else structure does.

If-else Structure

The if-else structure allows us to choose between different statements based on which condition is true. We can have an option of two sets of statements with an if-else statement, where the first group of statements (statementsA) is executed if the booleanExpression is true and the statementsB are executed if the booleanExpression is false:

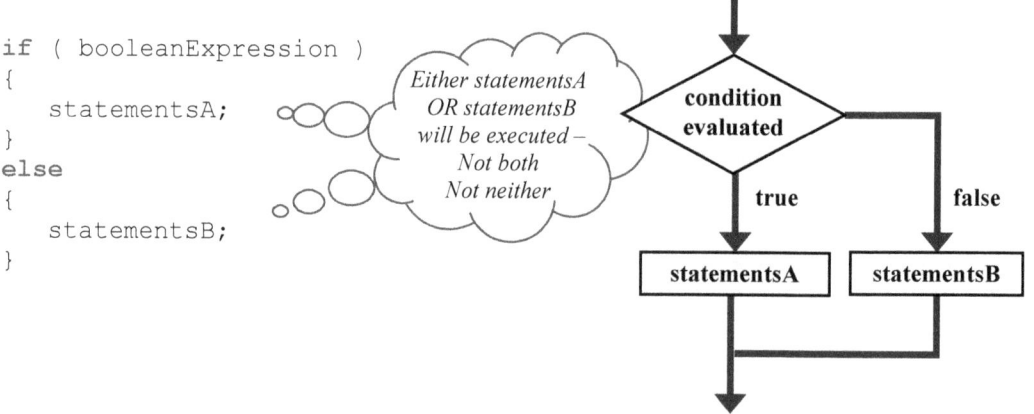

 Note: the squiggly braces optional for either the if or the else clause if there is only 1 statement but required if we want more than one statement.

```
import javax.swing.*;
import java.awt.*;
public class check extends JApplet
{
  JCheckBox isHappy;
  JTextArea textarea;

  public void init( )
  {
      setLayout( new FlowLayout( ) );
      isHappy = new JCheckBox( "Happy?", true );
      textarea = new JTextArea( 3,10);

      if ( isHappy.isSelected ( ) )
          textarea.setText ( "You're so happy!" );
      else
      {
          textarea.setText( "Why not happy?" );
      }
      add( isHappy );
      add( textarea );
  }
}
```

NOTE: we have not learned how to do events yet, so the saying doesn't change when we click on the checkbox. We can make more interesting programs once we learn events, but it is critical that we first learn how to use the if statement for processing events.

We can use the operators we learned in the previous chapter for our boolean expressions:

if A is greater than or equal to B, set the text area to say "A is great"	if (A >= B) textArea.setText("A is great");
if C is not equal to zero, then display "Good to Go" in the textarea	if (C != 0) textArea.setText("Good to Go");

If the text the user entered in the textField is equal to "Cookie Monster", then display "WELCOME Cookie Monster!" in the text area (2 separate lines) otherwise display "Who are you?" in the text area	String text = textField.getText( );
	if (text.equals("Cookie Monster")
	{
	    String display = "<HTML>WELCOME
" + name + "!";
	    textarea.setText(display);
	}
	else
	    textarea.setText("Who are you?");

Going back to our `JList` example from the previous section, we can incorporate the 3 if-statements into an if-else structure. To do so, we need to extend our `else` statement to an `else if`.

```
String selection = (String )myList.getSelectedValue( );
if ( selection.equals( "red" ) )
   msg.setText( "Red is HOT!" );
else if ( selection.equals( "blue" ) )
   msg.setText( "Blue is cool" );
else if ( selection.equals( "green" ) )
   msg.setText( "Green's my favorite color too!" );
else
   msg.setText( "Nothing's selected!" );
```

The if-else structure allows us to have a default else case to handle the situation where none of the options are selected. As we start at the top of the if-else structure, once one of the boolean expressions evaluates to true, the rest of the if statements and the final else within the if-else structure are skipped. If none of the boolean expressions evaluates to true, the final else clause will be executed.

Let's do an example. Let's write a method that determines whether or not the first character in a String is a vowel or not. First we need to determine how to layout the method, so let's start by defining the method header. We need to take a String as a parameter and return either true or false depending on whether the String begins with a vowel. We'll need a boolean variable since we'll need to return this value. So we start with the following method stub:

```
public boolean beginsVowel( String str )
{
        boolean  isVowel;

        return isVowel;
}
```

Now we need to implement the body of the method. We need to start by getting the first character in the String. Remember there is a method called charAt that we can call on strings and specify the index of the character we want. Java starts counting at zero, so the first character in the string is at index 0. This method returns a char to us. Our string is named **str** which we defined inside our method header parameters

```
char firstLetter = str.charAt( 0 );
```

There are several ways we could implement the if statement to check for each vowel. One way we can do this is by using lots of the OR operator ||. Checking for equality on char data types can be done with the == operator. For example:

```
public boolean beginsVowel( String str )
{
        char firstLetter = str.charAt( 0 );
        boolean  isVowel;
        if ( firstLetter == 'A' || firstLetter == 'a' ||
                     firstLetter == 'E' || firstLetter == 'e' ||
                     firstLetter == 'I' || firstLetter == 'i' ||
                     firstLetter == 'O' || firstLetter == 'o' ||
                     firstLetter == 'U' || firstLetter == 'u'  )
               isVowel = true;
        else
               isVowel = false;
        return isVowel;
}
```

Note: An easier way might have been to first convert the string to upper-case or lower-case letters then our if statement would have 5 less equality checks. Can you think of any other ways to implement this example?

Comparing Data Types

Usually when we want to compare two data values, we think of using the == to check for equality between two values. This works all the time on primitive data types (e.g. int, double, char, boolean, etc.) but when we're dealing with object data types we need to be careful about what we're actually comparing. To understand what's going on, we need to take a quick look at how these values are stored in memory. When we declare a variable, a spot in memory is reserved for us to put the value of the variable. Memory is accessed through address numbers, but that is difficult for us to remember; hence we use variable names to reference those spots in memory. If we declare a primitive data type, the value we assign to our variable goes directly into that spot in memory. However, all object variables are *references* to another spot in memory where the actual object is stored. Below is a figure depicting these two differences.

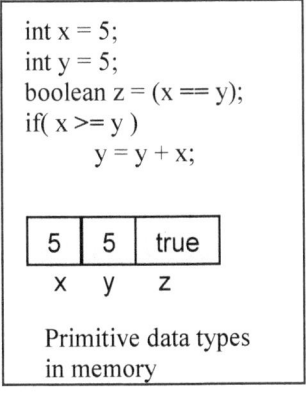

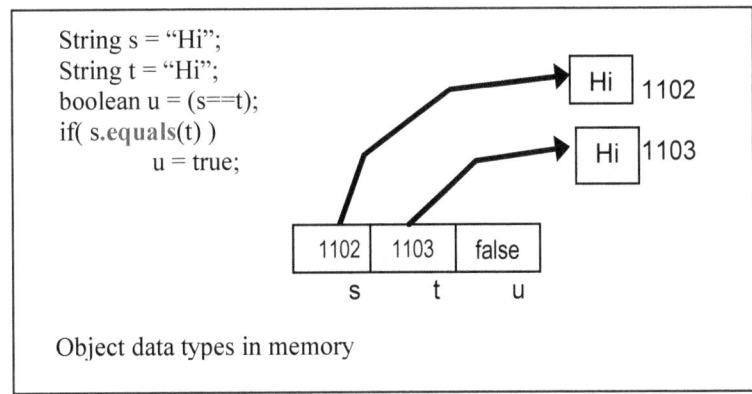

When we use the == operator, we are comparing if the spot in memory for the variable is equal to the other variable's value. In the case of primitive data types, this always results in evaluating whether the two variables contain the same value. When working with object data types, the == will return to us whether or not the variables are *referencing* the same spot in memory – in other words, is the address stored in the variable's spot in memory the same. This does *not* return whether the two objects happen to have the same value. This is an important distinction. Therefore, when we want to determine whether the two objects have the same *value*, we call the .equals method instead of using the ==.

So when do we use == versus using the .equals method? First rule is to always use == when comparing primitive data types. We can also use the == operator when we get to events and want to determine whether or not a particular component (JButton/JCheckBox/JRadioButton) triggered an event. However, when comparing two Strings we always want to use the .equals method. For example, let's say we have a JTextField named **tf_userName** and we want to see if the user typed in the value "Terry". We can call the **.getText( )** method on our JTextField component to get the String the user typed in, then call the **.equals** method on the string to see if it matches with "Terry". If it does match, we'll display a welcome back message in the same JTextField; otherwise we'll display an error message.

```
String userEntered = tf_userName.getText( );
if ( userEntered.equals( "Terry" ) )
        tf_userName.setText( "Welcome back Terry!" );
else
        tf_userName.setText( "Error: I don't know you!" );
```

Nesting if Statements

The statements inside an if statement can be almost any statement – including another if statement! This allows us to make another decision after the first decision is made. For example, if we need to find the max value between three numbers we could nest some if statements:

```
if ( x > y )
{
   if ( x > z )
   {
        maxValue = x;
   }
   else                     //  if x is bigger than y but not z, then z must be the biggest
        maxValue = z;
}
else if ( y > z )    // we only get here if y is >= to x
{
   maxValue = y;
}
else
   maxValue = z;
```

What happens if x is 5 and y is 5 and z is 8? If x is 5, y is 2 and z is 6? What happens if the squiggly braces are removed?

Switch Statements

The switch statement is another conditional structure we can use. It can be easier to read than an if-else structure, but has some limitations. The switch statement can only compare integer and character values to a set of *cases*. Therefore, we cannot use the switch statement for doubles, Strings or other objects.

The switch statement evaluates an expression in parenthesis that must be either an int or char. The structure requires squiggly braces around the set of cases. Each case identifier ends with a colon ':' before the statements are listed. The keyword break is used to transfer the flow of control of the program to the end of the switch statement, skipping all other statements and cases listed below. Without the break statement, the program will continue through the statements below until either a break statement is executed or the end of the switch structure is reached. The last case in the switch structure can be a default case to handle the situation when none of the cases above match to the expression in parenthesis at the beginning of the switch statement. Note that the break and default statements are not required within the switch structure.

In the example below, we take the numerical grade entered by the user in the JTextField named tf_grade, convert it to an integer and store that value in the variable grade. If the number is between 0 and 100, if we divide by 10 (integer division, so the remainder is truncated) then we end up with an integer value between 0 and 10. This makes it easy for us to display a custom message back to the user based on their achievement level. Notice that if the user got a 100% or anything in the 90's, we want to display the same message; therefore we do not need a break statement between those two case statements.

```java
        int grade = Integer.parseInt( tf_grade.getText() );
        switch( grade/10 )
        {
                case 100:
                case 90:
                        tf_grade.setText( "You ROCK!");
                        break;
                case 80:
                        tf_grade.setText( "Doin' good");
                        break;
                case 70:
                        tf_grade.setText( "Rather average" );
                        break;
                default:
                        tf_grade.setText( "Study More!" );
        }
```

Let's go back and re-do the example from the if-else section on writing a method that returns whether or not the first letter is a vowel. By using a switch statement, we can have each case of a vowel character fall through to the same statement to set the isVowel variable to true. The default case can be used to set the value to false.

```java
        public boolean beginsVowel( String str )
        {
                boolean  isVowel;
                char firstLetter = str.charAt( 0 );
                switch( firstLetter )
                {
                        case 'A':    case 'a':
                        case 'E':    case 'e':
                        case 'I':    case 'i':
                        case 'O':    case 'o':
                        case 'U':    case 'u':
                                isVowel = true;
                                break;
                        default:
                                isVowel = false;
                }
                return isVowel;
        }
```

Programming Tid-bits

When writing if-else structures, we want to avoid creating an empty if section just so we can use the else section. For example, in the example above if we only wanted to do something when the checkbox was not selected, we could write:

```java
        if ( isHappy.isSelected( ) )
        {

        }
        else
        {
            textArea.setText( "Why not happy?" );
        }
```

A better way to write this code is to make use of the not operator !

```
if ( ! isHappy.isSelected( ) )
{
    textArea.setText( "Why not happy?" );
}
```

Another example we'll see is when we want to see if something is true or not. We could write the code to see if a variable is equal to true or false, as such:

```
if ( myVariable == true )
    ...

if ( myVariable != false )
    ...
```

When we write an expression inside the parenthesis of the if statement, it has to evaluate to true or false. If our variable is already either true or false, then we needn't add code to see if it is == true or == false. For checking to see if it is true, we just put our variable inside parenthesis. For checking to see if it is false, we can use the not operator ! again. For example, we could change the above code to read as follows:

```
if ( myVariable )
    ...

if ( ! myVariable )
    ...
```

Comparing if and switch

When should we use an if instead of a switch, and vice versa? The first thing to determine is what the data type is that we're working with. Remember that the switch can only be used on expressions that evaluate to int or char. If the data type is anything other than int or char, then we'll need to use an if structure. If the data type is int or char, then we should next ask if the values are within a range such that an if statement may be easier to specify than listing each case value for a switch statement. For example, if we were to write a method to check if the user entered a proper number for the month in the year, the if structure is easier to write than the switch statement:

```
public String checkMonth( )
{
    String str = txtField_month.getText( );
    int month = Integer.parseInt( str );
    String result;
    if( month >=1 && month <= 12 )
        result = "Valid";
    else
        result = "Invalid";
    return result;
}
```

```
public String checkMonth( )
{
    String str = txtField_month.getText( );
    int month = Integer.parseInt( str );
    String result;
    switch( month )
    {
        case 1: case 2: case 3: case 4: case 5: case 6:
        case 7: case 8: case 9: case 10: case 11: case 12:
            result = "Valid";
            break;
        default:
            result = "InValid";
    }
    return result;
}
```

Example: Seasonal Weather

We can make use of some if statements to create an applet that changes based on the season and time of day. We'll display a house and if it's winter, have snow falling and snow on the ground. For spring, we'll have green grass and rain. In the summer we'll show green grass and blue skies. For fall we'll show our grass is brown. We'll also customize our sky to depict daytime or nighttime. The pictures below show what our applet should do depending on the season and time of day.

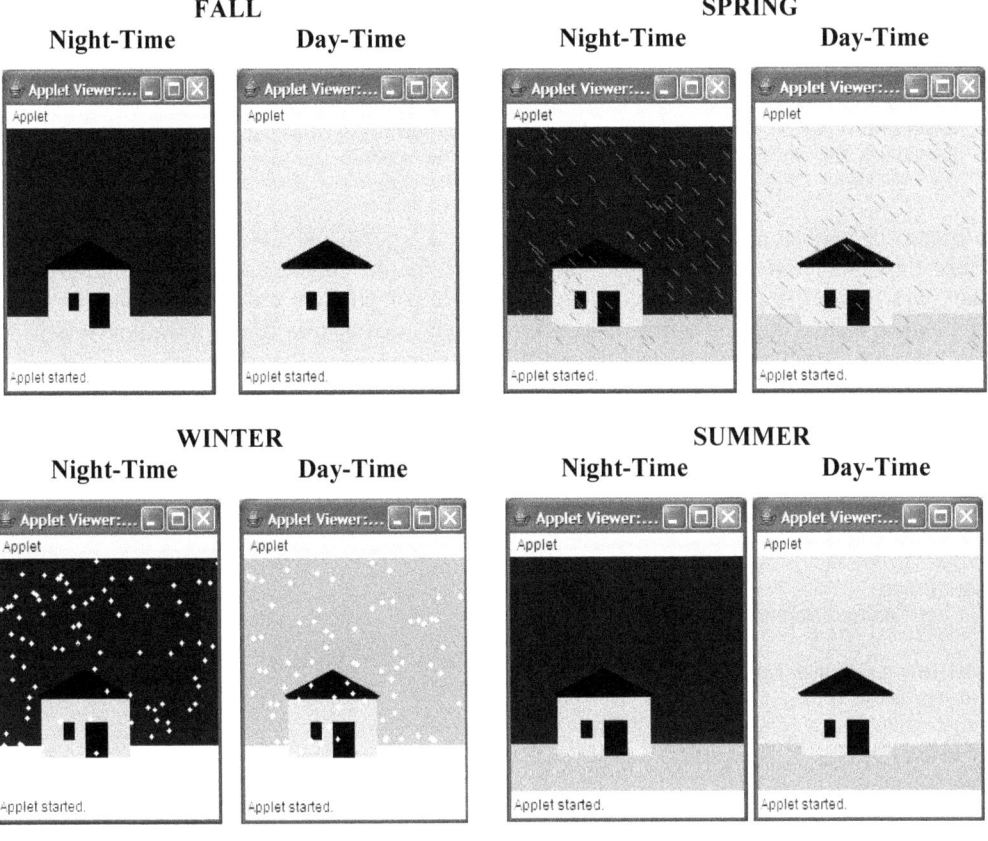

We can use the **Calendar** class to determine the time of the year to create a custom applet drawing. The Calendar class allows us to access the current date and time. The Calendar class is from the java.util package, so we also need an additional import statement at the top of our program.

```
import java.util.*;
```

To use the Calendar class, we can get the current time by calling **getInstance:**

```
Calendar rightNow;
rightNow = Calendar.getInstance( );
```

To get the current month or hour from our Calendar instance, we call:

```
int hour, month;
hour = rightNow.get( Calendar.HOUR_OF_DAY );
month = rightNow.get( Calendar.MONTH );
```

HOUR_OF_DAY returns a value betweeen 0 and 23 from the 24-hour clock

Other options in the Calendar class include:

Calendar.HOUR	hour on 12-hour clock
Calendar.MINUTE	the minutes
Calendar.SECOND	the seconds
Calendar.MILISECOND	the milliseconds
Calendar.HOUR_OF_DAY	hour based on 24-hour clock: 0..23
Calendar.TIME	time in milliseconds after Jan. 1, 1970 GMT
Calendar.DATE	the day within the month
Calendar.MONTH	the month
Calendar.YEAR	the year
Calendar.DAY_OF_MONTH	day of the month
Calendar.DAY_OF_YEAR	the day within the year
Calendar.WEEK_OF_MONTH	the week within the month
Calendar.WEEK_OF_YEAR	the week within the year

To create our weather program, we're going to create a separate class that extends the JPanel class. Inside this class, we need three instance variables: ints for the month and hour of the day, and a **Calendar** object to determine the current time. To make our program easier to manage, let's set up some methods to handle drawing different scenes. We need methods for drawing the house, sky, snow and rain. Let's get started with an outline for our WeatherClip class:

```java
import java.awt.*;
import javax.swing.*;
import java.util.*;
public class WeatherClip extends JApplet
{
   Calendar rightNow;
   int month, hour;
   public void paint( Graphics g )
   {
      rightNow = Calendar.getInstance( );
      hour = rightNow.get( Calendar.HOUR_OF_DAY );
      month = rightNow.get( Calendar.MONTH );
      drawSky( g );
      drawHouse( g );
   }
   public void drawHouse( Graphics g )
   {
      g.setColor( Color.BLACK );
      g.fillArc( 30, 50,  100, 90,  210, 120 );      // draw roof on house
      g.setColor( Color.PINK );
      g.fillRect( 40, 120, 80, 50 );                  // draw the main house
      g.setColor( Color.BLACK );
      g.fillRect( 60, 140, 10, 15 );                  // draw a window
      g.fillRect( 80, 140, 20, 30 );                  // draw the door
   }
   public void drawSnow( Graphics gr )   {
   }
   public  void drawRain( Graphics gr )   {
   }
   public void drawSky( Graphics g )   {
   }
}
```

Let's start by working on the drawSky method. In this method we need to check the hour of the day, which is one of our instance variables that we set. If this value is between 8am and 8pm inclusive, then it is daytime and we want our sky to be cyan. If the hour is before 8am or after 8pm, we should make our sky look dark with a dark blue. Once we set the color for the sky, then we can fill in a rectangular area for the sky. We can draw the sky with the following if statement:

```
public void drawSky( Graphics g )
{
   if ( hour >= 8 && hour <= 20 )
      g.setColor( Color.CYAN );
   else
      g.setColor( new Color( 25, 25, 112 ) );
   g.fillRect( 0,0, 200, 160 );
}
```

hour is an instance variable we declared at the top of our program, so we can access it inside our drySky method

Now we might want to customize daytime in winter with a gray sky. Winter months include December, January and February. So if it is daytime (if evaluates to true), then we'll nest another if statement to check to see if it is winter time. If it is, then we'll set the color to gray; if it is not, we'll set the color to cyan. Below is the final code for our drawSky method:

```
public void drawSky( Graphics g )
{
   if ( hour >= 8 && hour <= 20 )                       // daytime
   {
      if ( month == 12 || month ==1 || month==2)        // winter months
         g.setColor( new Color( 138,173, 217) );        // gray color
      else
         g.setColor( Color.CYAN );
   }
   else
      g.setColor( new Color( 25, 25, 112 ) );
   g.fillRect( 0,0, 200, 160 );
}
```

It's time we test our program to see if it works. It's important to work incrementally on a big program and make sure everything works as you go. Before we can test our code, we need to create the class that is the applet. Create a new class called Weather which extends the JApplet class. Inside the init method we'll draw our code in our paint method as we learned in Chapter 2.

To test that the sky really works, let's add some debugging lines in our WeatherClip class to test winter, summer, daytime and night. After we get the actual month and hour of the day, let's temporarily reassign these values so we can test our program. Let's set the month to January and the hour to 11. Run the program again and verify that the color is gray. Change the values again for month of May and hour set to 22. Run the program again and verify that the color is cyan. We'll use these temporary assignments to continue to check that our program is fully operational (since we don't want to wait a full year to keep checking it!). Once we're sure all the seasons and day/night settings paint correctly, we can comment out these two lines of code.

```
rightNow = Calendar.getInstance( );
hour = rightNow.get( Calendar.HOUR_OF_DAY );
month = rightNow.get( Calendar.MONTH );
month = 1;            // FOR DEBUGGING
hour = 12;            // FOR DEBUGGING
```

After we've drawn the sky and the house, we can draw in the ground and any rain or snow if appropriate. This is a good opportunity to make use of a switch statement. Since we have three cases (months) for each season, we could create three case statements that drop into the same set of statements.

```
switch( month )
{
    case 12:  case 1:  case 2:        // WINTER
                                      // ground is white
        drawSnow( g );
        break;
    case 3:  case 4:  case 5:         // SPRING
                                      // ground is green
        drawRain( g );
        break;
    case 6:  case 7:  case 8:         // SUMMER
                                      // ground is green
        break;
    case 9:  case 10:  case 11:       // FALL
                                      // ground is brown
        break;
}
```

Within each set of cases for a particular season, we add the code to draw in the ground: white for winter, brown for fall and green for spring and summer. In winter we'll also call the method drawSnow and in spring we'll call the method drawRain.

Implementing the drawSnow and drawRain methods are very similar. They both rely on selecting random numbers for (x, y) coordinates to draw a rain drop or snowflake. Using the Random class requires us to import the java.util package, but we've already added that to our code for the Calendar class. Now we can maintain an instance variable of type Random at the top of our WeatherClip class, and create an instance of the Random class at the beginning of our paintComponent method:

```
random = new Random( );
```

Inside our drawSnow and drawRain methods, we can get a random number for our coordinates by calling the nextInt method on our Random variable. To restrict the values it returns to ones that would fit within our dimensions of our applet, we'll send as a parameter the maximum value it should return (actually it will return a number between 0 and N-1 where N is the number we send as a parameter).

```
random.nextInt( 200 );
```

Now we can draw snow as many times as we like! Since we haven't covered loops yet, we'll have to copy and paste the line to randomly draw a rain drop or snowflake many times to get a lot of precipitation. Our drawSnow method now appears as follows:

```
public void drawSnow( Graphics gr )
{
    gr.setColor( Color.WHITE );
    random = new Random( );
    gr.fillOval( random.nextInt(200), random.nextInt(200), 5, 5 );
    gr.fillOval( random.nextInt(200), random.nextInt(200), 5, 5 );
    gr.fillOval( random.nextInt(200), random.nextInt(200), 5, 5 );
}
```

The drawRain method is similar except it draws lines in a gray color. Since lines require the (x, y) coordinates of the start and end of the line, we need to store the random numbers into a variable to be able to calculate the endpoint.

```java
public void drawRain( Graphics gr )
{
    gr.setColor( Color.GRAY );
    random = new Random( );
    int x = random.nextInt( 200 );
    int y = random.nextInt( 200 );
    gr.drawLine( x, y, x-5, y-5 );
    x = random.nextInt( 200 );
    y = random.nextInt( 200 );
    gr.drawLine( x, y, x-5, y-5 );
}
```

Our final program appears below

```java
import java.awt.*;
import javax.swing.*;
import java.util.*;
public class WeatherClip extends JApplet
{
    Calendar rightNow;
    int month, hour;
    Random random;

    public void paint( Graphics g )
    {
        rightNow = Calendar.getInstance( );
        hour = rightNow.get( Calendar.HOUR_OF_DAY );
        g.setColor( Color.GREEN );
        g.fillRect( 0,160, 200, 40 );
        month = rightNow.get( Calendar.MONTH );

// month=1;           // FOR DEBUGGING
// hour = 12;         // FOR DEBUGGING

        drawSky( g );
        drawHouse( g );

        switch( month )
        {
            case 12: case 1: case 2:          // WINTER
                g.setColor( Color.WHITE );
                g.fillRect( 0,160, 200, 40 ); // ground is white
                drawSnow( g );
                break;
            case 3: case 4: case 5:           // SPRING
                g.setColor( Color.GREEN );
                g.fillRect( 0,160, 200, 40 ); // ground is green
                drawRain( g );
                break;
            case 6: case 7: case 8:           // SUMMER
                g.setColor( Color.GREEN );
                g.fillRect( 0,160, 200, 40 ); // ground is green
                break;
```

continued

```java
          case 9: case 10: case 11:        // FALL
               g.setColor( new Color( 222, 184, 135 ) );
               g.fillRect( 0,160, 200, 40 );   // ground is brown
            break;
      }
   }
   public void drawHouse( Graphics g )
   {
      g.setColor( Color.BLACK );
      g.fillArc( 30, 50,  100, 90,  210, 120 );   // draw roof on house
      g.setColor( Color.PINK );
      g.fillRect( 40, 120, 80, 50 );              // draw the main house
      g.setColor( Color.BLACK );
      g.fillRect( 60, 140, 10, 15 );              // draw a window
      g.fillRect( 80, 140, 20, 30 );              // draw the door
   }

   public void drawSnow( Graphics gr )
   {
      gr.setColor( Color.WHITE );
      random = new Random( );       // right now draws only 3 snowflakes – use loops for more
      gr.fillOval( random.nextInt(200),  random.nextInt(200), 5, 5 );
      gr.fillOval( random.nextInt(200),  random.nextInt(200), 5, 5 );
      gr.fillOval( random.nextInt(200),  random.nextInt(200), 5, 5 );
   }

   public  void drawRain( Graphics gr )
   {
       gr.setColor( Color.GRAY );
       random = new Random( );
       int x = random.nextInt( 200 );
       int y = random.nextInt( 200 );
       gr.drawLine( x, y, x-5, y-5 );
       x = random.nextInt( 200 );
       y = random.nextInt( 200 );
       gr.drawLine( x, y, x-5, y-5 );
   }

   public void drawSky( Graphics g )
   {
      if ( hour >= 8 && hour <= 20 )
      {
         if ( month == 12 || month ==1 || month==2)    // winter
            g.setColor( new Color( 138,173, 217) );    // gray
         else
            g.setColor( Color.CYAN );
      }
      else
         g.setColor( new Color( 25, 25, 112 ) );       // night: dark-blue
      g.fillRect( 0,0, 200, 160 );
   }
}
```

When we learn loops, we'll make lots of rain and snow easily

Try adding to the program a tree that has a few leaves in spring, lots of green leaves in summer, multi-colored leaves in fall and no leaves in winter.

Summary

- Conditional statements allow us to choose which statements to execute.
- The if statement evaluates a boolean expression. If the boolean expression evaluates to true, the statements within the if statement are execute.
- Boolean expressions can include combinations of relational and logical operators as long as the final expression evaluates to either true or false.
- Squiggly braces are used to designate a block of statements attached to an if or else statement.
- An if-else structure executes the statements in the else block if the boolean expression evaluates to false.
- Each `else` requires a matching `if`.
- Strings and other objects should be compared to each other using the .equals method and not using the == operator.
- Switch statements evaluate either an integer or character value.
- Each case statement in a switch structure must be followed by a colon.
- The break and default statements in a switch structure are optional.
- If-else and switch structures can be nested inside each other.
- If a method returns a boolean value, it is not necessary to add a check: == true (e.g. `if ( btn.isVisible( ) )  )`
- The Calendar class can be used to get an instance of the current day/time stamp.

Exercises

1. True or False. An else clause is always matched to the nearest available unmatched if.
2. True or False. Curly braces are required with if structures.
3. True or False: An **else** clause is required with every **if** statement.
4. True or False. In Java, the statement **if (x = y)** is a valid construct of an if statement.
5. What is the value of the variable xyz after the following code segment?

   ```
   int x = 5;
   int y = -2;
   if ( x > 0 )
       if ( y > 0 )
           xyz = 1;
   else
       xyz = 2;
   ```

6. True or False: The statement **if (ale = bez)** evaluates to true if ale and bez have the same value.
7. True or False: Any if-else statement can be expressed in a switch structure.
8. True or False: Any switch statement can be expressed in an if-else structure.
9. True or False: The break statement is required for all cases in a switch structure.
10. True or False: The default statement is required for all cases in a switch structure.
11. Write a switch statement that takes an integer value for a student's grade out of 100 points and displays a label with their letter grade based on the following:

    | 90 – 100 | A |
    | 80 – 89 | B |
    | 70 – 79 | C |
    | 60 – 69 | D |
    | Anything else | F |

12. What would be a more descriptive name for the following method?

    ```
    public int myMethod( int a, int b )
    {
        if(  a >= b )
            return b;
        else
            return a;
    }
    ```

13. What is wrong in the following code?

    ```
    boolean isEqual;
    double m = 1.22 + 1.07;
    if( m == 2.29 )
        isEqual = true;
    else
        isEqual = false;
    ```

14. Does the ordering of `if-else if-else` segments matter? Why or why not?
15. Does the ordering of `switch case` segments matter? Why or why not?
16. Is the `break` keyword required in `switch` statements? What happens if the `break` statement is not in a `switch` statement?

17. Is the `default` keyword required in a `switch` statement?

18. Can you put the `default` keyword first in the `switch` statement? Try it and see how it works.

19. Why can't Strings be used in a switch statement?
    Hint: see the section on == vs. .equals( ) on objects.

20. Write a method named **isEven** that takes an int parameter between 1 and 10, and returns whether the number is even or odd. Implement both the if-else structure and a switch statement. Which is easier? Which is easier to implement if the int parameter could be between 1 and 10000?

21. Write a method named **getMin** that takes two int parameters and returns the minimum of the two values. Then write a second method that takes three int parameters that returns the minimum of all three values. In the second method, be sure to call your first method in your solution.

22. Write a method named **getMonth** that takes a number between 1 and 12 as a parameter and returns a String of the full name of the month (e.g. 3 should return "March"). Write it first with an if-else structure, then again with a switch.

23. We want to check a date entered by the user for validity. Write a program that prompts the user for the day as an integer between 1 and 31 and then an integer month between 1 and 12. We will assume the year is 2005 (which is not a leap year). Print out whether the month/day combination is valid or not.

24. Write a method called **getMonthAsString** that takes three integers as parameters (month, day, and year) and returns a String formatted as "Month day, year" (e.g., "November 25, 2005").

25. Write a method named **isEqual** that takes two double values as parameters, and returns true if they're essentially equal, or within 0.0001 of each other.

26. Extend the Weather program to draw a tree that is bare in winter, buds in spring, green leaves in summer and colored leaves in fall (for leaves, you can keep it simple by drawing lots of circles – abstractish art).

27. Write a class that maintains information about a date. The month, day, and year need to be stored as integer instance variables. Write a constructor that takes an int for each of these values, and initializes them. Add the following additional methods:

    a. **getEuropeanDate** that returns the date as "DD MMM YYYY" (e.g., "25 Nov 2007")

    b. **getAmericanDate** that returns the date as "MMM DD, YYYY" (e.g., "Nov 25, 2007")

    c. **getIntDate** that takes a char as a parameter to designate the delimiter, and returns the date as "MM-DD-YY" (e.g., "11-25-07" or "11/25/07")

Chapter 8

Events

*To listen, or not to listen
That is what we must decide...*

Objectives:

- Overview
- ActionEvents
- ItemEvents
- ListSelectionEvents
- KeyEvents
- MouseEvents
- MouseMotionEvents
- Method Stubs
- Adding/Removing components dynamically
- Case Study

Events

Finally we get to learn how to handle events! An event is when something triggers that we can decide to respond. Usually an event corresponds to actions by the user, but not always. For example, when the user clicks on a button, selects one of the radio buttons, selects or deselects a checkbox, selects an item from a list, types in text in a text field or text area, clicks on the mouse or even clicks on a key or combination of keys.

When working with events, we set up listeners to specify that we are interested in particular types of events. For example, if we want to listen to button clicks, we need to work with the ActionListener. If we're listening for mouse events, we implement either the MouseListener or the MouseMotionListener (or both). A list of common listeners is below:

Listener	Description
ActionListener	button clicks
ItemListener	selecting/deselecting a JCheckBox, selecting/deselecting a JRadioButton, selecting from JComboBox
ListSelectionListener	selecting from a JList
MouseListener	mouse entered the component, exited the component, mouse button pressed, mouse button released, mouse button clicked
MouseMotionListener	mouse moved, mouse dragged
KeyListener	any key on the keyboard pressed

We can capture this event and handle it by following the procedure listed below:
There are four things we need to do to get events to work in our applets:

1. **Import the events package**

   ```
   import java.awt.event.*;
   ```

2. **Implement the appropriate listener(s)**
   This is specified in the class header, using the keyword `implements`

   ```
   public class XYZ extends JApplet implements ActionListener
   ```

   You can specify multiple listeners by separating each with a comma.

   public class XYZ extends JApplet implements ItemListener, MouseListener

3. **Add listeners to the components**

   ```
   submitButton.addActionListener( this );
   combobox.addItemListener( this );
   panel.addMouseListener( this );
   textfield.addTextEvent( this );
   ```

143

The `this` java keyword specifies that the class that we're currently writing is the class that wants to listen for events from the component specified.

4. **Write the required listener method(s)**
   Each listener that we implement (from step 2) requires a particular set of methods that are <u>required</u> that we write.
   The list of methods for the common listeners are listed below:

ActionListener	public void actionPerformed(ActionEvent ae)
ItemListener	public void itemStateChanged(ItemEvent ie)
ListSelectionListener	public void valueChanged(ListSelectionEvent e)
MouseEvent	public void mouseClicked(MouseEvent me) public void mousePressed(MouseEvent me) public void mouseReleased(MouseEvent me) public void mouseEntered(MouseEvent me) public void mouseExited(MouseEvent me)
MouseMotionListener	public void mouseMoved(MouseMovedEvent me) public void mouseDragged(MouseMovedEvent me)
KeyListener	public void keyReleased(KeyEvent ke) public void keyTyped(KeyEvent ke) public void keyPressed(KeyEvent ke)

Implementing the required listener methods requires some thought and usually use of if-else structures. The first thing we want to do, no matter which method we are writing, is to figure out the source of the event.

First create a variable to store the object:

```
Object source = parameter.getSource( );
```

where *parameter* is the variable name we used in the method header. (For example: public void mousePressed(MouseEvent me) the variable is me so the line above would have `me.getSource( )`.

The next thing we want to do is determine which component caused the event. For example, if we have three buttons on our applet, it helps to know which button was the one that the user selected. We can do this by using the == operator.

ActionEvents

The `ActionListener` handles the button clicks on JButtons. Whenever the user clicks on a button, an `ActionEvent` occurs and the program automatically calls the `actionPerformed` method. If we do not write an `actionPerformed` method, the program will go to an `actionPerformed` method in the `JApplet` class (the class we extend or inherit) which does nothing. In order for us to do something based on a button click, we need to specify that our class implements the `ActionListener`, add our class as an `ActionListener` for each button we want to handle, and write the `actionPerformed` method.

Steps for ActionListener:

1. **Import the events package**

   ```
   import java.awt.event.*;
   ```

2. **Implement the appropriate listener(s)**

   ```
   public class XYZ extends JApplet implements ActionListener
   ```

3. **Add listeners to the components**

   ```
   submitButton.addActionListener( this );
   combobox.addItemListener( this );
   panel.addMouseListener( this );
   textfield.addTextEvent( this );
   ```

4. **Write the required listener method(s)**

   ```
   public void actionPerformed( ActionEvent ae )
   {
           Object src = ae.getSource( );
   }
   ```

```java
import javax.swing.*;
import java.awt.*;
import java.awt.event.*;
public class IfButton extends JApplet
                implements ActionListener
{
  JButton  go, stop;
  JTextField textf;
  public void init( )
  {
      setLayout( new FlowLayout( ) );
      setupButtons( );
      textf = new JTextField(10);
      add( textf );
  }
  public void setupButtons( )
  {
      go = new JButton( "Go!" );
      stop = new JButton( "Stop!" );
      //add events
      go.addActionListener( this );
      stop.addActionListener( this );
      add( go );     add( stop );       // add to applet
  }
  public void actionPerformed( ActionEvent ae )
  {
      Object obj = ae.getSource( );
      if( obj == go )
           textf.setText ( "Go GO GOOO!!!!" );
      else if ( obj == stop )
           textf.setText( "STOP." );
  }
}
```

First run:

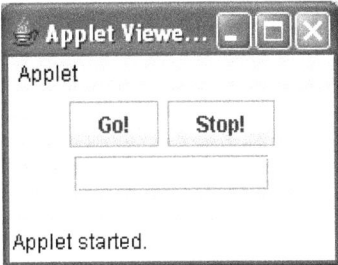

Click on Go!:

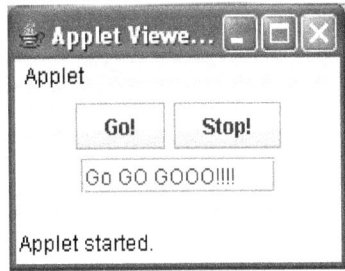

Click on Stop:

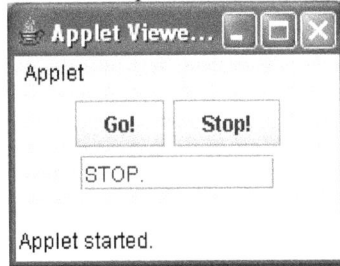

Example: using JButtons and changing images

```java
import javax.swing.*;
import java.awt.*;
import java.awt.event.*;
public class ButtonImages extends JApplet implements ActionListener
{
  JButton compButton, carButton, ideaButton;
  Image compImg, carImg, ideaImg;
  ImageIcon icon;
  JLabel imagelabel;
  JPanel butpanel;
  public void init( )
  {
    setLayout( new BorderLayout( ) );
    setupButtons( );
    compImg=getImage(getCodeBase( ), "oncomputer.png");
    carImg=getImage(getCodeBase( ),"gocart.png");
    ideaImg=getImage(getCodeBase( ),"idea.png");
    icon = new ImageIcon( );
    imagelabel=new JLabel( icon, JLabel.CENTER);
    add( imagelabel, BorderLayout.CENTER );
    setupImage( compImg );
  }
  public void setupButtons( )
  {
    compButton = new JButton( "Computer" );
    carButton = new JButton( "Go-cart" );
    ideaButton = new JButton( "Good Idea" );
    compButton.addActionListener( this );
    carButton.addActionListener( this );
    ideaButton.addActionListener( this );

    butpanel=new JPanel(new GridLayout(3,1));
    butpanel.add( compButton );
    butpanel.add( carButton );
    butpanel.add( ideaButton );
    add( butpanel, BorderLayout.WEST );
  }
  public void setupImage( Image img )
  {
          icon.setImage( img );
          imagelabel.setIcon( icon );
          repaint( );
  }
  public void actionPerformed(ActionEvent ae)
  {
          Object source = ae.getSource( );
          if( source == compButton )
                  setupImage( compImg );
          else if( source == carButton )
                  setupImage( carImg );
          else if( source == ideaButton )
                  setupImage( ideaImg );
  }
}
```

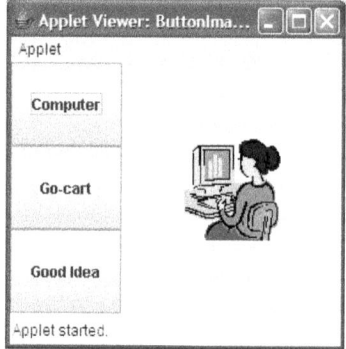

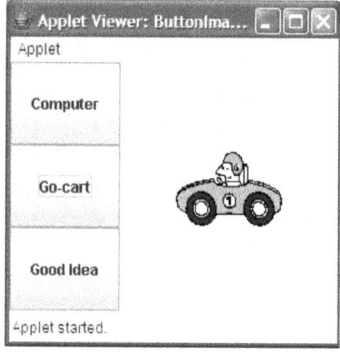

You must call repaint for it to work!

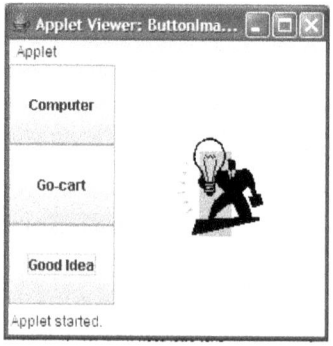

Searching a JList

In this example we want the user to enter something to search for, and if we find it in the list, we'll highlight it.

```java
import javax.swing.*;
import java.awt.*;
import java.awt.event.*;
import java.util.*;
public class SearchTFScroll extends JApplet implements ActionListener
{
    JLabel searchLabel;
    JTextField searchField;
    JPanel searchPanel;
    JButton searchButton;
    JList list;
    DefaultListModel model;
    JScrollPane scrollPane;
    public void init( )
    {
        setLayout( new BorderLayout( ) );
        searchLabel = new JLabel("Search for:");
        searchField = new JTextField(10);
        searchPanel = new JPanel( );
        searchButton = new JButton("search");
        model = new DefaultListModel( );
        list = new JList( model );
        addListItems( );
        scrollPane = new JScrollPane(list);
        searchButton.addActionListener( this );
        searchPanel.add(searchLabel);
        searchPanel.add(searchField);
        searchPanel.add(searchButton);
        add(scrollPane, BorderLayout.CENTER);
        add(searchPanel, BorderLayout.NORTH);
    }
    public void addListItems( )
    {
        model.addElement( "apples" );
        model.addElement( "bananas" );
        model.addElement( "blueberries" );
        model.addElement( "capers" );
        model.addElement( "cucumber" );
        model.addElement( "blackberries" );
        model.addElement( "carrots" );
        model.addElement( "cauliflower" );
        model.addElement( "kiwifruit" );
    }
    public void actionPerformed (ActionEvent e)
    {
        String field=searchField.getText( );
        if (field != null)
            findNode(field);
    }
    public void findNode(String field)
    {
        list.clearSelection( );
        list.setSelectedValue(field, true);
    }
}
```

ItemEvents

Itemlistener listens for events pertaining to selecting or deselecting a JCheckBox or JRadioButton, selecting from a JComboBox, and selecting from a JList.

Steps for ItemListener:

1. **Import the events package**

    ```
    import java.awt.event.*;
    ```

2. **Implement the appropriate listener(s)**

    ```
    public class XYZ extends JApplet implements ItemListener
    ```

3. **Add listeners to the components**

    ```
    combobox.addItemListener( this );
    ```

4. **Write the required listener method(s)**

    ```
    public void itemStateChanged( ItemEvent ie )
    {
          Object src = ie.getSource( );
    }
    ```

Example: using JCheckBox

```
import javax.swing.*;
import java.awt.*;
import java.awt.event.*;
public class CheckEvent extends JApplet
          implements ItemListener
{
  JCheckBox isHappy;
  JTextArea textarea;

  public void init( )
  {
      setLayout( new FlowLayout( ) );

      isHappy = new JCheckBox( "Happy?", true );
      textarea = new JTextArea( 3,10);
      // add listener
      isHappy.addItemListener( this );
      add( isHappy );
      add( textarea );
  }
  public void itemStateChanged( ItemEvent ie )
  {
      Object source = ie.getSource( );
      if( source == isHappy  && isHappy.isSelected ( ) )
            textarea.setText( "You're so happy!" );
      else if( source == isHappy  && ! isHappy.isSelected ( ) )
            textarea.setText( "Why not happy?" );
  }
}
```

Select checkbox:

Deselect checkbox:

Example: using JRadioButton and ButtonGroup

```java
import java.awt.*;
import java.awt.event.*;
import javax.swing.*;

public class JRadioEvent extends JApplet
                        implements ItemListener
{
  ButtonGroup grp;
  JRadioButton red, fuscia, pink;
  JTextArea ta;

  public void init( )
  {
    setLayout( new FlowLayout( ) );
    ta = new JTextArea(5, 10);
    setupButtons( );
    addListeners( );
    add( red );
    add( fuscia );
    add( pink );
    add( ta );
  }
  public void setupButtons( )
  {
    red = new JRadioButton( "red" );
    fuscia = new JRadioButton( "fuscia" );
    pink = new JRadioButton( "pink" );
    grp = new ButtonGroup( );
    grp.add( red );
    grp.add( fuscia );
    grp.add( pink );
  }
  public void addListeners( )
  {
    red.addItemListener( this );
    fuscia.addItemListener( this );
    pink.addItemListener( this );
  }

  public void itemStateChanged( ItemEvent ie )
  {
    Object o = ie.getSource( );
    if ( ie.getStateChange( ) == ItemEvent.DESELECTED )
        return;                 // ignore if deselecting
    if( o == red )
        ta.append( "we like RED \n" );
    else if( o == fuscia )
        ta.append( "We like fuscia \n" );
    else if( o == pink )
        ta.append( "We prefer pink \n" );
  }
}
```

When applet first run:

Select "fuscia":

Select "pink":

ListSelectionEvents

ListSelectionEvents occur when the user selects from a JList.
Steps for ItemListener:

1. **Import the events package**

    ```
    import javax.swing.event.*;
    ```

2. **Implement the appropriate listener(s)**

    ```
    public class XYZ extends JApplet implements ListSelectionListener
    ```

3. **Add listeners to the components**

    ```
    list.addListSelectionListener( this );
    ```

4. **Write the required listener method(s)**

    ```
    public void valueChanged( ListSelectionEvent le )
    {
            Object src = le.getSource( );
    }
    ```

Example: using JList

```
import java.awt.*;
import javax.swing.*;
import javax.swing.event.*;
public class JListEvent extends JApplet implements istSelectionListener
{
    JList list;
    DefaultListModel model;
    JLabel dessert;
    public void init( )
    {   model = new DefaultListModel( );
        list = new JList( model );
        model.addElement( "apple" );
        model.addElement( "banana" );
        model.addElement( "pear" );
        list.addListSelectionListener( this );
        JScrollPane pane = new JScrollPane( list );
        dessert = new JLabel( );
        setLayout( new FlowLayout( ) );
        add( pane );
        add( dessert );
    }
    public void valueChanged( ListSelectionEvent le )
    {   int index = list.getSelectedIndex( );
        if ( index == 0 )
            dessert.setText( "We're having apple pie!" );
        else if ( index == 1 )
            dessert.setText( "Banana split anyone?" );
        else if ( index == 2 )
            dessert.setText( "Pear for the pair?" );
    }
}
```

When applet first run:

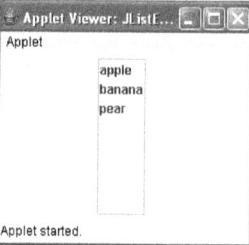

Select "apple":

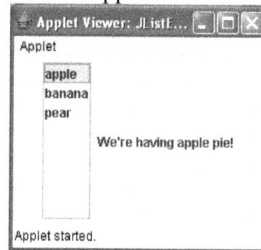

Select "banana":

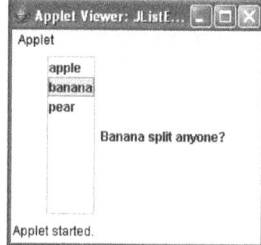

KeyEvents

Key events are used when we want to keep track of when the user types any keys on the keyboard. This is especially fun for controlling characters in a game environment. To listen for key events, we need the import statement as before and specify that we're implementing the KeyListener:

```
import java.awt.event.*;
import java.awt.*;
import javax.swing.*;
public class KeyEventEx extends JApplet  implements  KeyListener
```

We also need to state that we are interested in all key events performed on the applet. To do this, we add the key listener:

```
public void init( )
{
        addKeyListener( this );
}
```

Note that usually we want to listen for key events when the focus is anywhere within the applet, so we do not need to call the addKeyListener method on a specific object. Instead, we call addKeyListener on the entire applet. We could, however, listen for KeyEvents only when the focus is on a specific JPanel by calling the method on our JPanel:

```
JPanel pane = new JPanel( );
pane.addKeyListener( this );
```

Listening for key events requires us to write three methods:

```
public void keyReleased( KeyEvent ke )   { }
public void keyTyped( KeyEvent ke )      { }
public void keyPressed( KeyEvent ke )    { }
```

We'd probably be interested in only the `keyPressed` method, so we can leave the other two methods as *stubs*. A method stub contains the method header and the squiggly braces but nothing for the body of the method (inside the squiggly braces). We just list the method stubs as follows:

```
public void keyReleased( KeyEvent ke )   { }
public void keyTyped( KeyEvent ke )      { }
```

Inside the keyPressed method we'll do something basesd on which key was pressed. We don't need to get the source of the event like we do in the actionPerformed method – instead, we want to know which key was pressed. To figure this out, we ask for the key code:

```
public void keyPressed( KeyEvent ke )
{
        int code = ke.getKeyCode( );
}
```

Now we can check to see if it matches to a particular key. For example, we can look at:

up arrow	KeyEvent.VK_UP	left arrow	KeyEvent.VK_LEFT
down arrow	KeyEvent.VK_DOWN	right arrow	KeyEvent.VK_RIGHT

To see if a particular letter was pressed, check the KeyEvent.VK_[letter] where [letter] is any letter A through Z (in upper-case). For numbers on a keypad, use KeyEvent.VK_NUMPAD[#] where [#] is the numbers 0 through 9. Numbers not on the keypad can be accessed with KeyEvent.VK_[#]. Other useful key codes include: VK_ADD, VK_SUBTRACT, VK_MULTIPLY, VK_DIVIDE, VK_ENTER, VK_PERIOD, VK_SPACE, VK_TAB, VK_SHIFT, VK_ALT, VK_CONTROL.

One last thing we need to do is to set the applet as the focus so it can start listening for key events:

```
setFocusable(true);
```

In the following example, we can move around an animated gif by pressing arrow keys on the keyboard. Since we want to control where the image is, we'll use the null layout manager. This allows us to call the method setLocation on our JLabel with the image so we can specify the exact (x, y) coordinates for the image. The (x, y) coordinate specifies the upper-left corner of the label/image. To handle the key events, the user can press the arrow keys to get the image to move. The speed variable makes it easy for us to change how fast the image moves – how many pixels it should move in either the x or y direction each time an arrow key is pressed.

```java
import javax.swing.*;
import java.awt.*;
import java.awt.event.*;
public class KeyEventAnimation extends JApplet implements KeyListener
{
   Image img;
   JLabel penny;
   int x=0, y=0, speed=10;   // x,y coordinates and how many pixels move
   JPanel pane;
   public void init( )
   {
      pane = new JPanel( );
      pane.setLayout( null );
      pane.setBackground( Color.WHITE );
      img = getImage( getCodeBase( ), "pennyWalk.gif" );
      penny = new JLabel( new ImageIcon(img) );
      penny.setSize( img.getWidth(this), img.getHeight(this) );
      addKeyListener(this);
      pane.add( penny, 0, 0 );
      add( pane, BorderLayout.CENTER );
      setFocusable(true);
   }
   public void keyReleased( KeyEvent ke ) { }
   public void keyTyped( KeyEvent ke ) { }
   public void keyPressed( KeyEvent ke )
   {
      int code = ke.getKeyCode( );
      if ( code == KeyEvent.VK_UP )
         y -= speed;
      else if ( code == KeyEvent.VK_DOWN )
         y += speed;
      else if ( code == KeyEvent.VK_LEFT )
         x -= speed;
      else if ( code == KeyEvent.VK_RIGHT )
         x += speed;
      penny.setLocation(x,y);
   }
}
```

MouseEvents

There are two types of listeners to deal with mouse events:

LISTENER	METHODS REQUIRED	EVENT TYPES
MouseListener	mouseEntered mouseExited mousePressed mouseReleased mouseClicked	mouse entered the component exited the component mouse button pressed mouse button released mouse button clicked
MouseMotionListener	mouseMoved mouseDragged	mouse moved mouse dragged while button held down

All of the methods take a `MouseEvent` as a parameter.

To listen for mouse events, we need the import statement as before and specify that we're implementing either the MouseListener or the MouseMotionListener:

```
import java.awt.event.*;
import java.awt.*;
import javax.swing.*;
public class MouseEx extends JApplet implements MouseListener
{

}
```

We also need to state that we are interested in all mouse events performed on the applet. To do this, we add the mouse listener to the applet:

```
public void init( )
{
        addMouseListener( this );
}
```

Note that usually we want to listen for mouse events when the focus is anywhere within the applet, so we do not need to call the addMouseListener method on a specific object. Instead, we call addMouseListener on the entire applet. We could, however, listen for MouseEvents only when the focus is on a specific JPanel by calling the method on our JPanel:

```
JPanel pane = new JPanel( );
pane.addMouseListener( this );
```

Implementing the MouseListener requires us to write five methods:

```
public void mouseEntered( MouseEvent me )   { }
public void mouseExited( MouseEvent me )        { }
public void mousePressed( MouseEvent me )       { }
public void mouseReleased( MouseEvent me ) { }
public void mouseClicked( MouseEvent me )       { }
```

We probably don't want to use all the methods required, so we can leave the other methods as *stubs*.

153

Inside our methods that we do want to implement, we can find out the x and y coordinates of the mouse at the time of the event. To do this, we call the methods getX( ) and getY( ) on our MouseEvent variable.

```
public void mousePressed( MouseEvent me )
{
        int x = me.getX( );
        int y = me.getY( );
}
```

The example below shows the use of all of these mouse events:

```java
import java.awt.*;
import java.awt.event.*;
import javax.swing.*;
public class MouseEvents extends JApplet   implements MouseListener, MouseMotionListener
{
  JTextArea msg;
  JScrollPane spane;
  public void init( )    {
        addMouseListener( this );
        addMouseMotionListener( this );
        msg = new JTextArea( 10,20 );
        spane = new JScrollPane(msg);
        setLayout( new FlowLayout( ) );
        add( spane );
  }
  public void mouseEntered( MouseEvent me )
  {
        msg.append( "\nMouse entered applet at: x=" + me.getX( ) + " y=" + me.getY( ) );
  }
  public void mouseExited( MouseEvent me )
  {
        msg.append( "\nMouse exited applet at: x=" + me.getX( ) + " y=" + me.getY( ) );
  }
  public void mousePressed( MouseEvent me )
  {
        msg.append( "\nMouse button pressed at: x=" + me.getX( ) + " y=" + me.getY( ) );
  }
  public void mouseReleased( MouseEvent me )
  {
        msg.append( "\nMouse button released at: x=" + me.getX( ) + " y=" + me.getY( ) );
  }
  public void mouseClicked( MouseEvent me )
  {
        msg.append( "\nMouse button clicked at: x=" + me.getX( ) + " y=" + me.getY( ) );
  }
  public void mouseMoved( MouseEvent me )
  {
        msg.append( "\nMouse moved at: x=" + me.getX( ) + " y=" + me.getY( ) );
  }
  public void mouseDragged( MouseEvent me )
  {
        msg.append( "\nMouse dragged at: x=" + me.getX( ) + " y=" + me.getY( ) );
  }
}
```

Method Stubs

When our code states that we implement one of these listeners, we are required to write *all* of the required methods. Sometimes we don't care to handle any of the events for some of these methods. We can instead write a *method stub*. A **method stub** is a method with nothing in the body of the method.

For example, if we only wanted to print out when the mouse entered and exited the applet, we would change the code above to be the following:

```java
import java.awt.*;
import java.awt.event.*;
import javax.swing.*;
public class MouseEventsWithStubs extends JApplet implements MouseListener
{
   JTextArea msg;
   JScrollPane spane;
   public void init( )
   {
          addMouseListener( this );

          msg = new JTextArea( 10,20 );
          spane = new JScrollPane(msg);

          setLayout( new FlowLayout( ) );
          add( spane );
   }
   public void mouseEntered( MouseEvent me )
   {
          msg.append( "\nMouse entered applet at: x=" + me.getX( ) + " y=" + me.getY( ) );
   }
   public void mouseExited( MouseEvent me )
   {
          msg.append( "\nMouse exited applet at: x=" + me.getX( ) + " y=" + me.getY( ) );
   }
   public void mousePressed( MouseEvent me )   {  }
   public void mouseReleased( MouseEvent me )  {  }
   public void mouseClicked( MouseEvent me )   {  }
}
```

In the example above, we wrote *method stubs* for the mousePressed, mouseReleased and mouseClicked methods. We are required to have the methods written in the program, but we don't do anything inside the method.

Note that we can either listen to mouse events on the applet itself (as in the examples above), or on a particular component. This could be useful if we wanted to handle mouse events on a helper class that we create, such as the Smiley example where we extend the JPanel class.

Example – MouseListener and MouseMotionListener

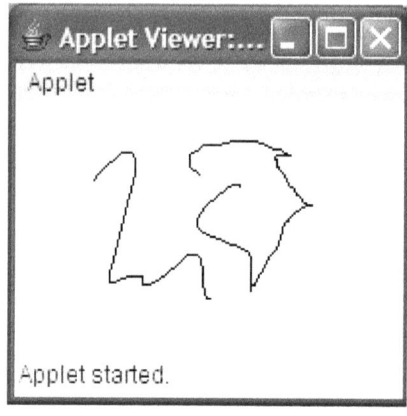

```
import javax.swing.*;
import java.awt.*;
import java.awt.event.*;

public class Scribble extends JApplet
     implements MouseListener, MouseMotionListener
{
   int last_x, last_y;

   public void init( )
   {
      addMouseListener( this );
      addMouseMotionListener( this );
   }

   public void mousePressed( MouseEvent me )
   {
      last_x = me.getX( );
      last_y = me.getY( );
   }

   public void mouseDragged( MouseEvent me )
   {
      Graphics g = this.getGraphics( );
      int x = me.getX( );
      int y = me.getY( );
      g.drawLine( last_x, last_y, x, y );
      last_x = x;
      last_y = y;
   }

   // Method stubs for methods we don't need
   public void mouseReleased( MouseEvent me ) {  }
   public void mouseClicked( MouseEvent me ) {  }
   public void mouseEntered( MouseEvent me ) {  }
   public void mouseExited( MouseEvent me ) {  }

   public void mouseMoved( MouseEvent e ) {  }
}
```

Another example using mouse events – eyeballs follow the mouse around the applet:

```java
import java.awt.*;
import java.awt.event.*;
import javax.swing.*;
public class MouseEyes extends JApplet implements MouseMotionListener
{
    int mouseX, mouseY;        // track current location of mouse

    public void init( )
    {
        addMouseMotionListener( this );
    }
    public void paint( Graphics g )
    {
        g.clearRect( 0,0,getWidth( ),getHeight( ) );
        int eyeWidth = 40;
        int eyeHeight = 80;
        g.setColor( Color.WHITE );                          // color the whites of the eyes
        g.fillOval( 0,0,eyeWidth,eyeHeight );
        g.fillOval( eyeWidth,0, eyeWidth, eyeHeight );
        g.setColor( Color.BLACK );                          // draw outline
        g.drawOval( 0,0, eyeWidth, eyeHeight );             // left eye
        g.drawOval( 1,1, eyeWidth-2, eyeHeight-2 );
        g.drawOval( eyeWidth,0,  eyeWidth, eyeHeight );     // right eye
        g.drawOval( eyeWidth+1,1, eyeWidth-2, eyeHeight-2);

        // eyes, x,y as percent of where mouse is
        int eyeX = (mouseX * 100 / getWidth( )) * eyeWidth / 100;       // eyeball
        int eyeY = (mouseY * 100 / getHeight( )) * eyeHeight / 100;
        g.fillOval( eyeX, eyeY, 10,10 );
        g.fillOval( eyeX+eyeWidth, eyeY, 10,10);
    }
    public void mouseMoved( MouseEvent me )                 // track current location of mouse
    {
        mouseX = me.getX();
        mouseY = me.getY();
        repaint( );
    }
    public void mouseDragged( MouseEvent me ) { }
}
```

157

The next example shows how we can be annoying:

```java
/** Program that moves a button whenever the mouse gets near it.
 * Shows example of MouseMotionListener events, null layout manager
 * @author : E.S.Boese
 */
import javax.swing.*;
import java.awt.*;
import java.awt.event.*;
import java.util.*;
                            // need to listen for mouseMoved events
public class Annoying extends JApplet implements MouseMotionListener
{
   JButton winner = new JButton( "Click me and win a million" );
                            // need a Random object to randomly select a new x and y coordinates
                            //   when we move the button to a new location
   Random random = new Random( );
                            // Rectangle object that determines the x and y coordinates
                            // that trigger a move of the button.
                            // The coordinates are 10 pixels bigger than the actual button,
                            // such that if the mouse gets within 10 pixels of the button, the button will move
   Rectangle rectangle = new Rectangle( );

   public void init( )
   {
                            // null layout so we can place the button in an exact location
         setLayout( null );
                            // since we're using the null layout, we have to set the bounds on our
                            // button.  x and y coordinates 100,200, width of 200 and height of 20
         winner.setBounds(100,200,200,20);
                            // rectangle holds the buffer area, 10 pixels bigger than than the button
                            // records the x and y coordinates 90,190, width 220 and height 40
         rectangle.setBounds( 90,190,220,40);      // "too close" boundary

         addMouseMotionListener(this);        // listen for mouse movements on the applet
         add(winner);                         // add button to applet

   }
   public void mouseMoved( MouseEvent me )
   {
         int x = me.getX( );                          // get x coordinate of the mouse location
         int y = me.getY( );                          // get y coordinate of the mouse location
         if ( rectangle.contains( x, y ) )      // method returns true if x,y inside rectangle
         {                                      // move the button to a new spot.
                                                // to make sure it doesn't go off screen, the max x is 300
            winner.setLocation( random.nextInt(300), random.nextInt(490) );
                                                // reset the boundary for the rectangle, such that it's 10 pixels
                                                // buffer from the new location of the button
            rectangle.setBounds( winner.getX( )-10, winner.getY( )-10,
                     winner.getWidth( )+20, winner.getHeight( )+20 );
         }
   }
   public void mouseDragged( MouseEvent me ) { }   // required method leave as stub
}
```

Adding and Removing Components Dynamically

Now that we can dynamically change things based on events, we can make bigger and more complex applets. This leads to the desire to change the main area of the applet based on a selection, such as a button or list option. To ensure the graphics are redrawn properly, the easiest way to this is to use a JPanel where you can remove all items by calling the removeAll method on it then add new items to it. We also need to call the validate and repaint methods to ensure the screen is redrawn with the new components. The following example illustrates how to achieve this.

```java
import java.awt.*;
import java.awt.event.*;
import javax.swing.*;
public class ClearPanel extends JApplet implements ActionListener
{
   JLabel title;
   JButton productInfo, aboutUs;
   JPanel  mainPanel;              // use this JPanel for everything in BorderLayout.CENTER
   JPanel productPanel, aboutUsPanel;
   public void init( )
   {   resize( 400, 400 );
       setLayout( new BorderLayout( ) );
       title = new JLabel( "<HTML><B><FONT COLOR=RED>Ski Wax For You!", JLabel.CENTER );
       add( title, BorderLayout.NORTH );
       setupButtons( );
       setupProductPanel( );
       setupAboutUsPanel( );
       mainPanel = new JPanel( new BorderLayout( ) );
       JLabel tmpMsg = new JLabel( "<HTML><CENTER>Welcome<BR> <BR> to our <BR> <BR> Home!", JLabel.CENTER);
       tmpMsg.setFont( new Font( "Serif", Font.BOLD, 18 ) );
       mainPanel.add(tmpMsg, BorderLayout.CENTER);
       add( mainPanel, BorderLayout.CENTER );
   }
   public void setupAboutUsPanel( )
   {
       aboutUsPanel = new JPanel( new GridLayout( 2, 1 ) );
       Image img = getImage( getCodeBase( ), "pennyWalk.gif" );
       ImageIcon icon = new ImageIcon( img );
       aboutUsPanel.add( new JLabel( icon ) );
       JLabel text = new JLabel( "<HTML><CENTER><B>About Us</B> <BR> <BR>"
           + "We are a family run business <BR>that has been making wax since 1997."
           + "<BR>We take pride in our work <BR>and guarantee you will love our wax.", JLabel.CENTER );
       aboutUsPanel.add( text );
   }
   public void setupProductPanel( )
   {
       productPanel = new JPanel( new BorderLayout( ) );
       JLabel prodinfo = new JLabel( "<HTML><CENTER><B>Product Info</B><BR> <BR>"
               + "Our ski wax is the best wax you'll ever find.<BR> Comes in two styles:<BR>"
               + " red:  warmer temperatures<BR>blue:  colder temperatures", JLabel.CENTER );
       productPanel.add( prodinfo, BorderLayout.CENTER );
   }
   public void setupButtons( )
```

```
    {
        productInfo = new JButton( "Info" );
        aboutUs = new JButton( "About Us" );
        productInfo.addActionListener( this );
        aboutUs.addActionListener( this );
        JPanel west = new JPanel( new GridLayout( 2,1 ) );
        west.add( productInfo );
        west.add( aboutUs );
        add( west, BorderLayout.WEST );
    }
    public void actionPerformed( ActionEvent ae )
    {
        Object src = ae.getSource( );
        if ( src == productInfo )
        {
            mainPanel.removeAll( );
            mainPanel.add( productPanel, BorderLayout.CENTER );
        }
        else if ( src == aboutUs )
        {
            mainPanel.removeAll( );
            mainPanel.add( aboutUsPanel, BorderLayout.CENTER );
        }
        mainPanel.validate( );
        mainPanel.repaint( );
    }
}
```

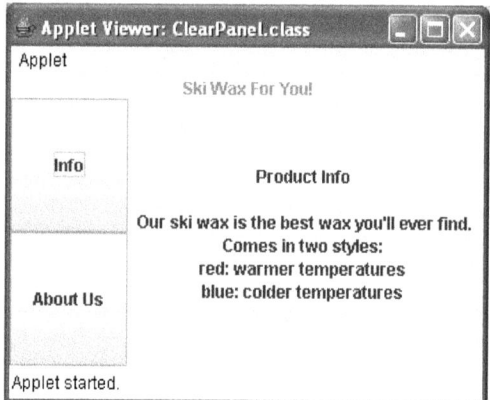
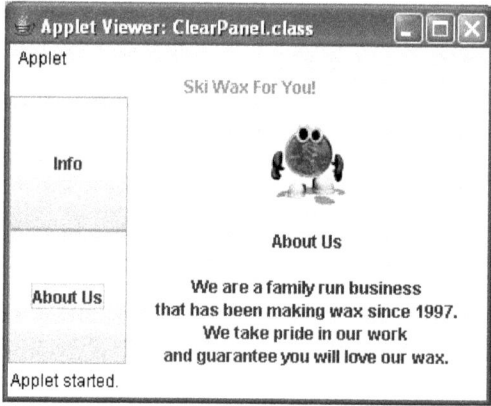

Case Study

Now we can add events to our case study of the coffee club applet. Similar to our last example, we want to click one of the buttons and use the extra layer panel to remove all components in the center region so we can add the new panel to be displayed. The following code is highlighted to show the new code added to get events to work on our coffee club example.

```java
import java.awt.*;
import javax.swing.*;
import java.awt.event.*;
public class CoffeeClubEvents extends JApplet  implements ActionListener
{
    JButton home, join, faq, contact;
    Image img;
    JLabel title, logo, copyright, ntbkImg, ntbkDesc, infoSheets, welcomeMsg;
    Color tanColor = new Color( 204, 153, 51 );
    Color darkColor = new Color( 51, 17, 0 );
    Color bkgrdColor = new Color ( 17, 8, 0 );
    JPanel leftside, top, center, welcomePanel, separator, freeNotebook, faqPanel;
    public void init( )
    {   setLayout( new BorderLayout( ) );
        doTitle( );
        doLeftSide( );
        doBottom( );
        doCenter( );
        setupFAQPanel( );
    }
    public void setupButton( JButton b )    // method makes it easier to do all method calls for each button
    {
            b.setContentAreaFilled( false );
            b.setBorderPainted( false );
            b.setFocusable( false );
            b.setForeground( tanColor );
            b.addActionListener( this );
            leftside.add( b );
    }
    public void doTitle( )
    {
        img = getImage( getCodeBase( ), "coffeeLogoMetal.png" );
        logo = new JLabel( new ImageIcon(img) );
        img = getImage( getCodeBase( ), "logoName.png" );
        title = new JLabel( new ImageIcon(img) );
        top = new JPanel( new FlowLayout( ) );
        top.add( logo );
        top.add( title );
        top.setBackground ( tanColor );
        add( top, BorderLayout.NORTH );
    }
    public void doLeftSide( )
    {
        // left side menu
```

```java
        leftside = new JPanel( new GridLayout(5,1 ) );
        leftside.setBackground ( darkColor );
        home = new JButton( "Home" );
        join = new JButton( "Join the Club" );
        faq = new JButton( "FAQ" );
        contact = new JButton( "Contact Us" );
        setupButton( home );
        setupButton( join );
        setupButton( faq );
        setupButton( contact );
        JLabel basket = new JLabel( new ImageIcon( getImage( getCodeBase( ), "coffeeBasket.png" ) ) );
        leftside.add( basket );
        add( leftside, BorderLayout.WEST );
    }
    public void doBottom( )
    {                              // String can go across multiple lines: use + to append
        copyright = new JLabel( "<HTML><SMALL>(c) 2008 by CoffeeClubOfTheWorld.com."
            + "  All Rights Reserved.", JLabel.CENTER );
        copyright.setForeground( tanColor );
        copyright.setOpaque(true);
        copyright.setBackground( darkColor );
        add( copyright, BorderLayout.SOUTH );
    }
    public void doCenter( )
    {
        center = new JPanel ( new BorderLayout( ) );
        center.setBackground( tanColor );
        // add the dark separator as a blank colored panel in the NORTH of the center panel
        separator = new JPanel( );
        separator.setBackground ( darkColor );
        separator.setPreferredSize( new Dimension( 10, 20 ) );
        center.add( separator, BorderLayout.NORTH );

        welcomePanel = new JPanel( new FlowLayout( ) );
        welcomePanel.setOpaque( false );
        welcomeMsg = new JLabel( "<html><center><H2>Welcome to our Coffee of the Month Club!"
            + "</h2><HR WIDTH=80%><I>Our coffee club is not just gourmet coffee – "
            + "<BR>it's an immersion of experience"
            + "<HR WIDTH=80%><BR>We personally select gourmet coffees from around the world. "
            + "<BR></CENTER>Each month a freshly roasted coffee is sent to your door "
            + "<BR>along with informative page about the coffee and other <BR>goodies related to the region."
            + "<BR><BR>Each month we send you"
            + "<UL><LI>12-16 oz. bag of fresh coffee beans (size depends on the roaster)"
            + "<LI>Information sheets about the coffee and region "
            + "<LI> Regional Gift each month (e.g. spices, nuts, chocolates, teas, etc.)"
            + "</UL><BR><B>FREE SHIPPING!</B><BR> <BR> ");
        welcomeMsg.setForeground( darkColor );
        welcomePanel.add( welcomeMsg );
        // create the bottom free notebook offer
        freeNotebook = new JPanel( new GridLayout( 1, 3 ) );
        freeNotebook.setOpaque(false);
        ntbkImg = new JLabel( new ImageIcon( getImage(getCodeBase( ), "ntbk.png")));
```

```java
            ntbkDesc = new JLabel( "<HTML><CENTER>Buy NOW and receive<BR> a FREE<BR>"
                + " leather binder notebook <BR>for collecting the articles<BR>and fact sheets!" );
            infoSheets = new JLabel( new ImageIcon( getImage(getCodeBase( ), "InfoSheets.png")));
            freeNotebook.add( ntbkImg );
            freeNotebook.add( ntbkDesc );
            freeNotebook.add( infoSheets );
            welcomePanel.add( freeNotebook, BorderLayout.SOUTH );
            center.add( welcomePanel, BorderLayout.CENTER );
            add( center, BorderLayout.CENTER );
        }
        public void setupFAQPanel( )
        {
            /* put this into a method so that it's only done once, and then
             * we only need one line inside the if statement in the actionPerformed method   */
            JLabel faqText = new JLabel( "<HTML><H1>FAQ</H1><H2>Can I get decaffeinated coffee?</H2>"
                + "No. Our selections are all caffeinated."
                + "<H2>Can I get ground coffee instead of the beans?</H2>"
                + "No. Coffee will stay fresher as whole beans than if pre-ground. "
                + "<BR>This gives you the best flavors to experience."
                + "<H2>Can I choose which coffees I get?</H2>"
                + "No. Each month we send the same coffee package to all current members."
                + "<H2>How do I store the coffee?</H2>"
                + "Coffee should be kept in a cool place in an air-tight container or bag. <BR>Do not freeze your coffee!");
            faqPanel = new JPanel( new FlowLayout( ) );
            faqPanel.setOpaque(false);
            faqPanel.add( faqText );
        }
        public void actionPerformed( ActionEvent ae )
        {
            Object src = ae.getSource( );
            center.removeAll( );
            // add the dark separator as a blank colored panel in the NORTH of the center panel
            separator = new JPanel( );
            separator.setBackground ( darkColor );
            separator.setPreferredSize( new Dimension( 10, 20 ) );
            center.add( separator, BorderLayout.NORTH );
            if ( src == home )
            {
                center.add( welcomePanel, BorderLayout.CENTER );
            }
            else if ( src == faq )
            {
                center.add( faqPanel, BorderLayout.CENTER );
            }
            center.repaint( );
            validate( );
            repaint( );
        }
}
```

Now you can add your own code to extend this program. Implement the other two buttons!

Summary

- An event is when something triggers and we have the option to handle it or not.

- Events require 4 steps to work: importing the java.awt.event package, specifying which listeners to implement in the class header, adding listeners to the applet or components, and writing the appropriate methods required of the implemented listener.

- Button clicks cause ActionEvents handled by the ActionListener and require the actionPerformed method to be written.

- ItemEvents are caused by selecting/deselecting a JCheckBox/JComboBox/JList/JRadioButton and require the itemStateChanged method.

- MouseEvents are caused by the mouse entering/exiting the component or the button being pressesd/released/clicked.

- MouseMotionEvents are caused by the mouse being moved or dragged.

- KeyEvents are from the user clicking on any key on the keyboard.

- TextEvents are caused by the user typing in a text component such as JTextField, JPassword, etc.

- For each event, a call to getSource( ) will return an Object reference to the object that caused the event.

- A *method stub* is a method with no body. Since many methods are required for implementing certain listeners, several methods may be listed in the code as a method stub.

Exercises

1. What are the four things you need to handle events?
2. What two things must your program do to respond to a particular type of event?
3. True or False. Clicking a mouse button generates a KeyEvent.
4. Which Listener is used to handle events for when the user changes the option in a drop-down list?
5. What is the method to get the text from the selected item in a **JTextField** component?
6. What method sets the text in a **JTextArea** component?
7. What is the difference between MouseEvent and MouseMotionEvent?
8. How many methods do you need to code when implementing the MouseListener?
9. How do you implement two listeners: e.g., ActionListener and ItemListener?
10. What do you do with methods that you don't care about when implementing a listener? For example, if you implement the MouseMotionListener and only want to do something when the mouse moved and not when the mouse is dragged, what do you do with the mouseDragged method?
11. Match the following events with the appropriate type of listener.
    a. ____ button clicks
    b. ____ mouse entered the component
    c. ____ user selects a new item from JComboBox
    d. ____ user drags the mouse
    e. ____ user deselects a JCheckBox

    m. ActionListener
    p. ItemListener
    s. MouseListener
    v. MouseMotionListener
    x. KeyListener

12. Write a mini version of the MasterMind game. Use three JButtons or JCheckBoxes with images. Allow three image options: a red, green and blue ball. As the user selects each ball, the color changes (display a different image on the button/checkbox from red to green, green to blue, and blue back to red. Randomly select an answer for each of the buttons/checkboxes. Once the user clicks on the "Try me!" button, check to see if the button colors match to the answer.

13. Write a Tic-Tac-Toe game. Set up a GridLayout with JButtons. Use images for the X, O and empty squares. Allow two users to play against each other. Notify the winner by setting text on a JLabel at the bottom of the applet.
14. Modify the KeyEventAnimation class to display different images based on the direction the figure is moving.
15. Create a "Where's Waldo" by dividing the screen into small images on buttons. Align the images so it looks like a seamless picture to the user.
16. Create a board game using a nullLayout manager. Move the pieces by calling setLocation on them.
17. Create a family tree as an image and use MouseClicked to display more information for each person.

Chapter 9

Loops

Why did the programmer get stuck in the shower?
Because the shampoo bottle said:
"Lather, Rinse, Repeat"

Objectives:

- Repeating Statements
    - While Loop
    - For Loop
    - Do Loop
    - Which Loop to Use?
- Animation
- Careful!

Repeating Statements

Loops allow us to execute statements multiple times. How many times the statement(s) are execute depend on the boolean expression. The statement(s) are executed over and over again while the boolean expression evaluates to true; once it evaluates to false the program continues with the rest of the program.

Java has three types of loops:

- while loop
- for loop
- do…while loop

Although we could probably get away with programming a loop with any of the loop types, there's a reason why there are three different types. As programmers, we should select the right kind of loop for the situation. Before we figure this out, let's first look at each one.

While Loop

The while loop is as follows:

```
while( booleanExpression )
    oneStatement;
```

OR if we want multiple statements within the while loop:

```
while( booleanExpression )
{
    statements;
    statements;
}
```

Before executing the statements inside the loop, the booleanExpression is evaluated. If it evaluates to false, then the statements inside the loop are skipped. If, however, the boolean expression evaluates to true, then the statements are executed and the boolean expression is evaluated again. This procedure is repeated until the boolean expression evaluates to false.

Procedure

1. Evaluate boolean expression.
2. If the boolean expression evaluates to `true`,
   a. Execute all the statements within the loop
   b. Go to step 1.
3. If the boolean expression evaluates to `false`, skip the statements in the loop and continue with the program.

Example:

```java
import java.awt.*;
import javax.swing.*;

public class DrawRectsLoop extends JApplet
{
  int x=0;
  int y=0;
  int width=300;
  int height=200;
  int spacing = 20;

  public void paint ( Graphics g )
  {
    while( width>spacing && height>spacing )
    {
            g.drawRect( x,y, width, height );
            x = x + spacing;
            y = y + spacing;
            width = width - 2*spacing;
            height = height - 2*spacing;
    }
  }
}
```

What would happen if you change the boolean expression such that the width and height are both greater than or equal to zero instead of spacing?

For Loop

The for loop is as follows:

```
for( initialization; booleanExpression; incrementer )
        statement;
```

OR if we want multiple statements within the for loop:

```
for( initialization; booleanExpression; incrementer )
{
        statement;
}
```

where the initialization is usually setting a variable to an initial value, such as:

```
int i = 0;
```

the booleanExpression is the same as the while loop, evaluates to either true or false, and the incrementer is used to either increment or decrement our initial value:

```
i = i+1;
```

```
import java.awt.*;
import javax.swing.*;
public class DropFor1to10 extends JApplet
{
  JComboBox list = new JComboBox( );
  public void init( )
  {
        setLayout( new FlowLayout( ) );
        setupList( );
  }
  public void setupList( )
  {
        for ( int i=1; i<10; i++ )
        {
           list.addItem( String.valueOf( i ) );
        }
        add( list );
  }
}
```

Example: populates a JComboBox with numbers 1 through 10

In the following example we use a for loop to fill the applet with alternating stripes. We need to make use of two methods on the applet to determine the size:

```
this.getWidth( );      // returns the width of the component or JApplet in this case
this.getHeight( );     // returns the height
```

```
import java.awt.*;
import javax.swing.*;
public class Stripes extends JApplet
{
  public void paint( Graphics g )
  {
        int stripes = 0;
        int width = 30;
        int height = this.getHeight( );
        int appletWidth = this.getWidth( );
        for (int x=0; x < appletWidth; x+=width)
        {
              if (stripes%2 == 0)
              {
                    g.setColor(Color.RED);
              }
              else
              {
                    g.setColor(Color.CYAN);
              }
              g.fillRect(x, 0, width, height);
              stripes = stripes + 1;
        }
  }
}
```

this.getHeight( ) returns the height of the component

use modules % operator to check if even (no remainder = 0) to alternate colors

In this next example, we make use of converting a String in a JTextField to a number, loop from 1 to that number, and convert each number in our loop to a String to display in the JTextArea.

```java
import java.awt.*;
import java.awt.event.*;
import javax.swing.*;

public class Conversions extends JApplet    implements ActionListener
{
   JTextArea textarea;
   JTextField enter;
   JLabel label;
   JButton go;
   JScrollPane spane;

   public void init( )
   {
        setLayout( new FlowLayout( ) );
        label = new JLabel("Enter the number you want me to count to");
        enter = new JTextField(5);
        textarea = new JTextArea(7,6);
        spane = new JScrollPane(textarea);
        go = new JButton( "GO!" );
        go.addActionListener( this );
        add(label);   add(enter);    add(spane);    add( go );
   }

   public void actionPerformed( ActionEvent ae )
   {
        Object src = ae.getSource( );
        if ( src == go )
        {
          String text = enter.getText( );
          if ( text.length( ) > 0 )
          {
               int num = Integer.parseInt( text );
               textarea.setText( "" );
               for ( int i=1; i<=num; i++ )
               {
                    textarea.append( String.valueOf(i) );
                    textarea.append( "\n" );
               }
          }
          else
               textarea.setText( "Please enter something first!");
        }
   }
}
```

Example populates a JTextArea with items copied from a JList

```java
import java.awt.*;
import javax.swing.*;
public class List2TA extends JApplet
{
  JList list;
  DefaultListModel model;
  JTextArea textarea;
  public void init( )
  {
          setLayout( new FlowLayout( ) );
          setupList( );
          textarea = new JTextArea( 5,10 );
          add(textarea);
          addListItemsToTextarea( );
  }
  public void setupList( )
  {
          model = new DefaultListModel( );
          list = new JList( model );
          model.addElement( "Milk" );
          model.addElement( "Cookies" );
          model.addElement( "Eggs" );
          add( list );
  }
  public void addListItemsToTextarea( )
  {       // getSize returns the number of items in the list
          for( int i=0; i<model.getSize( ); i++ )
          {
                  // grab the item at index i
             textarea.append( (String )model.get(i) );
             textarea.append( "\n" );
          }
  }
}
```

In this example we were able to copy the values in the JList into the JTextArea. To get this example to work, we need to re-look at some of the components introduced earlier. When working with the JList, remember that we have to add the items in the list in a `DefaultListModel` object.

JList and DefaultListModel

For us to find out how many items are in the JList, we call a method named `getSize( )` on the `DefaultListModel` object.

To get each item out of the list, we call the method `get( index )` on the `DefaultListModel`, where the parameter specifies which one in the list (Remember - Java starts counting at zero, so the first one in the list is at 0). Therefore our loop starts at 0 and continues while the i variable counter is less than the number of elements in the list. When we call the `get` method, it is returned to us as an `Object`. Since we want it to be a String specifically, we need to *cast* it to a String which is why the String in parenthesis is there.

```
(String ) model.get(i)
```

Do Loop

The do loop is as follows:

```
do
{
        statement(s);
} while( booleanExpression );
```

The do loop is similar to a while loop, except that it is guaranteed to execute the statements in the loop at least once. We're not going to cover the do loop in any more detail, since we can program any loop into a for or while loop.

Animation

We can also create our own animation by using loops in a paint method. By using the method **clearRect** on the Graphics object, we can erase a section that has been painted and then repaint it at a different x and y location.

The example below demonstrates animation using a while loop in the paint method:

```java
/* Demonstrate loops with animation */
import java.awt.*;
import javax.swing.*;
public class Animate extends JApplet
{
   int x, y, size, move, speed, count;
   public void paint ( Graphics g )
   {
      x = 0;
      y = 50;
      size = 20;           // width and height same
      move = 1;            //num pixels to move each time thru loop
      count = 0;
      speed = 10000000;    // slow down loop

      while ( count < 5000 )
      {
         g.clearRect ( x, y, size, size);    // erase space
         x = x + move;                        // new x coodinate, y stays same
         g.fillRect ( x, y, size, size );
                                              // did we hit the edge of the applet?
         if ( x + size > getWidth( ) )
            move = -move;                     // if so, go back
         for ( int i=0; i<speed; i++ )
            ;                                 // slow down painting so we can see it

         count = count + 1;
      }
   }
}
```

Although this example should make use of Threads and/or Timer to create the animation, this works for now. We could also draw an image instead of a square.

This looks really good with animated gifs of a character walking. Just be sure to use different images for each direction that the character is walking, so they're not walking backwards! There are plenty of images available to use on the Internet – look at the sprites at the Game Sprite Archives: http://www.gsarchives.net.

Which loop to use?

To determine which loop to use, the guideline is:

IF *you know the number of times to go through the loop,*
    USE *the for loop*
ELSE IF *you need to execute the statements in the loop at least once,*
    USE *the do loop*
ELSE
    USE *while loop*

Careful!

Some things to be careful with when working with loops:

- Off-by-one error:
  Example: want to add values 1 through 10 to the textarea.

  ```
  for( int i=1; i<10; i=i+1 )
          textarea.append( String.valueOf(i) );
  ```

- Squigglys for multiple statements:

  ```
  int i=10;
  while( i < 100 )
          textarea.append( String.valueOf(i) );
          textarea.append( "\n" );
          i = i + 10;
  ```

  the textarea.append("\n"); and i = i + 10; is not part of the while loop, even though the indentation makes it look like it is. Remember to use squiggly brackets if you want multiple statements as part of the loop.

- Semi-colon syntax:

  ```
  for( int i=1; i<=10; i=i+1 );
  {
          textarea.append( "Hello" );
  }
  ```

  You will not get an error message! However, because of the semi-colon at the end of the for loop declaration, this designates that there is nothing inside the loop! It will go through the loop 9 times doing nothing then go down and do the append to the textarea once!

- Infinite Loops

Example 1 no squigglys

```
int i=10;
while( i<100 )
        textarea.append( String.valueOf(i) );
        i=i+1;
```

Example 2 semi-colon

```
int i=10;
while( i<100 );
{
        textarea.append( String.valueOf(i) );
        i=i+1;
}
```

The semi-colon should not be at the end of the while loop declaration; this designates that the loop is empty - do nothing inside the loop! This example then ends up in an infinite loop, because the boolean expression `i<100` is always true!

Advanced Concept
Converting Binary to Decimal

Let's write a program named **BinToDec** that takes a binary number as a String variable consisting of 0's and 1's and convert it to a decimal value. First we need to learn how to convert a binary number to decimal before we can attempt to program it in Java. Let's start by looking at decimal representation. Decimal uses base 10, so values are based on multiples of 10.

$4096 = 4*1000 + 0*100 + 9*10 + 6*1$

This could also be represented as

$4096 = 4*10^3 + 0*10^2 + 9*10^1 + 6*10^0$

In binary we use base 2. So a binary number can be represented as:

$$\begin{aligned}
1011 &= 1*2^3 + 0*2^2 + 1*2^1 + 1*2^0 \\
&= 1*8 + 0*4 + 1*2 + 1*1 \\
&= 8 + 0 + 2 + 1 \\
&= 11
\end{aligned}$$

An algorithm for converting the number follows:

SET *numBits* to the number of bits in the binary number
    (HINT: how many characters in the string?)
SET *power* as the number of bits in the binary number minus one
SET *sum* to zero

LOOP for as many bits in the number
    SET *bit* be the value at the next position (as an integer)
    SET *term* be the value of the $bit * 2^{power}$
    ADD *term* to the *sum*
    SET *power* to *power* minus 1
END loop
RETURN decimal value of *sum*

An algorithm is a set of steps to solve a problem. The algorithm above is written in *pseudocode*, which is not quite proper English and not quite programming code. The words in upper-case are types of instructional statements. There are no steadfast rules on what these keywords should be, but we tend to use words that represent the process that should take place. Notice that the pseudocode could be useful for programming into any computer language – it's not specific to Java.

For our solution, based on the algorithm above we end up with:

```java
import java.awt.*;
import java.awt.event.*;
import javax.swing.*;
public class BinToDec extends JApplet implements ActionListener
{
    JTextField binaryNum;
    JLabel label, dec;
    JButton go;
    public void init( )
    {
        setLayout( new FlowLayout( ) );
        label = new JLabel( "Enter a binary number" );
        binaryNum = new JTextField( 10 );
        dec = new JLabel( "" );
        go = new JButton( "convert" );
        go.addActionListener( this );
        add( label );      add( binaryNum );
        add( go );         add( dec );
    }
    public void actionPerformed( ActionEvent ae )
    {
        String bin = binaryNum.getText( );
        int numBits = bin.length( );
        int power = numBits - 1;
        int sum = 0;
        for( int i=0; i<numBits; i++ )
        {
            int bit = Integer.parseInt( bin.substring( i, i+1 ) );
            int term = (int)(bit * Math.pow( 2, power ));
            sum += term;
            power--;
        }
        dec.setText( String.valueOf( sum ) );
    }
}
```

Now it's your turn – write a program that converts binary back to decimal or work with other bases such as octal or hexadecimal.

Summary

- Repetition statements (loops) allow us to repeat statements multiple times.
- There are three loops in Java: while, for and do while.
- We can use relational and conditional operators and complex expressions for our loops so long as the expression evalutes to a boolean value.
- Squiggly braces on while and for loops allow more than one statement to be executed in the body of the loop.
- The for loop is used when the number of iterations necessary is known or easily deciphered.
- The do while loop is used when we want the body of the loop to execute at least once.
- The squiggly braces are required for a do while loop.
- Semi-colons should not be placed after the while and for loops (but required at the end of a do while loop).
- Once the condition evaluates to false, the body of a loop is skipped and control of the program continues to the point after the loop.
- An *infinite loop* is a loop whose condition never evaluates to true, and the program is stuck executing inside the loop forever.
- Loops can be nested inside other loops or inside if-else/switch structures.
- To determine which loop to use, the guideline is:
    IF you know the number of times to go through the loop,
        USE the for loop
    ELSE IF you need to execute the statements in the loop at least once,
        USE the do loop
    ELSE
        USE while loop

Exercises

1. True or False. Curly braces are required with loop structures.

   Give the code below, answer the next two questions:
   ```
   int val = 1;
   for( int i=0; i<4; i++ )
        val += i;
   ```

2. How many times does the initialization part of the **for** loop get run?

3. What is the final value of the variable **val**?

4. What three types of loops does Java support?

5. True or False: A loop can be used to create animation.

6. True or False: Loops allow us to repeat statements until a condition evaluates to true.

7. List the values that are in the JComboBox based on the following code segment:
   ```
   JComboBox list = new JComboBox( );
   for( int   x=15; x<60; x = x+15 )
   {
           list.addItem( String.valueOf( x ) );
   }
   ```

8. How many times does the body of the following loop execute?
   ```
   int count = 10;
   while( count < 50 )
           count = count + 5;
   ```

9. True or False: you can you write a loop in the `paint` method but not the `init` method.

10. Write a code fragment that copies each element in a JList named **songs** to a JTextArea named **available** with each song from the JList displayed on a separate line inside the JTextArea.

11. Write a code fragment that creates a histogram inside a JTextArea named **histogram** based on the values listed in a JComboBox named **grades**. For example, if the values in **grades** are: 8, 8, 5, 9, 7 display a '*' for each point.

    ```
    8 : ********
    8 : ********
    5 : *****
    9 : *********
    7 : *******
    ```

12. What's wrong with the following code?
    ```
    int x = 5;
    while( x < 100 )
            textarea.append( String.valueOf(x) );
            x = x + 5;
    ```

13. What's wrong with the following code?
    ```
    for( int x=1; x<=10; x=x+1 );
    {
            textarea.append( "Hello" );
    }
    ```

14. What does the following code fragment do?
    ```
    int sum = 0;
    for( int i=0; i < 100; i++ )
            sum += i;
    ```

15. What is the final value of the variable **x** when the loop finishes?
    ```
    int  w = 4, x = 0, y = 3, z = 5;
    for (int i=0; i<z; i++)
        x = x + i;
    ```

16. What is the final value of the variable **x** when the loop finishes?
    ```
    int  w = 4, x = 0, y = 3, z = 5;
    for (int i=0; i<z; i++)
        x = x * i;
    ```

17. What is the final value of the variable **z** when the loop finishes?

    int z = 1999;
    do{
        z = z – 100;
    } while(z > 0);

18. Give an example of an off-by-one error when writing loops.

19. Which loop should you use in the following situations?
    d. display odd #'s between 1 and 100
    e. guessing game that prompts the user for a value, and ends when the user guesses the randomly chosen value.
    f. display the even numbers between 1 and 1000.
    g. Printing the characters in a string backwards (e.g., "Hello" prints as "olleH")

20. Write a code fragment that adds the numbers 1 through 10 to a JComboBox named **rating**.

21. Write a method named **power** that takes two integers: x and y and returns the value x^y.

22. Write a method named **spacer** that takes a String as a parameter and returns a new String with a space between each character (e.g. spacer("Java ROCKS!") returns "J a v a R O C K S !").

23. Write a method named **numReverse** which takes an integer as a parameter and returns the digits of the number in reverse (e.g. numReverse(1234) returns 4321). *Hint: make use of integer division and the remainder % operator.*

24. Write a method named **palindrome** which takes a String as a parameter and returns the boolean value `true` if the String is a palindrome and `false` if not (e.g. palindrome("racecar") returns `true`). A palindrome is when the string is exactly the same read forwards or backwards.

25. Write a method named **stripVowels** which takes a String as a parameter and returns the String without the vowels (e.g. stripVowels("Java is fun") returns "Jv s fn").

26. Write a method named **numVowels** which takes a String as a parameter and returns the number of vowels in the string (e.g. numVowels("Java") returns 2).

27. Modify the Weather program to use loops and have 100 snowflakes in winter and 100 rain drops in spring.

28. Create a program similar to the Weather program that draws a photo of your house and randomly chooses whether its raining or not. Be sure to make use of good methods to make it easier to program. Make the snowflakes randomly different sizes.

Chapter 10

Classes

Got class?

Objectives:

- Using Classes
- Extending JPanel
- Customizing Classes
- Font Fun
  - o Shadow Font
  - o Outline Font
- Background Images
- Customized Field

Using Classes

Java is an object-oriented language meaning that we organize our code into separate *classes* so we can instantiate *objects*. So far we've made use of many classes that someone else wrote and put together into either the `java.awt` package or the `javax.swing` package. Examples of these classes are: JButton, JLabel, Graphics and Color. Now we can learn how to create our own classes.

Remember when we started programming that each class needs to be in a file with the filename matching the name of the class and ending with the .java extension. So now we'll create two classes and reference one inside the other, just like how we reference Color and JLabel inside our applet classes. When we create our second class, however, we won't have it extend the JApplet. This means we won't be able to put it directly into a web page and view it – instead, we'll reference it in our other class that does extend JApplet. Because of this, we usually call this second class a *helper* class.

When we create our own class, many times we want it to be our own custom component. The easiest way to do this is to have our helper class extend the JPanel class. This enables our new class to have all the functionality of the JPanel class in addition to whatever customizations we add to it.

Extending JPanel

We've been using the JPanel class as a container to hold other components. But this class also allows us to create customized drawn components. We do so by writing a <u>separate class</u> that extends the **JPanel** class. Then we can create objects of this new class inside our applet program.

To set up this second class, create a new class that extends **JPanel**.

```
import java.awt.*;
import javax.swing.*;

public class Smiley extends JPanel
{

}
```

Inside this class, we can write a **paintComponent** method similar to the **paint** method from Chapter 2. One big difference is that inside this paintComponent method, we must first call our parent's (JPanel) `paintComponent` method. We can do this with a call to `super.paintComponent` and send it the variable for the Graphics object:

```
import java.awt.*;
import javax.swing.*;

public class Smiley extends JPanel
{
    public void paintComponent ( Graphics gr )
    {
        super.paintComponent( gr );

    }
}
```

NOTE: We must use the `paintComponent` method instead of the `paint` method.

Inside this paintComponent method, we can call methods on the Graphics object - just like we did in Chapter 2. We can also work with 2D graphics as introduced in Chapter 4:

```
Graphics2D  g2d = (Graphics2D )gr;
```

In the example below, we draw a smiley face.

```
import java.awt.*;
import javax.swing.*;
public class Smiley extends JPanel
{
    public void paintComponent ( Graphics g )
    {
        super.paintComponent( g );
        g.setColor( Color.yellow );     // face
        g.fillOval( 10,10, 200, 200 );

        g.setColor( Color.black );      // outline of face
        g.drawOval ( 10,10, 200,200 );

        g.fillRect ( 50,75, 50,5 );     // left eye
        g.setColor( Color.blue );       // right eye
        g.fillOval( 130,50, 30,50 );

        g.setColor( Color.red );        // mouth
        g.fillArc( 70, 100, 100, 70, 180, 180 );
    }
}
```

We can not run this class because it is not an applet – instead, create an instance of this in another class that does extend JApplet

Now we can use the Smiley class in our applet. We do so by first creating a Smiley object:

```
Smiley smiles;
smiles = new Smiley( );
```

*When you see: **new Smiley( )** that means we are creating an instance of the Smiley class*

Then we need to call a method **setPreferredSize(new Dimension(width, height))** on our Smiley object. If we do not call this method, the default width and height is zero. So even if we add it to the applet, we wouldn't be able to see it because the size is zero!

```
smiles.setPreferredSize( new Dimension(300, 300) );
```

Lastly, we can add it to the applet.

```
add( smiles );
```

The example below is the full applet code with other components as well.

```
import java.awt.*;
import javax.swing.*;

public class SmileyApplet extends JApplet
{
   Smiley smiles;
   JButton button;
   JTextField tf;

   public void init( )
   {
       smiles = new Smiley( );                            // create a Smiley object
       smiles.setPreferredSize( new Dimension( 300,300 ) );   // MUST set size or size will be zero!

       button = new JButton( "go!" );           // create button and text field
       tf = new JTextField(10);
       setLayout( new FlowLayout( ) );          // add to applet
       add( button );
       add( smiles );
       add( tf );
   }
}
```

JPanel is good for creating our own components, such as a thermometer, dial, fancy button, customized font, a smiley face or any other drawing that we want as a component among our other components on our applet. We can also create multiple smiley objects by declaring multiple variables of type Smiley and instantiating each as a separate object.

```
Smiley smiles1, smiles2, smiles3;
Smiles1 = new Smiley( );
smiles2 = new Smiley( );
smiles3 = new Smiley( );
smiles1.setPreferredSize( new Dimension(300, 300) );
smiles2.setPreferredSize( new Dimension(300, 300) );
smiles3.setPreferredSize( new Dimension(300, 300) );
add( smiles1 );    add( smiles2 );    add( smiles3 );
```

When adding a JPanel object to our applet, we must call the setPreferredSize method on the JPanel object otherwise it will display with a width and height of zero!.

Customizing our Class

Now that we can create multiple instances of our Smiley class and add them to our applet, it would be nice if we could customize each instance. For example, it would be nice if each instance could be a different size and change the colors. Let's start with the task of customizing the color of the face.

If we look back at our code for the Smiley class, inside the paintComponent method we *hard-coded* the face color of our smiley face. *Hard-coded* means we specified the actual values without making use of variables that are easily changed. We'll start by changing this value into a variable. This leads us to our first question – do we want to declare the variable as a *local* or *instance* variable? (Refer back to chapter 3) To answer this question, we need to decide what our solution will be. If we follow the conventions we've seen before where we can change colors on components by calling a method called `setColor`, then we will need to create our own method called `setColor`. The purpose of this method should be to simply set the variable for the color to the new value. Since it doesn't need to return any information to the caller, we will specify a return type of `void`. Our method should look like the following:

```
public void setColor( Color newColor )
{
    faceColor = newColor;
}
```

Now we need to have the variable faceColor declared somewhere. Remember, if we declare it as a local variable then we can only refer to it in the same method where it was declared. Since we want to be able to set its value within the setColor method and reference it to set the color in the paintComponent method, we will need to declare the variable as an instance variable. Our final version of the Smiley class with color customization is listed below.

```
import java.awt.*;
import javax.swing.*;
public class Smiley extends JPanel
{
    Color faceColor;         // declare variable as an instance variable
    public void paintComponent ( Graphics g )
    {
        super.paintComponent( g );
        g.setColor( faceColor );        // face
        g.fillOval( 10,10, 200, 200 );
        g.setColor( Color.black );      // outline of face
        g.drawOval ( 10,10, 200,200 );
        g.fillRect ( 50,75, 50,5 );     // left eye
        g.setColor( Color.blue );       // right eye
        g.fillOval( 130,50, 30,50 );
        g.setColor( Color.red );        // mouth
        g.fillArc( 70, 100, 100, 70, 180, 180 );
    }
    public void setColor( Color newColor )
    {
        faceColor = newColor;
    }
}
```

In our applet class we can now customize each Smiley object by calling the setColor method:

```
Smiley smiles1, smiles2;
Smiles1 = new Smiley( );
smiles2 = new Smiley( );
smiles1.setPreferredSize( new Dimension(300, 300) );
smiles2.setPreferredSize( new Dimension(300, 300) );
smiles1.setColor( Color.ORANGE );
smiles2.setColor( Color.MAGENTA );
add( smiles1 );   add( smiles2 );   add( smiles3 );
```

Now let's take a look at customizing the size. We could follow the same methodology we did for changing the color, but we could also use a different solution involving the *constructor* method. The constructor method is the method that automatically gets called when we create an instance, which is when the new operator is used (e.g. new Smiley ( )). So we can customize our constructor to take two parameters – one for the width, and one for the height. If we store this information in instance variables similar to our `faceColor` variable, we can reference them in the `paintComponent` method as well. The constructor method is shown below – note that constructors do not specify a return type and the name of the method must match the name of the class.

```
public Smiley( int w, int h )
{
    width = w;
    height = h;
}
```

We're not quite done yet. If we change the size of the smiley face, we need to change the location of our eyes, nose and mouth too! So now we need to calculate, with respect to the width and height, where these features should be located and how big they should be.

```java
import java.awt.*;
import javax.swing.*;
public class Smiley extends JPanel
{
    Color faceColor;          // declare variable as an instance variable
    int  width, height;
    public Smiley( int w, int h )
    {
        width = w;
        height = h;
        setPreferredSize( new Dimension( width, height ) );    // change size here instead of applet
    }
    public void paintComponent ( Graphics g )
    {
        super.paintComponent( g );
        g.setColor( faceColor );         // face
        g.fillOval( 0,0, width, height );

        g.setColor( Color.black );       // outline of face
        g.drawOval ( 0, 0, width, height );

        g.fillRect ( width/4,height/3, width/5, 6 );     // left eye
        g.setColor( Color.blue );                         // right eye
        g.fillOval(  width-width/3,height/4, width/10,height/6 );

        g.setColor( Color.red );         // mouth
        g.fillArc( width/4, height/2, width/2, height/3, 180, 180 );
    }
    public void setColor( Color newColor )
    {
        faceColor = newColor;
    }
}
```

The applet class would then be:

```java
import java.awt.*;
import javax.swing.*;

public class SmileyApplet extends JApplet
{
   Smiley smiles;
   JButton button;
   JTextField tf;
   public void init( )
   {
       smiles = new Smiley2( 200, 200 );      // create a Smiley object
       smiles.setColor( Color.MAGENTA );      // change the color

              // setPreferredSize accomplished in Smiley class so no need to do it here!
       // create button and text field
       button = new JButton( "go!" );
       tf = new JTextField(10);
       // add to applet
       setLayout( new FlowLayout( ) );
       add( button );
       add( smiles );
       add( tf );
   }
}
```

Advanced Concept

When creating methods, we can have more than one with the same name for even more flexibility in customization. This applies to our regular methods as well as constructors. This is called *overloading* methods. For example, we could define two constructors – one that takes two integer values for the size and another constructor with no parameters where we use default values for the size of the component. We've actually made use of this already in many calls to the add method to add our components to the applet. Sometimes we've sent a JButton as a parameter, sometimes a JTextField – yet everytime we called the same method: add. The following example is a modified snippet of the Smiley class with two constructors defined. If our applet program creates a Smiley object with two parameters, it will call the first constructor Smiley s = new Smiley (350, 350), and if we create a Smiley object with no parameters, it will call the second constructor defined below: Smiley s = new Smiley ( ) ;

```java
import java.awt.*;
import javax.swing.*;
public class Smiley extends JPanel
{
        Color faceColor;         // declare variable as an instance variable
        int  width, height;
        public Smiley( int w, int h )
        {
            width = w;
            height = h;
        }
        public Smiley( )
        {
            width = 300;
```

Overloaded constructor – 2 constructors with different # of parameters

```
            height = 300;
        }
        public void paintComponent ( Graphics g )
        {
            ....
            {
}
```

Method overloading is when we write multiple methods in the same class with the same name. There are three rules we need to follow to overload a method:
        1. Different <u>number</u> of parameters
        2. Different <u>data types</u> of parameters
        3. Different <u>ordering of the data types</u> of the parameters
An example is shown below:

```
public class Overloading
{
    public int add( int a, int b )
    {
        return a + b;
    }
    public int add( int a, int b, int c )
    {
        return   a + add( b, c );
    }
    public int add( int a, int b, int c, int d )
    {
        return add(a, b) + add(c, d);
    }
}
```

(Make use of methods you've already written)

We can also overload constructors by following the same rules:

```
public class Account
{
    String name;
    double balance;
    int ID;
    public Account( )
    {
        this( "unknown", -1, 0.0 );
    }
    public Account( String n, int id )
    {
        this( n, id, 0.0 );
    }
    public Account( String n, int id, double b )
    {
        name = n;
        ID = id;
        balance = b;
    }
}
```

*(**this**( ) calls another constructor in this class that match based on the parameters.)*

Font Fun

Now that we can create our own little components by extending the JPanel class, we can revisit some of the drawing techniques we learned in Chapter 2 and extend them. For example, we can learn how to create our own funky fonts by working with the drawString method. We will look at two font examples: a shadow font and an outline font.

Shadow Font

To create our own shadow font, we first need to create a separate class that extends the JPanel class:

```
public class FontShadow extends JPanel
{
    String txt;        // instance variable to hold the text to be displayed
    public FontShadow( String val )      // constructor, takes the text to display as a parameter
    {
        txt = val;
    }
    public void paintComponent ( Graphics g )
    {
        super.paintComponent( g );
                             // draw code here
    }
}
```

The name of our class is called `FontShadow`, and we will need to reference this in our applets whenever we want to create a shadow font text. The method **FontShadow** is called a *constructor* method, which gets called when our applet does the following:

```
FontShadow fs;
fs = new FontShadow( "text" );
```

To customize our component, we want to call the FontShadow with specific text to be displayed. We need to keep track of this information, so we store it into an *instance variable* named **txt**. Now we need to add some methods in our `paint` method to draw the shadow text. First we'll change the font by calling the `setFont` method. Then change the color to the shadow color. Next draw the shadow by calling the `drawString` method twice (for extra shadow effect). Then change the color for the text color, and `drawString` again for the text. The final class is displayed below:

```java
import java.awt.*;
import javax.swing.*;
public class FontShadow extends JPanel
{
  String txt;
  public FontShadow( String val )
  {
      setBackground( Color.yellow );  // change background color
      txt = val;
  }
  public void paintComponent( Graphics g )
  {
      super.paintComponent( g );
      g.setFont( new Font ( "SanSerif", Font.BOLD, 16 ) );
      g.setColor( Color.BLACK );      // can change shadow color
      g.drawString ( txt, 4,21 );
      g.drawString ( txt, 5,22 );
      g.setColor( Color.RED );         // can change text color
      g.drawString ( txt, 3,20 );
  }
}
```

Note: we can change the color for the background, shadow and text. A good exercise would be to make this class more customizable by allowing users to call methods to set the background color, text color and shadow color.

Now we need our applet to use this class we created. We can do this by creating `FontShadow` components just like we create JButtons and JLabels.

```java
import java.awt.*;
import javax.swing.*;
public class FontShadowEx extends JApplet
{
  FontShadow fshad;
  public void init( )
  {
      fshad = new FontShadow( "Elizabeth Sugar Boese" );
      fshad.setPreferredSize( new Dimension(190,30) );   // you have to define it's size

      setLayout( new FlowLayout( ) );
      add( fshad );
  }
}
```

Font Outline

Drawing an outline around the text is fairly similar, but this time we need to draw the text one pixel left and up, left and down, right and up, and right and down. This gives the effect of an outline around the text which is drawn last in a different color.

The example below is based on the same code as above but draws an outline

```java
import java.awt.*;
import javax.swing.*;
public class FontOutlineEx extends JApplet
{
  FontOutline fshad;
  public void init( )
  {
        fshad = new FontOutline( "Elizabeth Sugar Boese" );
        fshad.setPreferredSize( new Dimension(190,30) );   // we have to define it's size
        setLayout( new FlowLayout( ) );
        add( fshad );
  }
}
```

```java
import java.awt.*;
import javax.swing.*;
public class FontOutline extends JPanel
{
  String txt;
  public FontOutline( String val )
  {
        setBackground( Color.YELLOW );   // can change background color
        txt = val;
  }
  public void paintComponent( Graphics g )
  {
        super.paintComponent( g );
        g.setFont( new Font ( "SanSerif", Font.BOLD, 16 ) );
        g.setColor( Color.BLACK );       // can change shadow color
        g.drawString ( txt, 3,19 );
        g.drawString ( txt, 3,21 );
        g.drawString ( txt, 5,19 );
        g.drawString ( txt, 5,21 );
        g.setColor( Color.RED );         // can change text color
        g.drawString ( txt, 4,20 );
  }
}
```

How would you create a hollow font - just an outline of text?

Background Image

We can create a second class that extends `JPanel` and create a `paintComponent` method where we paint an Image or draw shapes (e.g. Chapter 2) as a background for the panel. In this class we can draw an image as a backdrop in the `paintComponent` method using the `drawImage` method. Then we can use this class in other classes, and add components to it like we do to any JPanel.

In the example below, it is written to center the image within the size of the panel.

NOTE: You cannot make a call to getImage inside a class that does not extend JApplet! This method is only accessible by classes that extend JApplet (via inheritance).

```java
import java.awt.*;
import javax.swing.*;
public class ImgBackground extends JApplet
{
    JLabel myplay, name;
    Image img;
    ImgPanel ipanel;
    public void init( )
    {
        myplay = new JLabel( "My Fun Playground" );
        name = new JLabel( "Java Rules" );
        myplay.setForeground( Color.YELLOW );
        name.setForeground( Color.RED );
        img = getImage( getCodeBase( ), "houseLake.png" );
        ipanel = new ImgPanel( img );

        myplay.setFont( new Font( "Serif", Font.BOLD, 20 ) );
        ipanel.setLayout( new GridLayout( 2,1 ) );
        ipanel.add( myplay );
        ipanel.add( name );
        add( ipanel );
    }
}
```

ImgPanel is just like JPanel – setLayout and add components to it

```java
import java.awt.*;
public class ImgPanel extends JPanel
{
    Image img;
    public ImgPanel( Image ic )
    {
        img=ic;
    }
    public void paintComponent( Graphics g )
    {
        super.paintComponent(g);
        if ( img != null )                                      // make sure the image exists
        {
            int imgWidth = img.getWidth(this);                  // find the width of the image
            int panelWidth = this.getWidth( );                  // find the width of the panel
            int x = (panelWidth - imgWidth ) / 2;               // calculate x to center the img
            int imgHeight = img.getHeight( this );              // find height of image
            int panelHeight = this.getHeight( );                // find height of panel
            int y = (panelHeight - imgHeight ) / 2;             // calculate y to center the img
            g.drawImage(img,x,y,img.getWidth(this),img.getHeight(this),this);   // paint the image
```

Use this separate class – send the Image when you create an instance

```
        }
    }
}
```

Customized Field Set

We can create a second class that extends `JPanel` and put a group of components inside it. Then we can reference this class whenever we want that group of components in our program. For example, a common set of fields is for a person's address. We could create a separate class that extends JPanel that handles creating all these fields for us. Then in our applet class, we could instantiate this new component twice – once for a person's mailing address and once for their billing address (or more times if they have work/school/home addresses, etc.).
The following code shows the class that extends JPanel with all these components. We named it AddressFields.

```
import java.awt.*;
import javax.swing.*;
public class AddressFields extends JApplet
{
    // instance variables
    JLabel name, street, city, state, zip;
    JTextField tf_name, tf_street, tf_city, tf_state, tf_zip;

    // constructor
    public AddressFields( )
    {
        // initialize the instance variables
        name = new JLabel( "Name:", JLabel.RIGHT );
        street = new JLabel( "Street:", JLabel.RIGHT );
        city = new JLabel( "City:", JLabel.RIGHT );
        state = new JLabel( "State:", JLabel.RIGHT );
        zip = new JLabel( "Zip:", JLabel.RIGHT );
        tf_name = new JTextField( 20 );
        tf_street = new JTextField( 20 );
        tf_city = new JTextField( 20 );
        tf_state = new JTextField( 20 );
        tf_zip = new JTextField( 20 );
        // add to the panel
        setLayout( new GridLayout( 5, 2 ) );
        add( name );       add( tf_name );
        add( street );     add( tf_street );
        add( city );       add( tf_city );
        add( state );      add( tf_state );
        add( zip );        add( tf_zip );
    }
}
```

The following is the applet code that makes use of our newly created AddressFields component.

```
import java.awt.*;
import javax.swing.*;
public class AddressApplet extends JApplet
{
    JLabel homeAddress, billingAddress;
    AddressFields home, billing;
    public void init( )
    {
        homeAddress = new JLabel( "Home Address" );
        billingAddress = new JLabel( "Billing Address" );
        home = new AddressFields( );
        billing = new AddressFields( );
        setLayout( new BoxLayout( getContentPane( ), BoxLayout.Y_AXIS ) );
        add( homeAddress );
        add( home );
        add( billingAddress );
        add( billing );
    }
}
```

Advanced Concept

Writing classes is the heart of object-oriented programming. Classes help us manage our programs into small modules. Each class maintains data specific for the class, and contains the methods that affect those data variables. Methods that return the value of a data variable are called *getters* or *accessor* methods. Methods that set or change the value of one of the data variables are called a *setter* or *mutator* methods. Constructor methods are called when we create an instance of the class via the new operator. Other methods in a class are called *helper* methods.

To properly set up a class, we should usually declare our instance variables *private*. This prevents other classes from having direct access to change their values; instead, these classes would have to go through one of the methods we define in our class to be able to change the data variable. This is a good practice because we could add error checking within the method which we couldn't do if the variable had public access.

The basic structure of a helper class is listed below:

```
public class <classname>     // class header
{
   // instance variables
   // constructors
   // getter methods
   // setter methods
   // helper methods
}
```

(Helper classes do not extend JApplet - therefore cannot be run. They can extend JPanel, JComponent, etc. or nothing at all.)

A more flushed out class structure follows:

```
public class <classname>   // class header
{
  // instance variables
  private <type> <instanceVariable1>;
  private <type> <instanceVariable2>;
       …
  // constructors
  public   <classname> ( <parameterList> )
  {
  }
  // getter methods
  public <returnType> get<instanceVariableName>( )
  {
        return <instanceVariableName>;
  }
  // setter methods
  public void set<instanceVariableName>( <type> <parameterValue> )
  {
        <instanceVariableName> = <parameterValue>;
  }
}
```

Instance variables should be private to adhere to encapsulation

Constructors have no return type!

Getter method return types must match the data type of the variable being returned

So let's build an example class. We want to develop a program that keeps track of the courses we're taking this semester. We need a class to keep track of each course we're taking. To keep it simple, we're just going to record the title of the course and the number of credits. In our Course class, we need getter and setter methods for our instance variables, since our instance variables should be private.

```
public class Course
{
  private int numCredits;           // instance variable
  private String title;             // instance variable
  public Course( String name, int nCredits )   // constructor
  {
        title = name;
        numCredits = nCredits;
  }
  public String getTitle( )         // getter method
  {
        return title;
  }
  public int getNumCredits( )       // getter method
  {
        return numCredits;
  }
  public void setTitle( String t )  // setter method
  {
        title = t;
  }
  public void setNumCredits( int nc )   // setter method
  {
        numCredits = nc;
  }
}
```

Constructor method name matches the name of the class and has no return type

*`title` is a String data type, so its getter method's return type is **String***

Note that we do not print things using System.out.println inside the toString method

```java
    public String toString( )            // returnStr is a local variable
    {
      String returnStr =  title;
      returnStr += " ( " + numCredits + " ) ";
      return returnStr;
    }
}
```

And the applet program:

```java
import java.awt.*;
import javax.swing.*;
public class CourseApplet extends JApplet
{
    Course math, history, cs;
    JList list;
    DefaultListModel model = new DefaultListModel( );
    public void init( )
    {
        math = new Course( "Calculus", 4 );        // call constructor method in Course
        history = new Course( "History", 3 );
        cs = new Course( "Java", 4 );
        list = new JList( model );
        model.addElement( math.toString( ) );
        model.addElement( history.toString( ) );
        model.addElement( cs.toString( ) );
        setLayout( new FlowLayout( ) );
        add( list );
    }
}
```

Summary

- We can create our own classes as helper classes to our programs. These helper classes to not extend JApplet but may extend JPanel or another component, or nothing at all.
- Each class we create can maintain its own list of instance variables and methods.
- When extending the JPanel, we can customize the background of the panel by using the Graphics methods inside a paintComponent method.
- Calling the new operator on a class will call the constructor method in the class.
- The constructor method header differs from other method headers. There is no return data type defined and the name of the method must match exactly to the name of the class.
- We can create several constructors depending on our needs. Therefore, we could have one constructor that takes no parameters and another constructor that takes an ImageIcon as a parameter. This is called *overloading* the method. The program can figure out which method to call based on the parameters sent to the method.
- When extending a component such as the JPanel, we need to set the preferred size of the component – otherwise it will default to a size of zero. We can set the preferred size either in the applet on our component variable, or inside the constructor of our custom component.
- We can extend almost any component, but the most common ones are JPanel and JComponent.

Classes Exercises

1. True or False: The JPanel component is useful for creating your own components, because you can use the paintComponent method to draw it any way you like.

2. On a JTabbedPane, what happens when you try to directly add two components to the same tab?

3. When creating a separate class using the JPanel, how does this class specify that it inherits from the JPanel class?

4. What happens to your program if you create a JPanel object (or use an extension such as the Smiley class), and you do NOT call the **setPreferredSize** method?

5. What other stylized fonts can you create by extending the JPanel class?

6. How would you put an image on the tab-top-part without any text?

7. When we use the **new** operator to create an object, what is the method that gets called?

8. When you call the method **setPreferredSize**, what do you need to send to it?

9. Take your drawings from Chapter 2 and put them into a separate class that extends the JPanel class, then add them to your applet with other buttons and labels, etc.

10. Create an applet that instantiates 3 FontOutline objects and add them to the applet.

11. Modify the ImgPanel class to stretch the image to fit the size of the JPanel instead of centering it.

12. Write a class that extends the JComponent class that keeps track of information for a movie. Maintain instance variables for the title, director, year released and an image. Write your own paintComponent method in this class that draws the image and then displays the title, director and release year. In your applet class, instantiate several Movie objects for different movies and add each to your applet.

13. Create a Logo class that displays your name with some shapes as your own personal logo. Add it to the bottom of all your applets.

14. Create an applet with 9 Smiley objects, each with different colors for face, eyes, and mouth. Use GridLayout to display in a 3x3 grid. Use a method for creating each Smiley that takes as parameters the various colors.

Chapter 11

Swing Components II

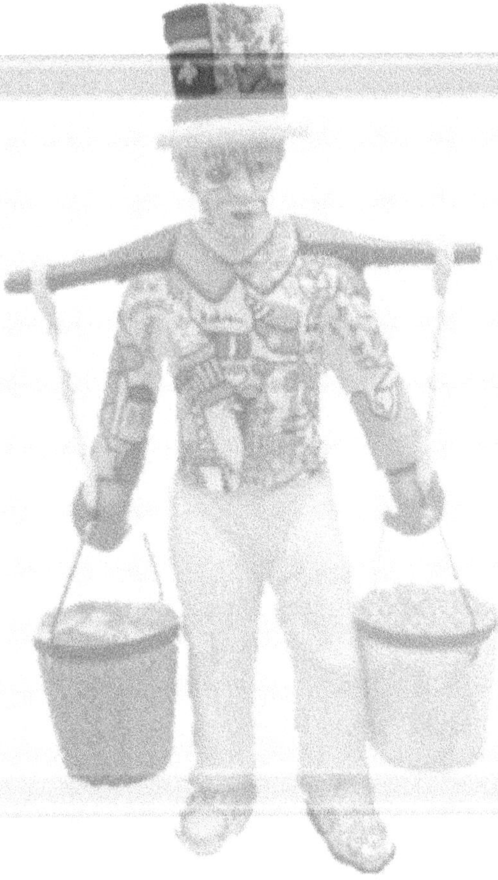

Objectives:
- JTabbedPane
- ToolTips
- Borders
- Audio
- JFrame
- MediaTracker

JTabbedPane

JTabbedPane allows us to have tabs for the user to click on to view different components. The tabs can be placed on any side - top, left, bottom or right by specifying the location when we create the JTabbedPane.

We can create a JTabbedPane two ways:

```
JTabbedPane tabpane;

tabpane = new JTabbedPane();
tabpane = new JTabbedPane( location );
```

The first one defaults the tabs on the top. The second one allows us to choose the location of the tabs, which can be one of the following:

- JTabbedPane.LEFT
- JTabbedPane.RIGHT
- JTabbedPane.TOP
- JTabbedPane.BOTTOM

When adding components to each tab, we call the method `addTab`. There are several formats for calling `addTab`:

```
JTabbedPane tabpane;
tabpane = new JTabbedPane();

tabpane.addTab( text, component );
tabpane.addTab( text, ImageIconOnTab, component );
tabpane.addTab( text, ImageIconOnTab, component, toolTipText );
```

The text is what is displayed on the actual tab. If an ImageIcon is specified, it will be displayed with the text on the tab. The component will be added to the pane for when the tab is selected - **only one component can be added to each of these panes**. This component is added to the pane as BorderLayout.CENTER (therefore, the component will be stretched both horizontally and vertically).

```
import java.awt.*;
import javax.swing.*;
public class JTabEx extends JApplet
{
   JButton b1, b2;
   JLabel b3;
   Image img1, img2, img3;
   ImageIcon iconCart, iconIdea, iconPC;
   JPanel p1;
   JTabbedPane tabpane;
   public void init( )
   {
      tabpane = new JTabbedPane( );
      img1 = getImage(getCodeBase( ), "gocart.png" );
      img2 = getImage(getCodeBase( ), "idea.png" );
      img3 = getImage(getCodeBase( ), "oncomputer.png" );
      iconCart = new ImageIcon(img1);
      iconIdea = new ImageIcon(img2);
      iconPC = new ImageIcon(img3);
      b1 = new JButton( "", iconCart );
      b2 = new JButton( "What an idea!", iconIdea );
      b3 = new JLabel( iconPC );
      p1 = new JPanel( );
      p1.add(b1);

      // add tabs
      tabpane.addTab( "Tab 1", iconCart, p1, "Hi there" );
      tabpane.addTab( "Second", b2 );
      tabpane.addTab( "third", b3 );

      // add tabbed pane to applet
      add( tabpane, BorderLayout.CENTER );
   }
}
```

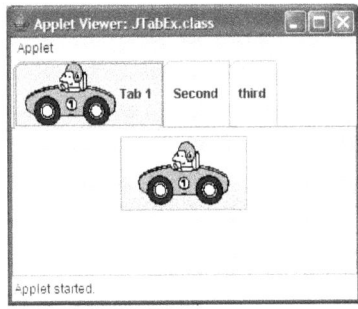

We can also have the tabs on the left, by specifying this when we create the JTabbedPane.

```
JTabbedPane tabpane;
tabpane = new JTabbedPane( JTabbedPane.LEFT );
```

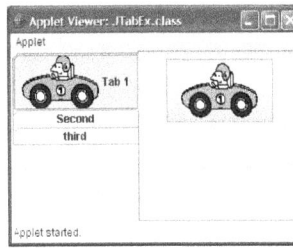

Using buttons to walk through tabs in a JTabbedPane

```java
import java.awt.*;
import java.awt.event.*;
import javax.swing.*;
public class JTabbedSwitch extends JApplet implements ActionListener
{
  JTabbedPane pane = new JTabbedPane( );
  JButton prev2 = new JButton( "Back" ), prev3 = new JButton( "Back" );
  JButton next1 = new JButton( "Next" ),  next2 = new JButton( "Next" );
  public void init( )
  {      // add listeners
        prev2.addActionListener( this );
        prev3.addActionListener( this );
        next1.addActionListener( this );
        next2.addActionListener( this );
        // first pane : no previous tab, has next tab
        JPanel panel1 = new JPanel( new FlowLayout() );
        JLabel label1 = new JLabel( "Here is some fine text " );
        panel1.add(label1);
        panel1.add( next1 );
        pane.add( "one", panel1 );
        // second pane : has previous tab, has next tab
        JPanel panel2 = new JPanel( new FlowLayout( ) );
        JLabel label2 = new JLabel( "Whhoooooeeeee!" );
        panel2.add( prev2 );
        panel2.add(label2);
        panel2.add( next2 );
        pane.add( "two", panel2 );
        // third pane : has previous tab, no next tab
        JPanel panel3 = new JPanel( new FlowLayout( ) );
        JLabel label3 = new JLabel( "yeaoswers!" );
        panel3.add( prev3 );
        panel3.add(label3);
        pane.add( "three", panel3 );
        add( pane );                    // add to applet
  }
  public void actionPerformed( ActionEvent ae )  /** handle events on the buttons, switching the current tab */
  {
        Object obj = ae.getSource( );              // get the object that caused the event
        int tabindex = pane.getSelectedIndex( );   // determine which tab index is currently selected
        if ( obj == prev2 || obj == prev3 )     // check which object caused the event - either previous button
              pane.setSelectedIndex( tabindex-1 );   // go back one tab
        else if ( obj == next1 || obj == next2 )    // check if the event was caused by a next button
              pane.setSelectedIndex( tabindex+1 );   // go forward one tab
  }
}
```

ToolTips

Tooltips are mini-pop-ups that display some information when the user's cursor hovers for a moment over a particular component.

All we need to do to set the tooltip information for a component is to call the method

```
component.setToolTipText( String )
```

Examples:

```
JButton submit;
submit = new JButton( "Submit" );
submit.setToolTipText( "Click button to email your message." );

Image img;
ImageIcon ic;
JLabel label;
img = getImage( getCodeBase( ), "me.gif" );
ic = new ImageIcon( img );
label = new JLabel( ic );
label.setToolTipText( "Image of me and friend" );
```

Change the background color of the tooltip box by changing GREEN to the color of your choice:

```
UIManager.put ("ToolTip.background", Color.GREEN);
```

JTabbedPane ToolTips

For JTabbedPane, we can specify the tool tip text when we add each tab with the `addTab` method.

tabbedpane.addTab(String title, Icon icon, Component component, String tip);

Example:

```
JTabbedPane tabs;
tabs = new JTabbedPane( );
tabs.addTab( "Title on tab", null, jpanel, "Hi there" );
```

where we specify `null` to designate no image on the tab and `jpanel` is the JPanel with the stuff that goes into the tab pane.

201

Borders

We can add borders to any JComponent that we create, including a JPanel. Borders don't add any functionality, it just adds decor to our applets. There are a couple of steps we need to do to get borders to appear, some dependent on the type of border that we want. For all borders, we have to import the javax.swing.border package:

```
import javax.swing.border.*;
```

Now we need to decide what type of border we want. We'll need to call a method on the BorderFactory class to create the actual Border object (these are explained in more detail below). There are many types of borders:

- line (in any color)
- etched (raised or lowered)
- bevel (raised or lowered)
- title (line, etched: raised or lowered, bevel: raised or lowerd)
- matte (uses an image)

Once we create the border, we can add it to a component by calling the `setBorder` method:

```
JPanel pane;
pane = new JPanel( );
pane.setBorder( Border );
```

The following example shows a basic line border:

```
import javax.swing.*;
import javax.swing.border.*;  // don't forget to include this!
import java.awt.*;
public class BorderLine extends JApplet
{
  JLabel label1, label2, label3;
  Image img;
  ImageIcon ic;
  JPanel panel;
  Border lineborder;
  public void init( )
  {
     setLayout( new FlowLayout( ) );
     label1 = new JLabel( "<HTML>Multiple<BR>Lines<BR>is<BR>fun" );
     label2 = new JLabel( "<HTML>Need<P>to<P>learn<P>HTML" );
     img = getImage( getCodeBase( ), "singer.gif" );
     ic = new ImageIcon(img );
     label3 = new JLabel( "Label with image", ic, JLabel.CENTER );
     panel = new JPanel( );                   // add labels to PANEL
     panel.add( label1 );
     panel.add( label2 );
     panel.add( label3 );
     lineborder = BorderFactory.createLineBorder( Color.RED );   // create red line border
     panel.setBorder(lineborder);            // set border to panel
     add(panel);
  }
}
```

Etched Border

Example changed with Etched Border - Raised

Border etchedBorder = BorderFactory.createEtchedBorder(EtchedBorder.RAISED);
panel.setBorder(etchedBorder);

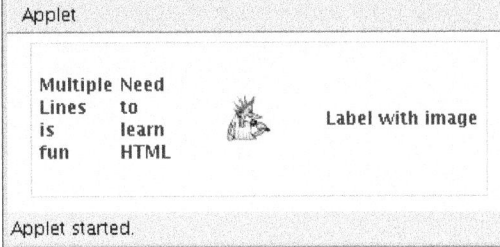

Example changed with Etched Border - Lowered

Border etchedBorder = BorderFactory.createEtchedBorder(**EtchedBorder.LOWERED**);
panel.setBorder(etchedBorder);

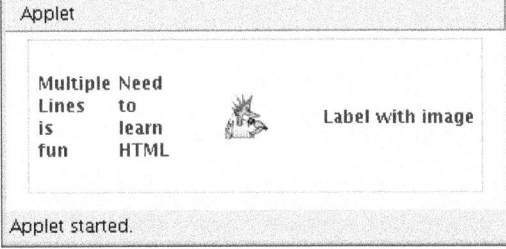

Bevel Border

Example changed with Bevel Border - Raised

Border bevelBorder = BorderFactory.createRaisedBevelBorder( );
panel.setBorder(bevelBorder);

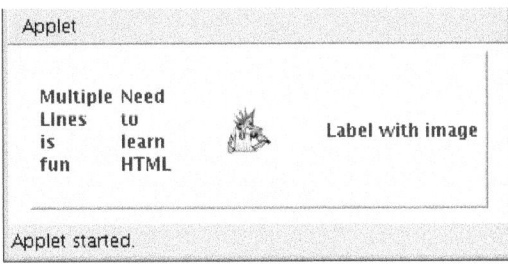

Example changed with Bevel Border - Lowered

Border bevelBorder = BorderFactory.createLoweredBevelBorder( );
panel.setBorder(bevelBorder);

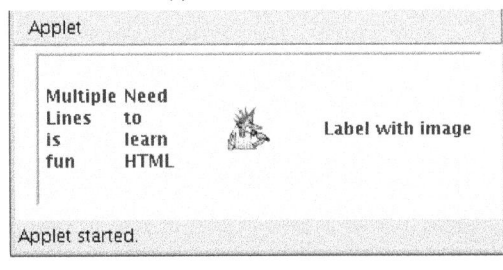

Titled Border

Example changed with Title Border

TitledBorder title = BorderFactory.createTitledBorder("Favorite Things");
panel.setBorder(title);

Matte Border

Matte borders allow us to specify an image to go around the component. Images can be any size, but some look better than others. A good idea for matte image is a pattern to create a sort of frame.

Example changed with Matte Border

Image borderimg = getImage(getCodeBase(), "bunny.gif");
ImageIcon bordericon = new ImageIcon(borderimg);
Border matteBorder = BorderFactory.createMatteBorder(-1, -1, -1, -1, bordericon);
panel.setBorder(matteBorder);

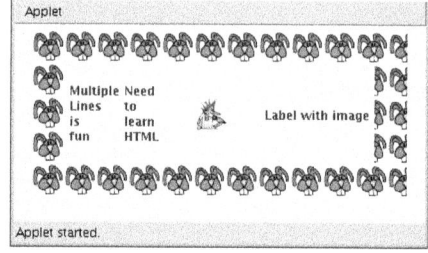

Audio

Java supports five different types of sound files:

- AIFF
- AU
- WAV
- MIDI
- RMF

Note: Java does not naturally support mp3 files, but you can download and install 3rd party software that does. This, however, takes some work.

To play sounds, we can simply get the sound file with the `getAudioClip` method and then play it by calling the `play` method.

```
AudioClip clip;
clip = getAudioClip( getCodeBase( ), audioFilename );
clip.play( );
```

```
import java.awt.*;
import java.applet.*;
import javax.swing.*;
public class AudioPlay extends JApplet
{
    String audioFilename = "mySounds.mid";
    AudioClip ac;
    public void init( )
    {
        ac = getAudioClip( getCodeBase( ), audioFilename );
        ac.play( );
    }
}
```

AudioClip is in the java.applet package

getCodeBase determines the file path location

There are three methods we can call on our AudioClip

play	play the sound file once through
loop	play the sound file continually
stop	stop playing the file

loop
 We can also have our audio file loop, so that it continually plays over and over again instead of playing through once and stopping. To continually loop, we call the `loop` method on our `AudioClip` object.

Example: *Based on the code above, replace*

```
ac.play( );
```
with
```
ac.loop( );
```

stop
 Whether playing a long audio file or looping an audio file, we should be sure we stop playing when the user leaves our applet page. To do this, we need to code a method named `stop` in our applet, which is automatically called when the user leaves our web page with our applet. In this method, we need to reference the `AudioClip` object. First we need to verify that it has been created by checking to see that it is not equal to `null`, and if it isn't equal to null, then we should call the `stop` method.

```java
import java.awt.*;
import java.applet.*;
import java.awt.event.*;
import javax.swing.*;
public class LoopAudio extends JApplet
{
   String audioFilename = "happyDaze.wav";
   AudioClip ac;

   public void init( )
   {
         ac = getAudioClip( getCodeBase( ), audioFilename );
         ac.loop( );              // loop instead of play
   }
   public void stop( )
   {
         if( ac != null )         // can't stop it if it isn't running
              ac.stop( );
   }
}
```

Note: This code will only work if you declare your AudioClip object at the top of your program!

 We need to write a stop( ) method if we're looping our audio – otherwise the audio will continue playing even after the user has left your applet website!

This next example is a guitar tuner. It would look much better with appropriate images.

```java
import java.awt.*;
import java.awt.event.*;
import javax.swing.*;
import java.applet.AudioClip;
public class GuitarTune extends JApplet implements ActionListener
{
   AudioClip  s1, s2, s3, s4, s5, s6;
   JButton E1, A, D, G, B, E2;
   public void init( )
   {
      setLayout( new FlowLayout( ) );
      setupSounds( );
      E1 = new JButton( "E" );
      A = new JButton( "A" );
      D = new JButton( "D" );
      G = new JButton( "G" );
      B = new JButton( "B" );
      E2 = new JButton( "E" );
      setupButton( E1);
      setupButton( A );
      setupButton( D );
      setupButton( G );
      setupButton( B );
      setupButton( E2 );
   }
```

continued

```
   public void setupSounds( )
   {
      s1 = getAudioClip( getCodeBase( ), "snd6.au" );
      s2 = getAudioClip( getCodeBase( ), "snd5.au" );
      s3 = getAudioClip( getCodeBase( ), "snd4.au" );
      s4 = getAudioClip( getCodeBase( ), "snd3.au" );
      s5 = getAudioClip( getCodeBase( ), "snd2.au" );
      s6 = getAudioClip( getCodeBase( ), "snd1.au" );
   }
   public void setupButton( JButton btn )
   {
      btn.addActionListener( this );
      add( btn );
   }
   public void actionPerformed( ActionEvent ae )
   {
      Object src = ae.getSource( );
      if ( src == E1 )
         s1.play( );
      else if ( src == A )
         s2.play( );
      else if ( src == D )
         s3.play( );
      else if ( src == G )
         s4.play( );
      else if ( src == B )
         s5.play( );
      else if ( src == E2 )
         s6.play( );
   }
}
```

JFrame

JFrame allows us to open a new window. The default JFrame has the following look to it:

```
import javax.swing.*;
public class JFrameDefault extends JApplet
{
   JFrame frame;
   public void init( )
   {
         frame = new JFrame( "Testing JFrame stuff" );
         frame.setSize( 200,100 );
         frame.setVisible( true );
   }
}
```
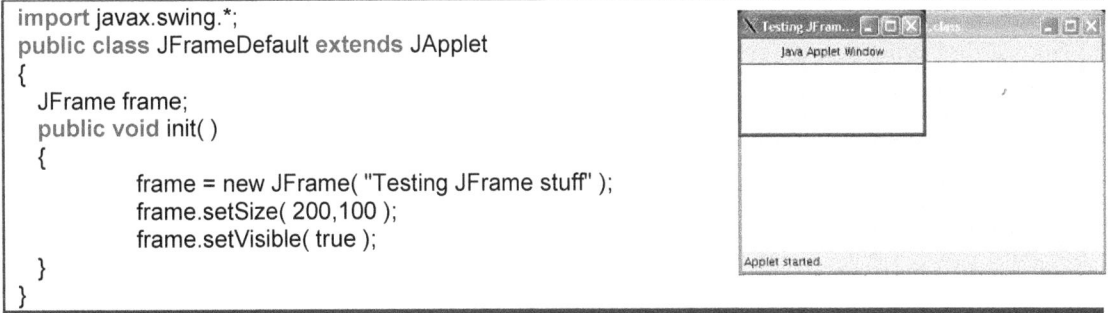

 We *must specify the size and visibility in order for us to see the frame!*
The setVisible method makes sure the frame is visible.

When we create the JFrame, we specify the title that is to appear in the top of the window (e.g., "Testing JFrame stuff");

```
JFrame frame;
frame = new JFrame( text );
```

For example:

```
JFrame newframe;
newframe = new JFrame( "Testing JFrame stuff" );
```

By default, we see that the new frame window appears in the top-left corner of our screen. We can specify a better location by calling the `setLocation` method on our frame object.
Example:

```
frame.setLocation( 500, 600 );
```

In this example, the frame will appear 500 pixels to the right and 600 pixels down from the upper-left corner of the screen.

The default layout manager for the frame is `BorderLayout`. We can change the layout manager as we've done before:

```
frame.setLayout( new FlowLayout( ) );
frame.setLayout( new GridLayout( 1, 2 ) );
```

Major Steps

There are five major steps to get the frames to work. Although there are additional things we could specify, these are the core steps we'll want to do at a minimum each time we use JFrame components.

1. Create the frame.

    ```
    JFrame frame;
    frame = new JFrame("FrameDemo");
    ```

2. Set layout manager

    ```
    frame.setLayout( new BorderLayout( ) );
    ```

3. Create components and put them in the frame.

    ```
    JButton go = new JButton( "Go for it!" );
    frame.add(universe, BorderLayout.SOUTH);
    ```

4. Size the frame.

    ```
    frame.pack();
    ```
    OR
    ```
    frame.setSize( 200, 500 );
    ```

    calling the .pack( ) method will size the frame based on the minimum size to fit all the components added to the frame.

5. Show it.

    ```
    frame.setVisible(true);
    ```

Other steps we may want to consider is to set the location of the frame, change the look-and-feel, add events, etc.

```java
import java.awt.*;
import javax.swing.*;
public class JFrameStuff extends JApplet
{
  JFrame frame;
  JLabel myname, universe;
  JButton go, skiing;
  public void init( )
  {
        //1. Create the frame.
        frame = new JFrame("FrameDemo");
        //2. Set layout manager
        frame.setLayout( new BorderLayout( ) );
        //3. Create components and put them in the frame.
        myname = new JLabel( "<HTML>My <BR>Stuff", JLabel.CENTER );
        go = new JButton( "Go for it!" );
        skiing = new JButton( "Do you like skiing too?" );
        universe = new JLabel( "I live at the borders of the universe where fact and fiction collide" );
        frame.add(myname, BorderLayout.NORTH);
        frame.add(go, BorderLayout.WEST);
        frame.add(skiing, BorderLayout.EAST);
        frame.add(universe, BorderLayout.SOUTH);

        //4. Size the frame.
        frame.pack( );
        //5. Show it.
        frame.setVisible(true);
  }
}
```

This next example uses events to trigger when to display the frame.

Upon starting the applet:

```java
import java.awt.*;
import java.awt.event.*;
import javax.swing.*;
public class JFrameEvents extends JApplet
           implements ActionListener
{
  JFrame frame;
  JPanel buttonspane;
  JButton pc, car, idea;
  Image pcimg, carimg, ideaimg;
  ImageIcon icon;
  JLabel label;

  public void init( )
  {
        setLayout( new BorderLayout( ) );
        setupImages( );
        setupButtons( );
  }

  public void setupButtons( )
  {
```

continued

```
            pc = new JButton( "<HTML>Lady on<BR>Computer" );
            car = new JButton( "Car" );
            idea = new JButton( "Great Idea!" );
            pc.addActionListener( this );          // add listeners
            car.addActionListener( this );
            idea.addActionListener( this );

            buttonspane = new JPanel( new GridLayout(3,1) );
            buttonspane.add( pc );
            buttonspane.add( car );
            buttonspane.add( idea );
            add( buttonspane, BorderLayout.CENTER );
    }
    public void setupImages( )
    {
            pcimg = getImage( getCodeBase( ), "oncomputer.png" );
            carimg = getImage( getCodeBase( ), "gocart.png" );
            ideaimg = getImage( getCodeBase( ), "idea.png" );
            icon = new ImageIcon( pcimg );    // start with the pc image
            label = new JLabel( icon );
    }
    public void actionPerformed( ActionEvent ae )
    {
            Object src = ae.getSource( );

            //1. Create the frame.
            frame = new JFrame("FrameDemo");
            //2. Set layout manager
            frame.setLayout( new BorderLayout( ) );
            //3. Create components and put them in the frame.
            if( src == pc )
            {
                    icon.setImage( pcimg );
                    label.setIcon( icon );
            }
            else if ( src == car )
            {
                    icon.setImage( carimg );
                    label.setIcon( icon );
            }
            else if ( src == idea )
            {
                    icon.setImage( ideaimg );
                    label.setIcon( icon );
            }
            frame.add(label, BorderLayout.CENTER);

            //4. Size the frame.
            frame.pack( );
            //5. Show it.
            frame.setVisible(true);
    }
}
```

Click on Lady:

Click on Car:

Click on Great Idea:

MediaTracker

When we create an applet with lots of images or some large images, it can take a while to load all the images. By default the applet will try to start to run even though the images are not all loaded yet. This can result in some of the images not appearing at all on our applets! The proper way to ensure our images are fully loaded before running our applets is to load them into a MediaTracker object and then tell the applet to wait for all the images to load before continuing. We can do this by loading the images into the MediaTracker with the addImage method call, then in the start method force our applet to ensure all images have loaded. This code can produce exceptions and therefore we need to put them inside something called a try…catch block. The example below shows how to work with the MediaTracker.

```java
import java.awt.*;
import javax.swing.*;
public class MediaTrackerEx extends JApplet
{
    Image one, two, three, four;
    MediaTracker imgTracker;
    public void init( )
    {
        loadImages( );
    }
    public void start( )
    {
        try
        {
            imgTracker.waitForAll( );
        }catch (Exception e )
        { }
    }
    public void loadImages( )
    {
        one = getImage( getCodeBase( ), "one.gif" );
        two = getImage( getCodeBase( ), "two.gif" );
        three = getImage( getCodeBase( ), "three.gif" );
        four = getImage( getCodeBase( ), "four.gif" );
        imgTracker.addImage( one, 1 );
        imgTracker.addImage( two, 2 );
        imgTracker.addImage( three, 3 );
        imgTracker.addImage( four, 4 );
    }
}
```

Summary

- Tabs can be added to a JTabbedPane on top, left, bottom or right.
- Only one component can be added to a tab in JTabbedPane. To have multiple components displayed in a tab, put them inside a JPanel and add the JPanel to the tab.
- The pack method on a JFrame will size the frame based on the minimum size required to fit all the components in the JFrame.
- Call the method setVisible on the JFrame when it is ready to be displayed.
- Add tooltips to Swing components by calling the **setToolTipText** mehod on the object we want a tooltip.
- Add tooltips to JTabbedPane panes when we call the **addTab** method by specifying the text on the tab, an ImageIcon (or null for none) for the tab, the panel to go inside the pane and the text for the tooltip.
- Create borders using the **BorderFactory** class in the **javax.swing.border** package.
- Add borders using the **setBorder** method.
- Types of borders: line, etched, bevel, titled, matte and empty.
- Etched and bevel borders can be either raised or sunk in.
- Java supports five types of audio files: AIFF, AU, WAV, MIDI, RMF
- To access an audio file, call the method **getAudioClip** in a similar way to getImage.
- To play audio files, either call **play** or **loop** on the AudioClip object.
- Call the **stop** method on the AudioClip object to stop it from playing.
- Write a **stop** method that stops all AudioClips running for when the user leaves your applet
- MediaTracker can be used to ensure all images load before the applet continues.

Exercises

1. True or False: On a **JTabbedPane**, you can put tabs on the top or left side of the panes.
2. What method is called to add a component to a JTabbedPane?
3. On a JTabbedPane, what happens when you try to directly add two components to the same tab?
4. What is the default placement for tabs in a JTabbedPane?
5. How do you add a button to a tab in JTabbedPane but keep the button's dimensions appropriate?
6. What does the **setForeground** method do on a JButton? on a JLabel?
7. What is the method to get the text a user entered in a JTextField?
8. How do you determine whether a JCheckBox is selected or not? a JRadioButton? a JButton?
9. How do you add text to a JTextArea?
10. What is the method **setEnabled** used for? Which components is this useful for?
11. How do you disable a JButton?
12. JFrames use what layout manager by default?
13. What is the purpose of the **pack( )** method for a JFrame?
14. What are the five steps to producing a window frame?
15. True or False: JFrames can pop-up based on a button-click.
16. True or False: You can program a JFrame to pop-up as soon as the applet loads.
17. What is the purpose of the method `setVisible` for JFrames? What happens if you don't call `setVisible(true)` on your JFrame?
18. Fill in the blanks so that this program displays a JFrame:
    ```
    import java.awt.*;
    import javax.swing.*;
    public class xyz extends JApplet
    {
      JFrame frame;
      JLabel  name;
      public void init( )
      {
        frame = new _____( "Title" );
        frame. _____( new FlowLayout( ) );
        name = new JLabel( "Cookie Monster" );
        frame. _____( name );
        frame.pack( );
        frame._____( true );
      }
    }
    ```
19. True or False: You can have tooltips on a JPanel object.
20. What method do you call on a component when you want to set the border to a matte border object you previously created?
21. True or False: You can make a border with an image.

213

22. True or False: You can make borders that look raised like a button or lowered like its carved into the component.

23. How do you add a tooltip to each pane in JTabbedPane?

24. True or False: You can change the color of a line border.

25. What three things do you need to do to get a border?

26. Can you add a border object (e.g., **border** from the examples) directly to an applet?

27. What sound file extensions can be played using the standard Java class libraries?

28. True or False: You cannot have two different audio files playing at the same time.

29. Why do we need to implement a stop method if we're running our audio file using loop?

30. Do we need a stop method if we just run the audio file with play?

31. Add images to the guitar tuner so it looks like the actual guitar strings. Add different images for when the user clicks on a string, to make it look like it is being "plucked".

32. Write an applet of quiz questions. When the user selects a particular difficulty and topic, pop up the quiz question inside a JFrame. When the user answers in the JFrame, pop up another JFrame letting the user know whether or not they answered the question correctly. Extend this to be a full Jeopardy style applet or Family Feud.

33. Add tooltips and borders to your applets that you made from the components and/or layouts chapter (Favorite movies/songs/party invitation/etc.).

34. Create an applet of your resume using JTabbedPane. Add tabs for your education, work experience and/or portfolio, contact information and photos.

35. Create an applet that loads 10 of your photos in a large size. Try to run the applet to display the images. Then implement the MediaTracker to ensure all the images load before running the applet.

Chapter 12

Collections

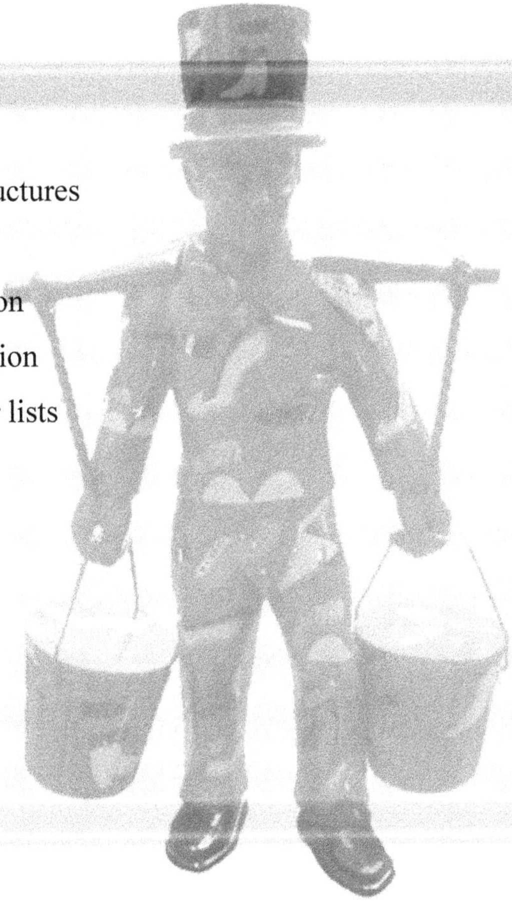

Objectives:

- List Data Structures
- Arrays
  - Declaration
  - Initialization
  - Initializer lists
  - 2-D
- JTable
- ArrayList
- Case Study

List Data Structures

Many times when we are programming we need to handle a group of items. Instead of creating separate variables for each one, it is more convenient for us to have one reference variable for all of them. This also enables us more flexibility to easily change the number of items in the group. We'll also see some clever code techniques that we can implement based on using one of these collections data data structures. The two data structures we'll look at are arrays and ArrayList.

Arrays

An array is a data structure that can hold a list of items. We can have a list of numbers, of Strings, of buttons, etc. One limitation is that when we create an array, all of the elements in the array must be the same data type. Therefore, we cannot have int values and buttons in the same array.

We can depict this list graphically as a bunch of boxes with the elements in each box. We can then number each box with an *index* value, to designate where the element is in the array.

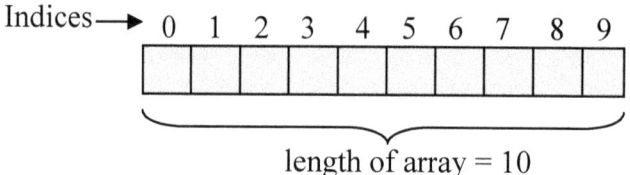

Note that the indices start at zero!
Therefore, if we have *n* elements in an array, the last element is at index *n-1*.

Array Declaration

We use brackets to declare an array. We can place the brackets either after the data type or after the variable name.
Example

```
int[ ] grades;         JButton[ ] buttons;        // after data type
int grades[ ];         JButton buttons[ ];        // after variable name
```

Note that declaration does not initialize the values!

Array Initialization

When instantiating an array, we need to specify the maximum size of our list. We do this by putting the size in brackets as follows:

```
grades = new int[3];
buttons = new JButton[4];
```

Note how this differs from creating a new JButton, where we say:

```
button = new JButton("txt").
```

Note also how we create a list of primitives, like the int.
This step initializes a list (array) of the specified size. We have not yet initialized each element in the list yet.

Arrays indices start at zero! The last element in an array is at the array.length – 1.

Array Element Initialization

Next we need to initialize each element in the array.
We can do this one of two ways: manually or with a loop.
Example manually:

```
grades[0] = 89;           buttons[0] = new JButton( "A" );
grades[1] = 92;           buttons[1] = new JButton( "B" );
grades[2] = 95;           buttons[2] = new JButton( "C" );
                          buttons[3] = new JButton( "D" );
```

Example with a loop:

```
for( int i=1; i<4; i++ )
       grades[i] = i;
```

What are the values in the array after the loop executes?

Short-cut Initializer List

We also have the option to declare and initialize our list all at once, if we know what we want in our list. We do this by using squiggly brackets to designate the values inside the list.
The following two examples illustrate this :

```
int[ ] grades = { 89, 92, 95 };

JButton buttons[ ] = {   new JButton( "A" ), new JButton("B"),
                         new JButton( "C"), new JButton("D")
                     };
```

Length

One of the most important things to know about arrays is the *length* of an array. We can access this information by referring to the constant `length` on the array.
For example, based on the above examples:

```
grades.length              <-- returns 3
buttons.length             <-- returns 4
```

NOTE: there is no parenthesis after length!

This is useful when we want to walk through all the elements in an array. For example, if we want to calculate the average of all the grades, we need to loop through the array to calculate:

```
int sum = 0;
for( int i=0; i < grades.length; i++ )
       sum = sum + grades[i];
double average = (double)sum / grades.length;
```

Another example, if we had an array of buttons we wanted to add to a JPanel:

217

```
            JPanel pane = new JPanel( new GridLayout(4,1) );
            for( int i=0; i<buttons.length; i++ )
            {
                    buttons[i].addActionListener( this );
                    pane.add( buttons[i] );
            }
            add( pane );
```

This first example prints a new quote each time the user clicks on the button.

```
import java.awt.*;
import javax.swing.*;
import java.awt.event.*;
import java.util.*;
public class RandomQuoter extends JApplet
   implements ActionListener
{
  JButton next;
  JLabel label;
  Random random = new Random( );
  String[ ] quotes =
    {
      "What's up doc?",
      "Have you any Grey Poupon?",
      "Can you hear me now?",
      "<HTML><CENTER>What is the average ground speed <BR> of an unladen swallow?",
      "As you wish"
    };
  public void init( )
  {
    setLayout( new BorderLayout( ) );
    next = new JButton( "Next!" );
    next.addActionListener( this );
    label = new JLabel( "Good morning!", JLabel.CENTER );
    label.setFont( new Font( "Serif", Font.BOLD, 16 ) );
    add( next, BorderLayout.NORTH );
    add( label, BorderLayout.CENTER );
  }
  public void actionPerformed( ActionEvent ae )
  {
    Object obj = ae.getSource( );
    if ( obj == next )
    {
            int index = random.nextInt( quotes.length );
            label.setText( quotes[index] );
    }
  }
}
```

This example shows the use of an array of images and buttons to walk through the images.

```java
import java.awt.*;
import java.awt.event.*;
import javax.swing.*;
public class SlideShowUsingButtons extends JApplet implements ActionListener
{
   Image[ ] photos;                              // array of all your images
   ImageIcon icon;                               // images need to be in an ImageIcon
   JLabel imgLabel;                              // and stored into a JLabel
   int currentIndex = 0;                         // which image index currently displayed
   JButton prev, next;
  public void init( )
  {
      setLayout( new FlowLayout( ) );
      photos = new Image[4];                    // load the images into memory
      photos[0] = getImage( getCodeBase( ), "houseLake.png" );
      photos[1] = getImage( getCodeBase( ), "idea.png" );
      photos[2] = getImage( getCodeBase( ), "gocart.png" );
      photos[3] = getImage( getCodeBase( ), "oncomputer.png" );
      icon = new ImageIcon( );
      imgLabel = new JLabel( );
      imgLabel.setHorizontalAlignment( JLabel.CENTER );  // center all images
      prev = new JButton( "Prev" );
      next = new JButton( "Next" );
      setupIcon( 0 );            // initialize setup to first display first image (index 0)

      add( prev );               // add components to applet
      add( imgLabel );
      add(next );
      prev.addActionListener(this);   // add listeners
      next.addActionListener(this);
  }
  public void setupIcon( int index )      // method changes the image in the label
  {                                       // & modifies next/prev buttons to be enabled/disabled
      currentIndex = index;
      icon.setImage( photos[index] );
      imgLabel.setIcon(icon );
      prev.setEnabled( true );            // default both buttons to enabled
      next.setEnabled( true );

      if( index == 0 )
         prev.setEnabled( false );
      if( index == photos.length-1 )
         next.setEnabled( false );
  }
  public void actionPerformed( ActionEvent ae )
  {
      Object obj = ae.getSource( );
      if ( obj == next )
         setupIcon( currentIndex+1 );    // otherwise just increment the index
      else
         setupIcon( currentIndex-1 );    // otherwise just increment the index
      repaint( );                        // Show the change.
  }
}
```

*We need **repaint** method call to ensure the applet updates the display.*

219

The following example is first listed (on left) without using arrays, and the second (right) uses an array for all the buttons. Notice the differences between the two. This example shows how using an array can save coding effort. How much code is necessary to expand each of these programs to handle 20 buttons? Which one would be easier to work with?

```java
import java.awt.*;
import javax.swing.*;
import java.awt.event.*;
public class ButtonNoArr extends JApplet
                    implements ActionListener
{
   JLabel label;
   JButton mybuttons1 = new JButton( "one" );
   JButton mybuttons2 = new JButton( "two" );
   JButton mybuttons3 = new JButton( "three" );
   JButton mybuttons4 = new JButton( "four" );
public void init( )
   {
      setLayout( new FlowLayout( ) );
      label = new JLabel( "Hello" );
      add( label ) ;
      mybuttons1.addActionListener( this );
      mybuttons2.addActionListener( this );
      mybuttons3.addActionListener( this );
      mybuttons4.addActionListener( this );

      add( mybuttons1 );
      add( mybuttons2 );
      add( mybuttons3 );
      add( mybuttons4 );
   }
   public void actionPerformed( ActionEvent ae )
   {
      Object obj = ae.getSource( );
      if( obj == mybuttons1 )
      {
         label.setText ( "first button" );
      }
      else if ( obj == mybuttons2 )
      {
         label.setText( "second button" );
      }
      else if( obj == mybuttons3 )
      {
         label.setText( "third" );
      }
      else if( obj == mybuttons4 )
      {
         label.setText( "fourth" );
      }
   }
}
```

```java
import java.awt.*;
import javax.swing.*;
import java.awt.event.*;
public class ButtonArr extends JApplet
                    implements ActionListener
{
   JLabel label;
   JButton[ ] mybuttons =
   {
      new JButton( "one" ),
      new JButton( "two" ),
      new JButton( "three" ),
      new JButton( "four" )
   };
   public void init( )
   {
      setLayout( new FlowLayout( ) );
      label = new JLabel( "Hello" );
      add( label ) ;
      for( int x=0; x < mybuttons.length; x++ )
         mybuttons[x].addActionListener(this);
         add( mybuttons[x] );
      }
   }
   public void actionPerformed( ActionEvent ae )
   {
      Object obj = ae.getSource( );
      if( obj == mybuttons[0] )
      {
         label.setText( "first button" );
      }
      else if ( obj == mybuttons[1] )
      {
         label.setText( "second button" );
      }
      else if( obj == mybuttons[2] )
      {
         label.setText( "third" );
      }
      else if( obj == mybuttons[3] )
      {
         label.setText( "fourth" );
      }
   }
}
```

Loop works no matter how many buttons in the array!

The example on the right can be optimized using another array for the text to be set in the label. Create a String array at the top of the class with "first button", "second button", "third" and "fourth". Then in the actionPerformed method, change it to loop through the buttons; once a match is found, the index of the matching button matches the index into our String array. Therefore, we can set the text on our label to the string matching the index of the selected button. The code is shown below:

```java
import java.awt.*;
import javax.swing.*;
import java.awt.event.*;
public class ButtonArr extends JApplet  implements ActionListener
{
   JLabel label;
   JButton[ ] mybuttons =    {   new JButton( "one" ),  new JButton( "two" ),
         new JButton( "three" ),
         new JButton( "four" )
   };
   String[ ] text =    {   "first button",   "second button",   "third",   "fourth"  };
   public void init( )
   {
      setLayout( new FlowLayout( ) );
      label = new JLabel( "Hello" );
      add( label ) ;

      for( int x=0; x < mybuttons.length; x++ )
      {
         mybuttons[x].addActionListener(this);
         add( mybuttons[x] );
      }
   }
   public void actionPerformed( ActionEvent ae )
   {
      Object obj = ae.getSource( );
      for( int x=0; x<mybuttons.length; x++ )
      {
         if ( obj == mybuttons[x] )
            label.setText ( text[x] );
      }
   }
}
```

This is a great example of clever programming. We can use this is a multitude of ways; for example, matching a button to an image, matching a button to an image and audio file and text! Create arrays for each item, where the indices match up within each array. Then when we figure out which button was selected, we know the index into each array: the image, the text, the audio to play!

x is the correct index for the button array as well as the String text array!

We can also create a sliding puzzle, with one "blank" spot. The user clicks on picture fragments adjacent to the blank spot to move them around, until they can finally produce the correct picture. This example will automatically divide up the image into a 4x4 grid.

```java
import java.awt.*;
import java.awt.event.*;
import java.awt.image.*;
import javax.swing.*;
public class SlidingPuzzle extends JApplet  implements ActionListener
{
   Image image;
   ImageIcon icon;
   JButton buttons[ ], blankButton;
   JPanel grid, spots[ ];
   int currentBlankSpot;
   public void init( )
   {
      setLayout( new FlowLayout() );
      buttons = new JButton[16];
      grid = new JPanel( new GridLayout(4,4) );
      setupPanels( );
      setupImage( );
```

continued

```java
      grid.setSize( 400, 400 );
      add( grid );
   }
   public void setupPanels( )
   {
      spots = new JPanel[16];
      blankButton = new JButton( " " );
      blankButton.setBackground( Color.BLACK );
      for ( int i=0; i<spots.length; i++ )
      {
         spots[i] = new JPanel( new BorderLayout( ) );
         grid.add( spots[i] );
      }
   }
   public void setupImage( )
   {
      image = getImage( getCodeBase( ), "GalapagosTurtlesSquare.gif" );
      MediaTracker tracker = new MediaTracker( this );
      tracker.addImage( image,1);
      try { tracker.waitForAll( );
      } catch( Exception e ) { }
BufferedImage bimage = new BufferedImage(image.getWidth(null),image.getHeight(null),BufferedImage.TYPE_INT_ARGB);
      Graphics g = bimage.getGraphics( );
      g.drawImage(image,0,0,this);

      int width=image.getWidth(this);
      int height=image.getHeight(this);
      System.out.println( width + " h = " + height );
      int count = 0;
      for ( int i=0; i<4; i++ )
       for ( int j=0; j<4; j++ )  // don't display the last one, this is the blank spot
       {
          BufferedImage window = bimage.getSubimage(i*width/4,j*height/4,width/4,height/4);
          setupButton( count++, window );
       }
      // override the last button with the blank spot
      spots[ spots.length-1 ].add( blankButton );
      currentBlankSpot = spots.length-1;
   }
   public void setupButton( int id, Image img )
   {
      buttons[id] = new JButton( new ImageIcon( img ) );
      buttons[id].addActionListener( this );
      buttons[id].setMargin(new Insets( 0,0,0,0) );
      buttons[id].setContentAreaFilled( false );
      spots[id].add( buttons[id],BorderLayout.CENTER );
   }
   public void actionPerformed( ActionEvent ae )
   {
      Object src = ae.getSource();
      for ( int i=0; i<buttons.length; i++ )
      {
         if ( buttons[i] == src )
         {
            if ( currentBlankSpot - 1 == i || currentBlankSpot - 4 == i
               || currentBlankSpot + 1 == i || currentBlankSpot + 4 == i )
            {
                                        // exchange spots with blank
```

continued

```
                    spots[ currentBlankSpot ].removeAll( );
                    spots[ i ].removeAll( );

                    spots[ currentBlankSpot ].add( buttons[ i ] );
                    spots[ i ].add( blankButton );

                    buttons[ currentBlankSpot ] = buttons[ i ];
                    buttons[ i ] = blankButton;
                    currentBlankSpot = i;
                    repaint( );
                    return;                      // must have this here
                }
            }
        }
    }
}
```

Handle buttons with different images, holding state if selected

```
import java.awt.*;
import java.awt.event.*;
import javax.swing.*;
public class JButImg extends JApplet implements ActionListener
{
  JButton[ ] buttonArray = new JButton[3];

  public void init( )
  { setLayout( new GridLayout( 3, 1 ) );
    setupButton( 0, "About Me" );  // set up each of the buttons by calling the setupButton method
    setupButton( 1, "Resume" );    // send it the number of the button in the buttonArray array and
    setupButton( 2, "Hobbies" );   // text to display on the button
  }
  public void setupButton( int buttonNum, String name )
  {
      Image img = getImage(getCodeBase( ), "buttongr.gif" );  // get the main image for the button
      ImageIcon ic = new ImageIcon( img );
      buttonArray[buttonNum] = new JButton( name, ic );   // create the button
                                                // place the text on top of the image
      buttonArray[buttonNum].setHorizontalTextPosition( SwingConstants.CENTER );
                                                // turn the border off around the button
      buttonArray[buttonNum].setBorderPainted(false);
                          // no spacing between the contents of the button and the edge
      buttonArray[buttonNum].setMargin( new Insets(0,0,0,0) );
      buttonArray[buttonNum].setForeground( Color.white );      // set the font color to white
      buttonArray[buttonNum].addActionListener( this );   // listen for clicks
      // when the user pressed the button, have the icon color change
      buttonArray[buttonNum].setPressedIcon(
                          new ImageIcon( getImage(getCodeBase( ), "buttonbrite.gif" ) ) );
      // when the user selects the button, have the icon color change
      buttonArray[buttonNum].setSelectedIcon(
                          new ImageIcon( getImage(getCodeBase( ), "buttongray.gif" ) ) );
      // when the user rolls the mouse over the button, have the icon color change
      buttonArray[buttonNum].setRolloverIcon(
                          new ImageIcon( getImage(getCodeBase( ), "buttonred.gif" ) ) );
      // when the user rolls the mouse over a SELECTED button, have the icon color change
      buttonArray[buttonNum].setRolloverSelectedIcon(
```

```
                               new ImageIcon( getImage(getCodeBase( ), "buttondim.gif" ) ) );
    // don't draw the regular button background
    buttonArray[buttonNum].setContentAreaFilled(false);
    buttonArray[buttonNum].setFocusPainted(false);
    add(buttonArray[buttonNum]);              // add to applet
 }
 public void actionPerformed( ActionEvent ae )
 {
    Object obj = ae.getSource( );
    if ( obj instanceof JButton )
    {
       for ( int i=0; i<buttonArray.length; i++ )   // de-select the button that is currently selected
          if ( buttonArray[i].isSelected( ) )
                    buttonArray[i].setSelected( false );
       JButton button = (JButton) obj;   // set the button that was just clicked to selected mode
       button.setSelected( true );
    }
 }
}
```

Arrays and JTable

Arrays are going to help us display graphical tables in our applets, which sort of look like spreadsheets. Before we can learn how to create tables in applets, we first need to expand our knowledge of arrays. So far, we have looked at single-dimensional arrays. We also need to look at 2-D arrays.

2-D Arrays

A 2-D array is similar to a 1-D array, but we now have two dimensions. We still designate using the brackets [and], but we have two sets of brackets.
Example:

```
        int[ ][ ] grades;         String data[ ][ ];
```

Similar to the 1-D arrays, we still need to create the actual array and specify the dimensions - the number of rows and columns. The first set of brackets is used to designate the number of rows, and the second set of brackets for the number of columns.
Example:

```
        grades = new int[2][3];    // two rows three columns
        data = new String[5][4];   // five rows four columns
```

Remember - Java starts counting at zero!

We can assign values to each cell in the array manually, by again specifying the exact row and column for a particular cell:
Example:

```
        grades[0][1] = 89;         // row zero, column 1
        data[4][3] = "Good";       // last row 4, last column 3
```

Like the 1-D array, we can also initialize the entire thing all at once using the squiggly braces, the outer squigglys for the row and the inner sets of squigglys for each column:

```
            int[ ][ ] grades = {      {1, 2, 3},
                                      {4, 5, 6}
                                };
```
creates the following array:

1	2	3
4	5	6

If we reference:

```
            grades[1][2]
```

we would be referring to the value 6

This next example shows an array of Strings:

```
            Object data[ ][ ] = {  { "Liz",   "Skiing",   "Fort Fun", "21" },
                                   { "C. M.", "Cooking",  "Denver",   "56" },
                                   { "Oscar", "Mtn Biking","Mars",    "19" },
                                };
```
creates the following array:

Liz	Skiing	Fort Fun	21
C. M.	Cooking	Denver	56
Oscar	Mtn Biking	Mars	19

If we reference:

```
            data[2][1]
```

we would be referring to "OK"

JTable

Now that we can do both 1-D and 2-D arrays, we can put together a JTable. A table requires both a 1-D and a 2-D array - the 1-D array for the column headings displayed at the top of the table, and a 2-D array for the actual data inside the table. The column headings have to be Strings, but our data array can be of type `Object` where we could put Strings or checkboxes or even images inside them. Of course, adding different types add to the complexity of creating the table, but it's great to have such flexibility available.

Let's start with a simple example creating a table with just Strings. We'll use the data example listed above. First we need to create the column headings:

```
            String[ ] colHeadings = {  "Name", "Sport", "Location", "Age" };
```

Then we can use the data variable listed above:

```
            Object data[ ][ ] = {  { "Liz",   "Skiing",    "Fort Fun", "21" },
                                   { "C. M.", "Cooking",   "Denver",   "56" },
                                   { "Oscar", "Mtn Biking","Mars",     "19" },
                                };
```
Note: we can not store an int directly into a JTable - convert to String first!

225

To create our table:

```
JTable table;
table = new JTable(data, colHeadings);
```

In order to get the headings to display properly, we also have to do two more things. The first is to set the viewable area of the table (based on pixels - width and height):

```
table.setPreferredScrollableViewportSize(new Dimension(500, 70));
```

Then we need to put the table into a scroll pane so that users can view all of it, in case the rows and columns do not fit within the viewport size:

```
//Create the scroll pane and add the table to it.
JScrollPane scrollPane = new JScrollPane(table);

//Add the scroll pane to this panel.
add(scrollPane);
```

 Put JTables into a JScrollPane and add the JScrollPane to the applet to ensure the JTable displays properly.

The following is our complete example:

```
import java.awt.*;
import javax.swing.*;
public class JTableData extends JApplet
{
  String[ ] colHeadings = { "Name", "Sport", "Location", "Age" };

  Object data[ ][ ] = { { "Liz",  "Skiing",   "Fort Fun", "21" },
                        { "C. M.", "Cooking", "Denver", "56" },
                        { "Oscar", "Mtn Biking","Mars", "19" },
                      };
  JScrollPane scrollPane;
  JTable table;

  public void init( )
  {
    table = new JTable( data, colHeadings );
    table.setPreferredScrollableViewportSize(new Dimension(400, 70));
    //Create the scroll pane and add the table to it.
    scrollPane = new JScrollPane(table);.
    add(scrollPane);
  }
}
```

Coloring

We can also have too much fun with colors on our tables. The following example explores a bunch of opportunities for coloring different aspects of our tables:

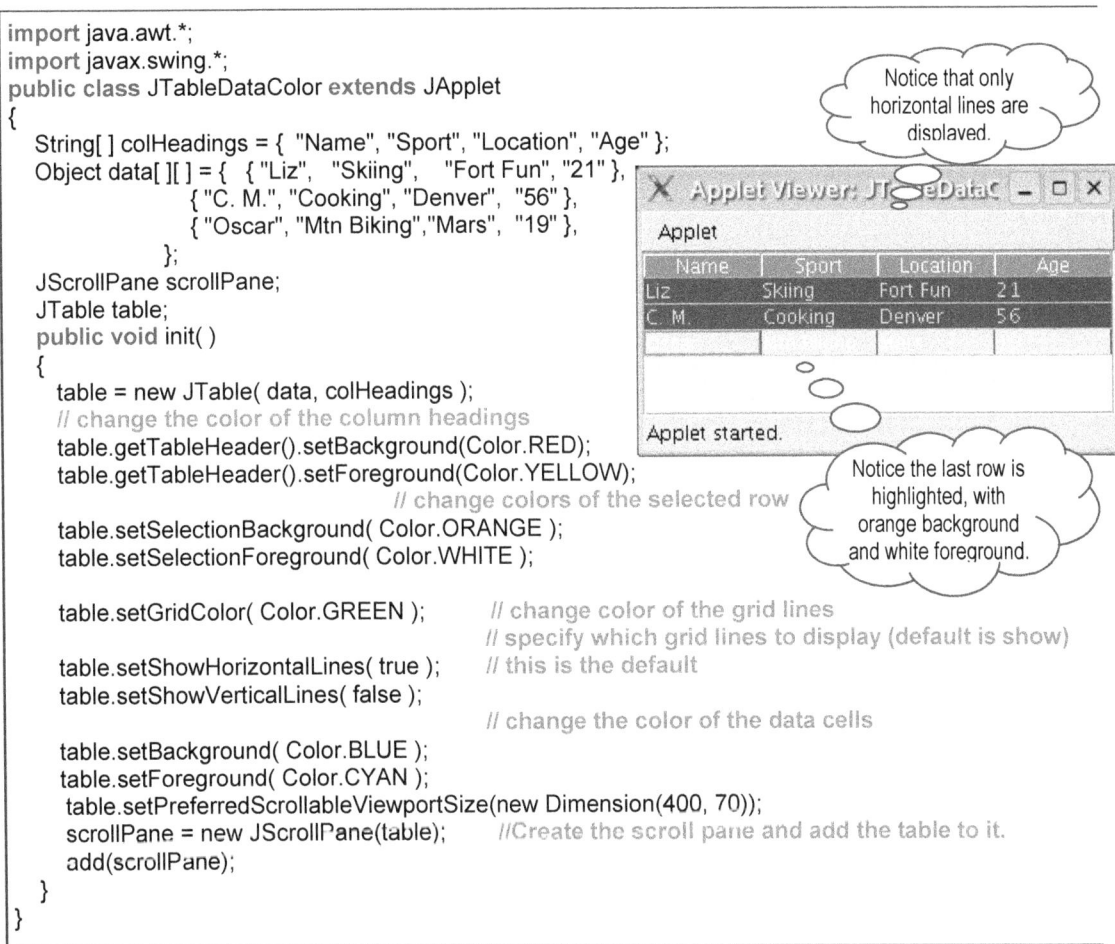

```java
import java.awt.*;
import javax.swing.*;
public class JTableDataColor extends JApplet
{
  String[ ] colHeadings = {  "Name", "Sport", "Location", "Age" };
  Object data[ ][ ] = {  { "Liz",   "Skiing",    "Fort Fun", "21" },
              { "C. M.", "Cooking", "Denver",   "56" },
              { "Oscar", "Mtn Biking","Mars",   "19" },
            };
  JScrollPane scrollPane;
  JTable table;
  public void init( )
  {
    table = new JTable( data, colHeadings );
    // change the color of the column headings
    table.getTableHeader().setBackground(Color.RED);
    table.getTableHeader().setForeground(Color.YELLOW);
                // change colors of the selected row
    table.setSelectionBackground( Color.ORANGE );
    table.setSelectionForeground( Color.WHITE );

    table.setGridColor( Color.GREEN );    // change color of the grid lines
                      // specify which grid lines to display (default is show)
    table.setShowHorizontalLines( true );  // this is the default
    table.setShowVerticalLines( false );

                // change the color of the data cells
    table.setBackground( Color.BLUE );
    table.setForeground( Color.CYAN );
    table.setPreferredScrollableViewportSize(new Dimension(400, 70));
    scrollPane = new JScrollPane(table);   //Create the scroll pane and add the table to it.
    add(scrollPane);
  }
}
```

Change the color of the grid lines

        table.setGridColor(Color.GREEN);

Change the width of each column

        table.setAutoResizeMode(JTable.AUTO_RESIZE_OFF);
        table.getColumnModel().getColumn(0).setPreferredWidth(50);
        table.getColumnModel().getColumn(1).setPreferredWidth(200);
        table.getColumnModel().getColumn(2).setPreferredWidth(100);

Fix the width to a set size

        table.getColumnModel().getColumn(0).setPreferredWidth(50);
        table.getColumnModel().getColumn(0).setMinWidth(50);
        table.getColumnModel().getColumn(0).setMaxWidth(50);

Make the cells uneditable

```
JTable table;
DefaultTableModel dfmodel = new DefaultTableModel(data, roster)
{
        public boolean isCellEditable(int row, int column)
        {
        return false;
        }
};
table = new JTable(dfmodel);
```

Change the colors of the column headings

```
DefaultTableCellRenderer head = new DefaultTableCellRenderer( );
head.setBackground( Color.YELLOW );
head.setForeground( Color.BLUE );
table.getColumnModel().getColumn(0).setHeaderRenderer(head);
table.getColumnModel().getColumn(1).setHeaderRenderer(head);
table.getColumnModel().getColumn(2).setHeaderRenderer(head);
// continue for each column
```

Other Features

There are a lot of additional features for JTables, but it starts to get very complex very fast. We learned the basics for most uses of tables, which should suffice.

ArrayList

ArrayList is a data structure that also allows us to keep track of a group of items. Similar to the array, we do not add the ArrayList to the applet as a display component. It is a data structure to help organize our program, not a component we add to an applet. However, it is quite different than arrays. For instance, we can only store objects inside an ArrayList – so we cannot put int, double, boolean or char types in an ArrayList. Another difference is that we do not have to specify the maximum size of the list. ArrayList will dynamically grow and shrink as needed. To create an ArrayList, we need to reference the java.util package:

```
import java.util.*;
```

We create an instance of ArrayList by calling the new operator. We should also specify what type of objects we are going to put into the ArrayList by designating the data type in angle brackets. For example, if we are creating a list of String objects, we would use the <String> notation:

```
ArrayList<String>  mylist;
mylist = new ArrayList<String>( );

ArrayList<ImageIcon> iconList;
iconList = new ArrayList<ImageIcon>( );

ArrayList<JButton> buttonList;
buttonList = new ArrayList<JButton>( );
```

We can add any Object data type to an ArrayList. Therefore, primitive data types need to be wrapped inside an Object data type. To add items to the list, we call the add method.

```
mylist.add( aButton );
iconList.add( anImageIcon );
buttonList.add( aJButton );
intlist.add( new Integer( intVal ) );
dbllist.add( new Double( doubleVal ) );
chrlist.add( new Character( charVal ) );
```

To access elements in the list, call the get method. The get method takes the index as a parameter (remember – Java starts counting at zero).

```
String s = mylist.get( index );
JButton b = buttonList.get( index );
int i = (intlist.get( index ) ).intValue( );            // get int value
double j = (doublelist.get( index ) ).doubleValue( );
```

To remove items from the list we can call the `remove` method with either the object we want removed or the index of the element we want to remove from the list:.

```
iconList.remove(0);      // remove first element
buttonList.remove( aJButton );
```

When we walk through the list of elements in the ArrayList, we need to know the size of the list. We can call the .size( ) method on the ArrayList variable to tell us the exact number of elements in the list.

.size( ) on ArrayList returns the # of elements in list
.length on an array returns max size of the list

```
int numElements = iconList.size( );
```

When considering whether to use an array or an ArrayList, determine whether or not the items in the list are going to change through the course of the program. For example, if we have a program that randomly selects a qote to display (eg. the example RandomQuoter earlier this chapter) then using an array is the better option (arrays are faster than manipulating an ArrayList). If, however, we modify this quote program to only display each quote once, then we might prefer to use an ArrayList and remove the quote from the list after we display it to the user. The example below demonstrates this new version of the program:

```java
import java.awt.*;
import javax.swing.*;
import java.awt.event.*;
import java.util.*;
public class RandomQuoterAL extends JApplet
   implements ActionListener
{
  JButton next;
  JLabel label;
  Random random = new Random( );
  ArrayList<String> quotes;
  public void init( )
  {
    setLayout( new BorderLayout( ) );
    quotes = new ArrayList<String>( );
    quotes.add( "What's up doc?" );
    quotes.add( "Have you any Grey Poupon?" );
    quotes.add( "Can you hear me now?" );
    quotes.add( "<HTML><CENTER>What is the average ground speed <BR> of an unladen swallow?" );
    quotes.add( "As you wish" );

    next = new JButton( "Next!" );
    next.addActionListener( this );
    label = new JLabel( "Good morning!", JLabel.CENTER );
    label.setFont( new Font( "Serif", Font.BOLD, 16 ) );
    add( next, BorderLayout.NORTH );
    add( label, BorderLayout.CENTER );
  }
  public void actionPerformed( ActionEvent ae )
  {
    Object obj = ae.getSource( );
    if ( obj == next )
    {
       if ( quotes.size( ) > 0 )
       {
           int index = random.nextInt( quotes.size( ) );
           label.setText( quotes.get( index ) );
           quotes.remove( index );
       }
        else
           label.setText( "I have nothing more to say." );     // ran out of quotes
    }
  }
}
```

Differences Between Arrays and ArrayList

What are the differences between arrays and ArrayList? Remember that an ArrayList is implemented using arrays; the difference is that the ArrayList provides us with a bunch of methods that implement features that would be otherwise a lot of code for us to write if we were using an array. Generally, if we are using a list of a fixed size we would want to use an array for efficiency. If our list is going to change a lot – especially through inserting and deleting elements, it would make our life much easier if we chose to implement with an ArrayList.

arrays		ArrayList
static	**Size**	dynamic
.length	**Method to access size**	.size( )
arrayname[i]	**Get/remove elements**	cast result from .get(i) or .remove(i)
Objects and primitives	**Data type**	Objects only
you program it	**Insert/remove element**	method call
faster	**Speed**	slower
	Implementation	with arrays

Case Study

One of the best situations for implementing arrays is when we have a bunch of buttons in our applet. Usually there are a lot of method calls we need on each individual button, so setting up an array can make it a lot easier to implement. The following example is based on a ski wax DVD tutorial website. First we need to think through the design. They are providing a full image for the backdrop which we can make as a background image using the ImgPanel we worked with earlier in the chapter on classes. Then we need to display the buttons in the top-right corner, in a JPanel using GridLayout inside the ImgPanel in BorderLayout.NORTH. For the text, we can display that in the BorderLayout.WEST region. If we set the preferred size of our ImgPanel, we won't need to put anything inside BorderLayout.CENTER.

Background image:

Screen shot:

```java
import java.awt.*;
import javax.swing.*;
import javax.swing.border.*;
import java.awt.event.*;
public class Tuning2 extends JApplet implements ActionListener
{
    Image background;
    ImgPanel mainPanel;
    JButton[ ] buttons;
    Color redColor = new Color( 189, 33, 38 );
    JLabel theText;
    JPanel menu, menuNorthPanel;
    String [ ] texts =
    {
        "<HTML><B><U>Chapters</U></B><BR><BR>Chapter 1: Equipment"
            + "<BR><BR>Chapter 2: Base Prep"
            + "<BR><BR>Chapter 3: Edge Sharpening"
            + "<BR><BR>Chapter 4: Waxing"
            + "<BR><BR>Chapter 5: Brushing and Polishing"
            + "<BR><BR>Chapter 6: Extras",
        "<HTML><B><U>Guarantee</U></B><BR><BR>"
            + "If you are not completely satisfied that this DVD "
            + "<BR> tutorial explains how to properly tune your gear,"
            + "<BR>simply return it and we will refund 100% of the "
            + "<BR>purchase price, and we can still be friends.  The "
            + "<BR>information contained in this material has been "
            + "<BR>compiled from 25 years of professional tuning "
            + "<BR>experience.  Sharp edges and fast wax cocktails "
            + "<BR>have allowed us to outrun the masses for years, "
            + "<BR>and we're certain you will be able to do the same.",
        "<HTML><B><U>Contact Us</U></B><BR><BR>http://www.tuning101dvd.com"
            + "<BR><BR>If you have any questions, <BR>feel free to contact us at:"
            + "<BR><BR>info@tuning101dvd.com"
    };
    public void init( )
    {
        doBackground( );
        doMenu( );
        doText( );
    }
    public void doBackground( )
    {
        background = getImage( getCodeBase( ), "tuning101website.jpg" );
        mainPanel = new ImgPanel( background );
        mainPanel.setLayout( new BorderLayout( ) );
        mainPanel.setPreferredSize( new Dimension( 800, 600 ) );
        setLayout( new BorderLayout( ) );
        add( mainPanel, BorderLayout.CENTER );
    }
    public void doMenu( )
```

```java
    {
        menu = new JPanel( new GridLayout( 3,1, 50, 10 ) );
        buttons = new JButton[3];
        buttons[0] = new JButton( "Chapters" );
        buttons[1] = new JButton( "Guarantee" );
        buttons[2] = new JButton( "Contact Us" );
        for ( int i=0; i<buttons.length; i++ )
        {   buttons[i].addActionListener( this );
            buttons[i].setFocusable( false );
            buttons[i].setForeground( redColor );
            menu.add( buttons[i] );
        }
        menuNorthPanel = new JPanel( new FlowLayout( FlowLayout.RIGHT ) );
        menuNorthPanel.add( menu );
        menu.setOpaque( false );
        menuNorthPanel.setOpaque( false );
        mainPanel.add( menuNorthPanel, BorderLayout.NORTH );
    }
    public void doText( )
    {
        theText = new JLabel( texts[0] );                    // display chapters when applet starts
        theText.setFont( new Font( "Serif", Font.PLAIN, 14 ) );
        theText.setForeground( redColor );
        Border margins = BorderFactory.createEmptyBorder( 0,50,0,0 );
        theText.setBorder( margins );
        mainPanel.add( theText, BorderLayout.WEST );
    }
    public void actionPerformed( ActionEvent ae )
    {
        Object src = ae.getSource( );
        if ( src == buttons[0] )
            theText.setText( texts[0] );
        else if ( src == buttons[1] )
            theText.setText( texts[1] );
        else if ( src == buttons[2] )
            theText.setText( texts[2] );
    }
}
```

Summary

- An array is a data structure than can hold a list of items.
- All elements in an array must be of the same data type.
- Indices are used to reference each item in an array. Indices start at zero.
- Arrays are declared with the data type of the elements to be stored in the array and square brackets.
- When initializing an array, the maximum size must be specified.
- The .length on an array gives the size of the array.
- The last element in an array can be accessed at index: array.length – 1
- An initializer list is when the array is declared and initialized in one step, specifying each element within squiggly braces.
- 2-D arrays contain rows and columns of data.
- JTable is made up of a 1-D array for the column headings and a 2-D array for the cells in the table.
- JTables must be stored in a JScrollPane and the method setPreferredScrollableViewportSize called to display correctly.
- The JTable can be customized heavily, though some features get very complex to implement.
- The ArrayList is also a data structure to maintain a list of items, but the size is dynamic.
- Stepping through an array or ArrayList is usually done using a for loop.

Exercises

1. The indices of an array always start with what value?
2. Which of the following are legal? Circle **ALL** that apply!!
    a. int vals[ ] = (4, 2, 1);
    b. char vals[ ] = new char[3];
    c. Button controls[ ] = { "Up", "Down", "Left", "Right" };
3. Which loop should you use to walk through an array?
4. True or False. You can have an array of primitive values.
5. What is the index of the last element in any array? e.g., array named **values**.
6. In the slide-show example in the lecture notes, how does the program know when it's at the end of the list of photos?
7. True or False: The column headings for a **JTable** are stored in a **String** variable.
8. True or False: Column headings in a JTable are in a 2-D array.
9. What is the index of Vail in the following array?
    ```
    String[ ] skiing = { "Beaver Creak",
            "Breckenridge", "Copper", "Jackson Hole", "Vail" };
    ```
10. Write an expression that refers to the string Copper within the array.
11. What is the value of the expression skiing.length?
12. What is the index of the last item in the array?
13. What is the value of the expression skiing[3]?
14. Which loop should you use to access each item in an array?
15. In the Slideshow example presented, remove the call to the **repaint** method. What happens?
16. In the Slideshow example presented, add comments explaining how the **setupIcon** method works.
17. Change the Slideshow example presented such that the buttons are never disabled. Instead, once the user selects the "next" button and the slideshow is at the end of the list of images, have it start over with the first image.
18. Change the Slideshow example presented to store an array of ImageIcon objects with the appropriate Images instead of an array of Image objects.
19. True or False: You can store integers and booleans directly into cells of a **JTable.**
20. How would you create an array of three buttons containing the numbers 1 through 3?
21. How would you create a new **JTable** with your column headings in the variable named *colHeadings* and your data in a variable named *data*?
22. Why is it preferred to use an array than an ArrayList for the slideshow?
23. Would you use an array or ArrayList for a program that maintains an inventory of your mp3s?
24. Write a method called **find** which takes an ArrayList of Strings and a String keyword, and returns the index into the ArrayList where the keyword appears in the ArrayList.
25. Write a method called **sort** which takes an int array and returns a new array with the list in sorted order.

26. Write a method named **getMaximum** that takes an int array and returns the maximum value in the array.

27. Write a method named **getMaximum** that takes an ArrayList containing Integer objects and returns the maximum value in the list.

28. Write a method named **getAvgLength** that takes an array of Strings as a parameter, and returns the average length of all the Strings.

29. Write a method named **getAverage** that takes an array of ints as a parameter, and returns the average of all the numbers.

30. Write a method that takes an int array and returns a new array with the values in reverse order.

31. Write a method that takes an array of ints as a parameter and prints out each value on the same line with each value separated with a semi-colon (e.g., 10, 4, 9, 5, 1)

32. Write a method that takes an int array and reverses the elements in this array. This method should not return anything.

33. Write a method that takes an ArrayList of Strings and returns a new ArrayList with the values in reverse order.

34. Write a method that takes an ArrayList of Integer objects and reverses the elements in this ArrayList. This method should not return anything.

35. Modify the slide puzzle to have a button that, when clicked, will solve the puzzle. This can either just display the correct ordering (easy problem), or go through the motions following the rules of clicking on adjacent tiles to the blank spot (very difficult problem).

36. Convert the following code from using an ArrayList to an array:

```
public class ArrayListEx1
{   ArrayList<String> names = new ArrayList<String>( );
    public void addName( String n )   { names.add( n ); }
    public String getName( int index )
    {
        return names.get(index);
    }
    public void printList( )
    {
        for( int i=0; i<names.size( ); i++ )
        {
            if( i != 0 )
                System.out.print( ", " );
            System.out.print(  names.get(i) );
        }
    }
}
```

Suggestion: Write a class named **Toolbox** that contains all your methods, so if you ever need to use one of these methods, you can simply reference to this class you've written!

Chapter 13

Threads and Timer

Objectives:

- Threads
  - Slideshow
  - Animation
- Timers

Threads

Threads allow us to have multi-processing occur: when two or more things can be occurring at the same time. When we run a program, a single thread automatically starts to run the program. To run two or more things simultaneously, we need to create a second (or more) thread(s). For example, if we want to perform a slideshow while the user is typing inside a JTextArea, we need to use a separate thread for the slideshow. If we didn't use a second thread, the applet would hang while we ran through the code for the slideshow.

There are four steps to get Threads to work:

1. **The class needs to implement the Runnable interface.**
   ```
   implements Runnable
   ```
2. **Create a Thread**
   ```
   Thread runner;
   runner = new Thread( this );
   ```
3. **Start the Thread**
   ```
   runner.start( );
   ```
4. **Create a method named run**
   ```
   public void run( )
   {
   }
   ```

When we use Threads we put the code inside the **run** method. Usually we want the code to loop. We can set up the loop as an infinite loop.

```
public void run( )
{
    while( true )
    {
        // code
    }
}
```

We can also use the method **sleep** in the **Thread** class to simulate a delay:

```
Thread.sleep( delayInMilliseconds );
```

To use this method, we need to put it within a **try ... catch** block to catch any exceptions (errors) that may occur (usually put the `try...catch` around the `while(true)` loop):

```
try {
    Thread.sleep( delayInMiliseconds );
} catch( Exception exc )   {  }
```

(However, we can also use a Timer – see next section).

When working with threads we also need to handle the different states that the applet may be in. Since applets are intended to be run embedded within a web page, the user may leave our applet to go to another web page. It is our responsibility to ensure that our applet stops using resources we reserved for our applet to run. We also need to ensure our applet will display correctly again if the user were to return to our applet page. To keep track of all these different states of our applet, Java applets provide specific methods for each situation. When we first run our applet, we need to initialize it by calling the init method. The init method is only executed once – when the applet first loads. Then the start method is called. This is where we should start our threads. The start method is called each time our applet is to run. We also need to implement a stop method which is called when the user leaves our applet page. We need to stop our threads from running inside this stop method.

Method Header	Description
public void init( )	Initialize our applet; called only once
public void start( )	Starts our applet running; start up necessary threads
public void stop( )	Applet is no longer being displayed; stop our threads from running

An outline sketch of a program using Threads is listed below:

```java
import java.awt.*;
import javax.swing.*;
public class className extends JApplet implements Runnable
{
  Thread thread;
  public void init( )
  {
  }
  public void start( )
  {
      if ( thread == null )
          thread = new Thread( this );
      thread.start( );
  }
  public void run( )
  {
    while( true )
    {
      // put code here
      try {
        Thread.sleep(500);
      }
      catch( Exception e ) { }
    }
  }
  public void stop( )
  {
      if ( thread != null )
      {
          thread.stop( );
          thread = null;
      }
  }
}
```

If you are using more than one Thread there are possibilities of synchronization issues if two or Threads are trying to access the same component. There are ways of synchronizing methods to handle these situations but are beyond the scope of this book

Slideshow

We will look at two examples of a slideshow that automatically displays the next image. The first example adds the slideshow code within an applet with other stuff as well. The second example shows how we can separate the slideshow into a separate class and reference it within our applet class (e.g. extend JPanel class).

```java
import java.awt.*;
import java.awt.event.*;
import javax.swing.*;
public class SlideShow extends JApplet implements Runnable
{
    int SPEED = 1000;           // how fast to rotate through images
    Image[ ] photos;            // array of all your images
    ImageIcon icon;             // images need to be in an ImageIcon
    JLabel imgLabel;            // and stored into a JLabel
    int currentIndex = 0;       // which image index currently displayed
    Thread runner;
    public void init( )
    {
            photos = new Image[4];                      // load the images into memory
            photos[0] = getImage( getCodeBase( ), "oncomputer.png" );
            photos[1] = getImage( getCodeBase( ), "gocart.png" );
            photos[2] = getImage( getCodeBase( ), "idea.png" );
            photos[3] = getImage( getCodeBase( ), "houseLake.png" );
            icon = new ImageIcon( );
            imgLabel = new JLabel( );
            imgLabel.setHorizontalAlignment( JLabel.CENTER );
            setupIcon( 0 );       // initialize setup to first display first image (index 0)
            add( imgLabel );      // add label to applet
    }
    public void start( )
    {
            runner = new Thread(this);      // start a thread to time it
            runner.start( );
    }
    public void setupIcon( int index )    /** changes the image in the label */
    {
            currentIndex = index;
            icon.setImage( photos[index] );
            imgLabel.setIcon(icon );
            validate( );
    }
    public void run( )
    {
      try {
          while ( true ) {
             if ( currentIndex == photos.length-1 )     // if we're at the last one,
                     setupIcon( 0 );                    // start over with index 0
             else
                     setupIcon( currentIndex+1 );       // otherwise just increment the index
             repaint( );  // Show the change.
             Thread.sleep(SPEED);
          }
      } catch (InterruptedException ie) { }
    }
}
```

> We need our code in the run method inside a *try...catch* block to handle errors.

> The **Thread.sleep** waits for x number of milliseconds.

Another way to work with a slideshow is to put the code for the slideshow in a separate class, and add this class to the applet. This makes the code more manageable, with everything related to the slideshow in it's own separate file and simplifies the code required inside the applet.

```java
import java.awt.*;
import javax.swing.*;
public class SlidesApplet
                extends JApplet
{
  Slides  myslideshow;
  public void init( )
  {
    myslideshow = new Slides( );
    myslideshow.init( this );
    setLayout(new FlowLayout( ));
    add( myslideshow ) ;
  }
}
```

```java
import java.awt.*;
import java.awt.event.*;
import javax.swing.*;
public class Slides extends JPanel implements Runnable
{
    int SPEED = 1000;      // how fast to rotate through images
    Image[ ] photos;       // array of all your images
    ImageIcon icon;        // images need to be in an ImageIcon
    JLabel imgLabel;       // and stored into a JLabel

    int currentIndex = 0;  // which image index currently displayed

    public void init( JApplet app )
    {
        photos = new Image[4];    // load the images into memory
        photos[0] = app.getImage( app.getCodeBase( ), "house.png" );
        photos[1] = app.getImage( app.getCodeBase( ), "gocrt.png" );
        photos[2] = app.getImage( app.getCodeBase( ), "idea.png" );
        photos[3] = app.getImage( app.getCodeBase( ), "cmput.png" );
        icon = new ImageIcon( );
        imgLabel = new JLabel( );
        imgLabel.setHorizontalAlignment( JLabel.CENTER );
        setupIcon( 0 );       // initialize to display first img (index 0)

        add( imgLabel );       // add label to applet
    }
    public void start( )
    {
        Thread runner = new Thread(this);  // start a thread to time it
        runner.start( );
    }
    /** changes the image in the label    */
    public void setupIcon( int index )
    {
        currentIndex = index;
        icon.setImage( photos[index] );
        imgLabel.setIcon(icon );
        validate( );
    }
    public void run( )                       /** time the slideshow   */
    {
      try {
        while(true) {
           if( currentIndex == photos.length-1 )   // if at the last one,
              setupIcon( 0 );                      // start over with index 0
           else                     // otherwise just increment the index
              setupIcon( currentIndex+1 );
           repaint( );              // Show the change.
           Thread.sleep(SPEED);
        }
      } catch (InterruptedException ie) { }
    }
}
```

Animation

This next example shows how we can animate our own drawings. We'll put our drawing code in a separate class that extends JPanel that implements threads, then add it to our applet. To prevent it from redrawing the whole thing each time, we'll only draw over a small area where the eye is. To do this, when we wink we first fill in the eye with yellow then draw the wink.

```java
import java.awt.*;
import javax.swing.*;
public class Smiley extends JPanel implements Runnable
{
  int size=50;
  int leftEyeX = (int)(size*0.25);
  int eyeWidth = size/7;
  int eyeHeight = size/6;
  int rtEyeX = (int)(size*0.75-eyeWidth);
  int eyeY = (int)(size/3);
  boolean winking = false;
  public void run( )
  {
    while( true )
    {
        repaint( );
        try {
           Thread.sleep(500);
        }
        catch( Exception e ) { }
    }
  }
  public void paintComponent ( Graphics g )
  {
      super.paintComponent( g );
     g.setColor( Color.YELLOW );
     g.fillOval( 0,0,size,size );
     g.setColor( Color.BLACK );
     g.drawOval ( 0,0,size,size );            // outline
     g.fillOval( leftEyeX, eyeY,eyeWidth,eyeHeight);    // left eye
      if( winking )
      {
           g.setColor( Color.YELLOW );
           g.fillOval( rtEyeX, eyeY,eyeWidth,eyeHeight);  // rt eye
           g.setColor( Color.BLACK );
           g.fillRect ( rtEyeX, eyeY+eyeHeight,eyeWidth,2);
           winking = false;
      }
      else
      {
           g.fillOval( rtEyeX, eyeY,eyeWidth,eyeHeight);   // rt eye
           winking = true;
      }
     g.setColor( Color.RED );
     g.fillArc( 10,eyeY+eyeHeight,size-20,20, 180,180 );
  }
}
```

Thought bubbles:
- sleep for 500 miliseconds then redraw
- First color over the black eye in yellow, then draw the wink
- Decide what to draw – either a wink or a full eye

```
import javax.swing.*;
import java.awt.*;
public class Wink extends JApplet
{
  Smiley sm;
  Thread t;
  JLabel title, leftside;
  public void init( )
  {
      setLayout( new FlowLayout( ) );
      title = new JLabel( "<HTML><FONT SIZE=+2 COLOR=BLUE>Gooood Mornin'!" );
      leftside = new JLabel( "<HTML>This goes <BR>to show<BR>some fun<BR>animation!" );
      add( title );
      add( leftside );
      sm = new Smiley( );        // work the smile
      sm.setPreferredSize( new Dimension(55,55) );
      add( sm );
  }
  public void start( )
  {
      t = new Thread(sm);
      t.start( );
  }
}
```

Notice that we do not need to do any thread code in the Wink applet class. All the thread work is done in the Smile class. This makes it easy for us to add two smile faces on our applet, both animated.

Timers

Timers are useful for for repeating steps at particular intervals. Timers can be used to to create progress bars, custom clocks and timed animation, similar to using Threads. Timers are based on event processing, so it is important that the code to be run from a Timer event can be executed quickly to enable the system to handle the next event. Threads do not have this limitation and therefore are ideal for more time-intensive code processing.

We create a Timer object by specifying the delay count as an integer in miliseconds and the listener for the ActionEvent:

```
Timer timer;
timer = new Timer( delay, this );
```

Similar to threads, we then need to start the timer:

```
timer.start( );
```

After the delay in miliseconds, the **actionPerformed** method is called. Therefore, just like when we listen for events on buttons, we need to implement the ActionListener.

There are five steps to get Timers to work:

1. Import the package to handle ActionEvent events:

    ```
    import   java.awt.event.*;
    ```

2. Specify that we're listening for events:

   ```
   public class xyz extends JApplet   implements ActionListener
   ```

3. Add an actionListener method:

   ```
   public void actionPerformed( ActionEvent ae )
   ```

4. Create a Timer object

   ```
   Timer timer;
   timer = new Timer( delay, this );
   ```

5. Start the timer:

   ```
   timer.start( );
   ```

6. (Optional) Stop the timer: If you want the timer to stop, call the stop method.

   ```
   timer.stop( );
   ```

If we are listening for ActionEvents from multiple objects (e.g. buttons), recall that we can use the **instanceof** operator to differentiate between them:

```
Object src = actionEvent.getSource( );
if ( src instanceof  Timer )
    ...
else if ( src instanceof JButton )
    ...
```

We can also check to see if the source that caused the event is a specific timer by checking for equality with ==. For example, if we have two Timer object variables named **timer1** and **timer2**:

```
Object src = actionEvent.getSource( );
if ( src == timer1 )
    ...
else if ( src == timer2 )
    ...
```

Note that we may have other code to handle buttons in the same actionPerformed method. This works by setting up an if-else structure and either use the instanceof operator to differentiate between Timer and JButton or JList events, or check for the source of the event matching to one of your variables. For example, the actionPerformed method may have the following:

```
public void actionPerformed( ActionEvent ae )
{
    Object src = ae.getSource( );
    if ( src == timer )
        myLabel.setText( "Time out!" );
    else if ( src == button1 )
        myLabel.setText( "Submitting your results" );
    else if ( src == buttonStopTimer )
        timer.stop( );
}
```

An example of using a Timer is to perform a countdown. In the example below, every 800 miliseconds the JLabel is updated with the next lower number. Once the countdown reaches zero, the label displays "Blast-off!"

```java
import java.awt.*;
import java.awt.event.*;
import javax.swing.*;
public class TimedClock extends JApplet  implements ActionListener
{
    JLabel countdown;
    int count = 10;
    Timer timer;
    int DELAY = 800;          // delay in miliseconds
    public void init( )
    {
         setLayout( new FlowLayout( ) );
         countdown = new JLabel( String.valueOf( count ) );
         countdown.setFont( new Font( "Serif", Font.BOLD, 46 ) );
         add( countdown );
         timer = new Timer( DELAY, this );
         timer.start( );
    }
    public void actionPerformed( ActionEvent ae )
    {
         Object src = ae.getSource( );
         if ( src == timer  && count > 0 )
         {
              count = count - 1;
              countdown.setText( String.valueOf( count ) );
         }
         if ( count == 0 )
              countdown.setText( "Blast-off!" );
    }
}
```

The following example displays an image or drawing traveling around the applet.

```java
import java.awt.*;
import javax.swing.*;
import java.awt.event.*;
public class TimerEx extends JApplet implements ActionListener
{
   Image img;
   ImageIcon icon;
   int x, y, moveX, moveY;
   Timer timer;
   int DELAY = 20;
    public void init( )
    {
       x=5;  y=5;
       moveX = 10;
       moveY = 5;
       img = getImage( getCodeBase( ), "gocart.png" );
       timer = new Timer( DELAY, this );
       timer.start( );
    }
    public void paint ( Graphics g )
    {              // clearRect clears a small portion of the screen to prevent flicker
       g.clearRect( x, y, img.getWidth(this), img.getHeight(this) );
       x = x + moveX;
       y = y + moveY;
       g.drawImage( img, x, y, this );
    }
    public void actionPerformed( ActionEvent ae )
    {
       if ( x <= 0 || x >= this.getWidth( ) - img.getWidth(this) )
          moveX = moveX * -1;
       if ( y <= 0 || y >= this.getHeight( ) - img.getHeight(this) )
          moveY = moveY * -1;
       repaint( );          // force a call to the paint method
    }
}
```

Summary

- Threads allow us to process multiple things at the same time.
- There are 4 steps required for adding threads: 1) specify the class implements Runnable interface, 2) create a Thread 3) start the thread and 4) write a method named run to handle what happens.
- Use Thread.sleep to create a delay in the animation.
- Put the code in the run method within a *try...catch* block to handle errors that may occur.
- Slideshows can be written within the applet class or inside a separate class that extends the JPanel class.
- Timers are useful for repeating steps at particular intervals.
- Threads are preferred over Timers when the processing will take a while.
- Timers create ActionEvents, so we handle the Timer delay inside the actionPerformed method.

Exercises

1. Animate one of the drawings from chapter 2 or chapter 7.
2. Animate the Smiley face to speak consistent with sound.
3. Change the Wink animation such that it redraws the whole screen instead of just the eye each time. What is the difference on performance when you run the program now?
4. Implement the Wink animation with a Timer instead of Threads. How does this affect the performance?
5. True or False: A slideshow of images could be implement with either a Thread or a Timer.
6. True or False: Using Threads triggers ActionEvent events.
7. True or False: We send the amount of seconds we wish to delay to the Thread.sleep method.
8. True or False: Threads allow us to process multiple things at the same time.
9. True or False: Timers are useful for repeating steps at particular intervals.
10. What is the interface we need to implement to get Threads to work?
11. What is the name of the method you are required to write if you implement the Runnable interface?
12. What type of code block do you need to put your call to Thread.sleep in?
13. When calling Thread.sleep, what unit of measurement is the delay?
14. What method do you call on your thread to get the thread to begin running?
15. What listener does the Timer use?
16. Write an applet that shows a clock, which updates the second-hand every second, the minute-hand every minute, and the hour hand every hour. Make use of the Calendar class to figure out the current time.
17. Create an applet that is a stopwatch where the user can enter an amount of time before the alrm should go off. Either play sound for an alarm bell and/or pop open a JFrame with flashing text.

Chapter 14

Game Programming

*If life's a game,
why not create your own?*

Objectives:

- Overview
    - Game World
    - Player Control
    - Brains
- Breakout Game Example
- Dungeon Game Example

Overview

There are many different types of games we could program, and they all fall into different styles for development. Arcade games, tic-tac-toe, pin-ball, pong, adventure, point-and-shoot are various game types that use different programming structures to develop. We're going to introduce game programming here to give you some of the basics to get you started.

Most games deal with three essential ingredients: a game world, player control and brains for intelligent behavior. The game world involves the backdrop, borders/walls, objects that may either be consumed or held and entities that may be either good or bad for the player. Player control is the method of interaction for the player to be involved in the game. This can include keyboard keys, mouse movements, joystick actions, etc. The last ingredient for a game is the brains – intelligent behavior for entities that the computer must control in the game.

When we develop a game, we should use multiple classes to help simplify development and maintain modularity. This will help us test small portions of code to ensure they work correctly, and also enable us to reuse code in multiple games. For example, if we first write a Breakout game that makes use of a Ball object, when we want to develop a Pong game we can reuse our code for the Ball class with minimal if any changes.

Game World

The Game World provides the fundamental view of the game for the player. It is responsible for displaying the world with the walls and boundaries defined. It should also maintain information about the entities and objects in the game, as well as an instance of the player object.

The design of the base world can be done with drawing methods on the applet or working with components and using a null layout structure. In the examples provided in this chapter, we will look at building a world based on drawing to the applet. When we draw to the applet, we'll need to prevent flicker from occurring, so we will make use of a BufferedImage to draw all the items first before overlaying the current applet screen with the final version of our image drawn off-screen.

There are multiple ways to keep track of the entities in the game, as we'll discuss during our exploration of creating a dungeon game. Arrays and ArrayLists are good data structures for keeping track of items in our game including monsters, weapons, coins, etc.

Player Control

We need to handle the users' interaction to control the player in the game. Usually we implement the KeyListener to handle different key strokes the user types to move the player. The code to maintain information about the player is usually implemented in a separate class, called a Sprite (we'll see this in the dungeon example). Based on the key that was pressed, we need to move the player on the screen.

Brains

Each game needs to define some objective the player is trying to accomplish to 'win' the game. Part of the 'brains' of a game is coordinating this effort – has the player rescued the princess and escaped to to the exit with her safely? Has the player knocked out all blocks in the BreakOut game? Some games have monster enemies that can harm the player if they collide or fight. Monsters that don't move at all are not very interesting to play against, so its best if we can somehow program each monster to move differently around the game world.

Flicker

Before we begin writing games, we need to learn how to get rid of the flicker problem. What happens is when the screen is to be redrawn, it is first cleared before the program attempts to redraw the screen. This clearing and redrawing is usually not fast enough – so our eyes detect what we call a 'flicker' of white as the screen is cleared before it is completely redrawn. The fix to this is to work on an offscreen image where we update the screen as we want it, then draw on top of the current screen instead of erasing it first. The example below demonstrates this by having an offscreen image where the backdrop and player image is drawn before redrawing on the viewing screen. The applet moves the player's image wherever the user's mouse roams.

```java
import javax.swing.*;
import java.awt.*;
import java.awt.event.*;
public class BufImages extends JApplet implements MouseMotionListener
{
    Image offscreen;              // offscreen image to prevent flicker
    Graphics offscreenGrp;        // graphics for offscreen image - draw to here first
    Image player;                 // image for player - moves where mouse is
    int x, y;                     // coordinates for player - where mouse is
    public void init( )
    {   resize(300,300);
        offscreen = createImage( 300, 300 );        // create offscreen image
        offscreenGrp = offscreen.getGraphics( );    // get graphics for drawing on offscreen image
        player = getImage( getCodeBase( ), "lightning-bolts.gif" );   // get image for player)
        addMouseMotionListener(this);
    }
    public void paint( Graphics g )
    {
        // draw to the offscreen image first
        offscreenGrp.setColor( Color.CYAN );
        offscreenGrp.fillRect( 0, 0, 300, 300 );
        offscreenGrp.setColor( Color.GREEN );
        offscreenGrp.fillRect( 0,290, 300, 10 );
        offscreenGrp.drawImage( player, x, y, this );
        g.drawImage( offscreen, 0, 0, this );
    }
    public void mouseMoved( MouseEvent me )
    {
        x = me.getX( ) -50;
        y = me.getY( ) - 50;
        repaint( );
    }
    public void mouseDragged( MouseEvent me ) { }
}
```

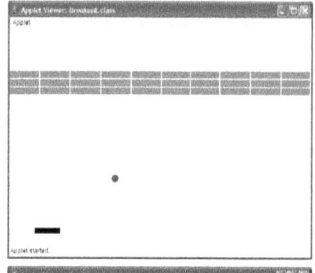
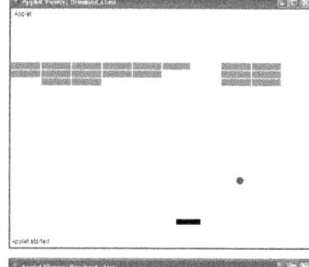
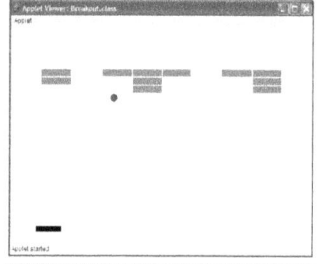

Breakout Game

We'll start with a simple old game called Breakout. Breakout is a form of the Pong game, where the user has a paddle that can go horizontally across the bottom of the screen. The objective of the game is to knock out all the blocks. Let's build this incrementally, the way a programmer would approach it.

Note that there are multiple different solutions to this same program, but we'll explore one way here. Let's start off by programming the blocks. Our initial program will look similar to what we did in Chapter 2. However, we'll need to keep track of each block so we can remove it when it is hit by the ball. To keep track of each block, we'll create a Rectangle object:

Rectangle rec = new Rectangle(x, y, width, height);

We'll need to store them all inside a list. This will make it easy for us to repaint the screen each time, by writing a loop through the list and drawing each Rectangle object. Since our list will be dynamic, in that we want it to shrink as we remove Rectangle objects from the list when hit, we should use a data structure called **ArrayList** over choosing an array. Arrays do not allow us to easily remove things from the list; ArrayList makes it very easy.

To create an ArrayList object, we declare an instantiate it similar to other objects:

```
ArrayList  blocks;
blocks = new ArrayList( );
```

To populate the list with all our blocks, we'll need to write a loop inside a loop. The outer loop should create each of the rows in our game – notice in the top image that we start with three rows of blocks. The inner loop will keep track of our columns – in our game, we have 10 columns across. Since inside the loop we need to create our Rectangles for each block, we can make our loops keep track of the x and y coordinates of where the next block should begin. To do this, we'll need to also figure out what the size of each block should be. That gives us a loop that looks like:

```
public void buildBlocks( )
{
    int sizeOfBlock = width / numBlocks;
    int heightOfBlock = 15;
    for( int rows=0; rows<width; rows += sizeOfBlock )
    {
      for( int cols=0; cols<numRows*heightOfBlock; cols += heightOfBlock )
      {
        Rectangle r = new Rectangle( rows,80+cols, sizeOfBlock-2, heightOfBlock-2 );
        blocks.add(r);
      }
    }
}
```

The 80 is how low from the top we want the first row to be displayed

Inside our paint method, we can walk through our list of blocks and display each one by calling the **fillRect** method on the Graphics object.

The code for Part I of our Breakout game appears below:

```java
import java.awt.*;
import javax.swing.*;
import java.util.*;            // for ArrayList
public class BreakoutPart1 extends JApplet
{
   ArrayList blocks;
   int width, height;          // dimensions of applet
   int numBlocks = 10;         // # of blocks horizontally
   int numRows = 3;            // # of rows
   public void init( )
   {
      blocks = new ArrayList( );
      width = getWidth( );
      height = getHeight( );
      buildBlocks( );
   }
   public void buildBlocks( )
   {
      int sizeOfBlock = width / numBlocks;
      int heightOfBlock = 15;
      for ( int rows=0; rows<width; rows += sizeOfBlock )
         for ( int cols=0; cols<numRows*heightOfBlock; cols += heightOfBlock )
         {
            Rectangle r = new Rectangle( rows,80+cols, sizeOfBlock-2, heightOfBlock-2 );
            blocks.add(r);
         }
   }
   public void paint( Graphics g )
   {
       g.clearRect(0,0,width,height);       // clear screen
       g.setColor( Color.RED );
       for (int i=0; i<blocks.size( ); i++ )    // color remaining blocks
       {
          Rectangle r = (Rectangle )blocks.get(i);
          g.fillRect( r.x, r.y, r.width, r.height );
       }
   }
}
```

The next step we'll do is to create a ball and have it move around the screen, bouncing off the walls. When we create a ball, we're going to need to know about the x, y coordinates of the ball's location, the size (ball has same size for width and height), speed in pixels which is how many pixels the ball moves each time it is redrawn, and the width and height of the screen so we can bounce off the walls of the screen.

To create a bounce off a wall, we'll create a method named **move** that first adjusts the x and y coordinates of the ball, then checks to see if these coordinates are beyond the area of the screen. If the ball is past the left side of the wall, then the x is less than zero. If it is greater than the applet's width, it's past the right side. Usually in a real Breakout game, once the ball drops below the screen the ball is "out" and the game either ends or a new ball comes into play (depending on the exact rules of this game's variation). We're going to keep the ball in play for now, bouncing off the bottom of the screen as well. You can configure this program differently however you like. When the ball bounces off a wall, we'll change the direction of the ball by inversing the direction: direction = (-1) * direction; This way, whenever we move, we'll add the speed * direction which will direct the ball for us.

```java
import java.awt.*;
public class Ball
{
   int x, y, size, speed;
   int dirX, dirY;
   int appletWdt, appletHgt;
   public Ball( int _x, int _y, int _size, int _speed, int w, int h )
   {
      x = _x;                          // (x, y) coordinates of ball
      y = _y;
      size = _size;                    // width and height are same size
      speed = _speed;                  // speed is number of pixels to move each time
      dirX = 1;                        // direction is either +1 go right or -1 go left
      dirY = 1;                        // direction is either +1 go down or -1 go up
      appletWdt = w;                   // applet width
      appletHgt = h;                   // applet height
   }
   public void paint( Graphics g )     // called from applet
   {
      g.setColor( Color.BLUE );
      g.fillOval( x, y, size, size );
   }
   public void move( )
   {                                   // move ball based on speed and direction
      x = x + speed * dirX;
      y = y + speed * dirY;
      if ( x < 0 )                     // hit left boundary, change direction
         dirX = 1;
      else if ( x > appletWdt )        // hit right boundary, change direction
         dirX = -1;
      if ( y < 0 )                     // hit top boundary, change direction
         dirY = 1;
      else if ( y > appletHgt )        // hit bottom boundary, change direction
         dirY = -1;
   }
}
```

To use this Ball class in our program, we'll add some code to create the Ball object and to paint it. To keep the ball moving, we'll need a Thread running that continually moves and repaints the ball. We also need to check to see if the Ball collides with one of our Rectangle blocks.

```java
import java.awt.*;
import javax.swing.*;
import java.util.*;
public class BreakoutPart2 extends JApplet  implements Runnable
{
   ArrayList blocks;
   int width, height;   // dimensions of applet
   int numBlocks;       // number of blocks horizontally
   int numRows;         // number of rows - 1 least difficult, 5 more difficult
   // Part II
   Thread thread;
   Ball ball;
   public void init( )
   {
      numBlocks = 10;
      numRows = 3;
      blocks = new ArrayList( );
      width = getWidth( );
      height = getHeight( );
      buildBlocks( );
      // PART II
      ball = new Ball( 50, 120, 15,  5, width, height );
   }
   public void start( )
   {
      thread = new Thread(this);
      thread.start( );
   }
   public void buildBlocks( )
   {
      int sizeOfBlock = width / numBlocks;
      int heightOfBlock = 15;
      for ( int rows=0; rows<width; rows += sizeOfBlock )
         for ( int cols=0; cols<numRows*heightOfBlock; cols += heightOfBlock )
         {
            Rectangle r = new Rectangle( rows,80+cols, sizeOfBlock-2, heightOfBlock-2 );
            blocks.add(r);
         }
   }
   public void paint( Graphics g )
   {
      g.clearRect(0,0,width,height);        // clear screen
      ball.paint( getGraphics( ) );         // paint ball
      g.setColor( Color.RED );
      for (int i=0; i<blocks.size( ); i++ )  // color remaining blocks
      {
         Rectangle r = (Rectangle )blocks.get(i);
         g.fillRect( r.x, r.y, r.width, r.height );
      }
   }
   public void run( )
   {
      while( true )
      {
         ball.move( );
         checkForCollision( );
         repaint( );
         try {
```

continued

```
          Thread.sleep(15);
        }catch( Exception ex ) { }
      }
    }
    public void checkForCollision( )
    {
      Rectangle ballR = new Rectangle( ball.x, ball.y, ball.size, ball.size);
      for( int i=0; i<blocks.size( ); i++ )
      {
        Rectangle r = (Rectangle )blocks.get(i);
        if ( r.intersects( ballR ) )
        {
          blocks.remove(r);
          ball.dirX = -1 * ball.dirX;
          ball.dirY = -1 * ball.dirY;
          return;
        }
      }
    }
}
```

The next step would be to add the user's paddle, and allow the user to move left or right based on the arrow keys. This is similar to the code from example of the penny character walking around.

One thing you might notice is that there is a lot of flicker occurring when we run our game applet. We can fix this by first drawing to a **BufferedImage** then drawing the BufferedImage to the applet. The only difference is inside the paint method: Start with the paint method as follows:

```
public void paint( Graphics grph )
{
        BufferedImage buffer = new BufferedImage( width, height, BufferedImage.TYPE_INT_RGB);
        Graphics g = buffer.getGraphics( );
```

keeping the rest of the code in the paint method the same, then at the end of the paint method,

```
        grph.drawImage(buffer,0,0,this);
```

```
/* Breakout - Final version  -   add paddle and remove flicker problems  */
import java.awt.*;
import javax.swing.*;
import java.util.*;
import java.awt.event.*;
import java.awt.image.*;
public class Breakout extends JApplet  implements Runnable, KeyListener
{
   ArrayList blocks;
   int width, height;    // dimensions of applet
   int numBlocks;        // number of blocks horizontally
   int numRows;          // number of rows - 1 least difficult, 5 more difficult

   Rectangle paddle;
   int speed;
   Thread thread;
   Ball ball;
   Image buffer;
   public void init( )
   {
```

```java
      resize(600, 400 );
      numBlocks = 10;
      numRows = 3;
      blocks = new ArrayList( );
      width = getWidth( );
      height = getHeight( );
      buildBlocks( );
      paddle = new Rectangle( 50, height-30, 50, 10 );
      addKeyListener( this );
      speed = 10;
      buffer = createImage( width,height );
      ball = new Ball( 50, 120, 15, 5, width, height );
   }
   public void start( )
   {
       if ( thread == null )
           thread = new Thread(this);
      thread.start( );
      setFocusable(true);
   }
   public void buildBlocks( )
   {
      int sizeOfBlock = width / numBlocks;
      int heightOfBlock = 15;
      for( int rows=0; rows<width; rows += sizeOfBlock )
         for( int cols=0; cols<numRows*heightOfBlock; cols += heightOfBlock )
         {
            Rectangle r = new Rectangle( rows,80+cols, sizeOfBlock-2, heightOfBlock-2 );
            blocks.add(r);
         }
   }
   public void paint( Graphics g )
   {
      Graphics bg = buffer.getGraphics( );
      bg.setColor(Color.WHITE);
      bg.fillRect(0,0,width,height);
      ball.paint( bg );
      bg.setColor( Color.RED );
      for (int i=0; i<blocks.size( ); i++ )
      {
         Rectangle r = (Rectangle )blocks.get(i);
         bg.fillRect( r.x, r.y, r.width, r.height );
      }
      bg.setColor( Color.BLACK );
      bg.fillRect( paddle.x, paddle.y, paddle.width, paddle.height );
      g.drawImage(buffer,0,0,this);
   }

   public void run( )
   {
      while( true )
      {
         ball.move( );
         checkForCollision( );
         repaint( );
         try {
            Thread.sleep(15);
         }catch( Exception ex ) { }
```

continued

```java
      }
   }
   public void checkForCollision( )
   {
      Rectangle ballR = new Rectangle( ball.x, ball.y, ball.size, ball.size);
      for( int i=0; i<blocks.size( ); i++ )
      {
         Rectangle r = (Rectangle )blocks.get(i);
         if ( r.intersects( ballR ) )
         {
            blocks.remove(r);
            ball.dirX = -1 * ball.dirX;
            ball.dirY = -1 * ball.dirY;
            return;
         }
      }
      if ( ballR.intersects( paddle ) )       // check for paddle collision
      {
         ball.dirX = -1 * ball.dirX;
         ball.dirY = -1 * ball.dirY;
      }
   }
   public void keyTyped( KeyEvent ke ) {  }
   public void keyReleased( KeyEvent ke ) {  }
   public void keyPressed( KeyEvent ke )
   {
      int code = ke.getKeyCode( );
      if( code == KeyEvent.VK_LEFT )
         paddle.x -= speed;
      else if( code == KeyEvent.VK_RIGHT )
         paddle.x += speed;
   }
}
```

This is the basics to programming games similar to pong, missile command/asteroids, etc. A good exercise would be to modify this program down to a two-person pong game.

Dungeon Games

There are different styles of dungeon games: full-screen view of dungeon (e.g. Pac Man), scrolling to different rooms via top-down view (e.g. Zelda) or via first-person view (e.g. Doom) or a scrolling left-right background (e.g. Super Mario Brothers). Some of the core programming for any style is the same, such as using something called Sprites to maintain information about the player. There are two different approaches to drawing the scene for any game: use painting techniques with a buffered image or use components (classes that extend JComponent to create custom components). We're going to explore the use of the painting methods and a buffered image.

As we saw during the Breakout game, the BufferedImage is important to prevent a flicker in the drawing of the graphics. In our dungeon game we will also first draw the image to a BufferedImage object before drawing on the applet screen.

We're going to create a dungeon game where we can see the full maze from the top. For the first step in developing our game, we'll define the walls where the player cannot go as Rectangle objects (like the Breakout game) stored in an ArrayList and check for collisions of the player with each wall every time we move. The code below is our starting point where we draw the walls and set up the thread for processing the graphics:

```java
import java.awt.*;
import java.awt.image.*;
import javax.swing.*;
import java.util.*;
public class Game extends JApplet implements Runnable
{
    int width, height;                          // dimensions of game
    ArrayList<Rectangle> walls;
    Image backgroundBuf, screenBuf;    // screenBuf = draw backgrd then player and entities in layers
    Graphics2D background;
    Thread thread;
    public void init( )
    {
        resize( 300, 300 );
        width = this.getWidth( );
        height = this.getHeight( );
        walls = new ArrayList<Rectangle>( );
        buildWalls( );
    }
    public void start( )
    {
        if ( thread == null )
            thread = new Thread( this );
        thread.start( );
    }
    public void stop( )
    {
        if ( thread != null )
            thread.interrupt( );
        thread = null;
    }
    public void buildWalls( )
    {
        // create Rectangle objects and store in ArrayList walls
        int wallThickness = 10;
        walls.add( new Rectangle( 0,0, width, wallThickness ) );                    // top
        walls.add( new Rectangle( 0,0, wallThickness, height ) );                   // left
        walls.add( new Rectangle( width-wallThickness,0, wallThickness, height ) );     // right
        walls.add( new Rectangle( 0,height-wallThickness, width, wallThickness ) );     // bottom

        walls.add( new Rectangle( 0,100, 100, wallThickness ) );                    // left
        // bottom wall structure
        walls.add( new Rectangle( 50,height-wallThickness-120, wallThickness, 70 ) );       // vert on left
        walls.add( new Rectangle( 50,height-wallThickness-120, width-150, wallThickness ) );    // horiz top
        walls.add( new Rectangle( 50,height-wallThickness-50, width-120, wallThickness ) );     // horiz bottom
        walls.add( new Rectangle( 200,height-230, wallThickness, 130 ) );                       // vert on rt
    }
    public void paintWalls( )
    {
        backgroundBuf = createImage( width, height );                       // backdrop and walls
        background = (Graphics2D )backgroundBuf.getGraphics( );
        background.setColor( Color.black );
        background.fillRect( 0,0, width, height );
        background.setColor( Color.gray );
        for ( int i=0; i<walls.size( ); i++ )
        {
            Rectangle r = (Rectangle )walls.get( i );
            background.fillRect ( r.x, r.y, r.width, r.height );
```

continued

```
            }
        }
        public void paint( Graphics g )
        {
            g.drawImage( screenBuf,0,0,this);
        }
        public void run( )
        {
            paintWalls( );
            screenBuf = createImage( width, height );
            Graphics gapplet = (Graphics2D )screenBuf.getGraphics( );

            while( true )
            {
                gapplet.drawImage( backgroundBuf, 0,0,  this );     // first draw background on buffer

                        // then draw player on buffer
                repaint( );                                           // draw buffer to applet
                try {
                    Thread.sleep(10);
                } catch( Exception ex ) { stop( ); }
            }
        }
    }
```

Our next step is to add the player. To maintain information about the player, such as the image to display and the location, direction and speed, we'll set up a separate class called Sprite (this generic class is not called 'Player' because we can use the same class to create monsters and other entities we want in our game). The following is the code for setting up a Sprite and incorporating it into our main applet.

```
import java.awt.*;
import javax.swing.*;
public class Sprite
{
  Image image, up, down, left, right, stand;
  int x, y, lastX, lastY;
  int speed=5;
  int directionX = 1, directionY = 1;
  public Sprite( Image i )                            // all images are the same
  {
    image = i;  stand = i; up = i; down = i; left = i; right = i;
    x = 10;  lastX = 10;
    y=10;   lastY = 10;
  }
  public Sprite( Image i, Image u, Image d, Image l, Image r )
  {
    image = i;  stand = i;  up = u; down = d; left = l; right = r;
    x = 10;  lastX = 10;
    y=10;   lastY = 10;
  }
  public void setLocation( int _x, int _y )
  {
        lastX = x;  lastY = y;
        x = _x;
        y = _y;
```

> Separate image objects allow us to customize the look of the character (player or monster). Use animated gifs to make it look like it's walking/flying.

continued

```java
        }
        public Rectangle getDimensions( )
        {
                return new Rectangle( x, y, image.getWidth(null), image.getHeight(null) );
        }
        public void stopMoving( )
        {
           image = stand;
        }
        public void moveUp( )
        {
                image = up;
                lastX = x;  lastY = y;
                y -= speed;
        }
        public void moveDown( )
        {
                image = down;
                lastX = x;  lastY = y;
                y += speed;
        }
        public void moveLeft( )
        {
                image = left;
                lastX = x;  lastY = y;
                x -= speed;
        }
        public void moveRight( )
        {
                image = right;
                lastX = x;  lastY = y;
                x += speed;
        }
        public void paintComponent( Graphics g )
        {
                g.drawImage( image, x, y, null );
        }
        public void undoMove( )
        {
                x = lastX;
                y = lastY;
        }
}
```

Keep track of the last (x, y) coordinates when moving in case an undo is necessary due to a collision

```java
import java.awt.*;
import java.awt.event.*;
import java.awt.image.*;
import javax.swing.*;
import java.util.*;
public class Game extends JApplet implements Runnable, KeyListener
{
     int width, height;                    // dimensions of game
     ArrayList<Rectangle> walls;
     Image backgroundBuf, screenBuf;       // screenBuf = draw backgrd then player and entities in layers
     Graphics2D background;
     MediaTracker track;
```

```java
    Sprite player;
    Thread thread;
    public void init( )
    {
        resize( 300, 300 );
        loadImages( );
        width = this.getWidth( );
        height = this.getHeight( );

        walls = new ArrayList<Rectangle>( );
        buildWalls( );

         player.setLocation( 50, 50 );

        addKeyListener(this);
    }
    public void start( )
    {
        try {
                track.waitForAll( );
         } catch ( Exception e ) { };
        if ( thread == null )
                thread = new Thread( this );
        thread.start( );
        setFocusable(true);
    }
    public void loadImages( )
    {
        track = new MediaTracker( this );
        Image img = getImage( getCodeBase( ), "stand_front.gif" );
        Image back = getImage( getCodeBase( ), "walk_back.gif" );
        Image front = getImage( getCodeBase( ), "walk_front.gif" );
        Image right = getImage( getCodeBase( ), "walk_right.gif" );
        Image left = getImage( getCodeBase( ), "walk_left.gif" );

        track.addImage(img, 2);    track.addImage(back, 6 );
        track.addImage( front, 3 ); track.addImage( left, 4 );
        track.addImage( right, 5 );

        player = new Sprite( img, back, front, left, right );
    }
    public void buildWalls( )
    {
        // create Rectangle objects and store in ArrayList walls
        int wallThickness = 10;
        walls.add( new Rectangle( 0,0, width, wallThickness ) );                       // top
        walls.add( new Rectangle( 0,0, wallThickness, height ) );                      // left
        walls.add( new Rectangle( width-wallThickness,0, wallThickness, height ) );    // right
        walls.add( new Rectangle( 0,height-wallThickness, width, wallThickness ) );    // bottom

        walls.add( new Rectangle( 0,100, 100, wallThickness ) );                       // left
                                                                                       // bottom wall structure
        walls.add( new Rectangle( 50,height-wallThickness-120, wallThickness, 70 ) );          // vert on left
        walls.add( new Rectangle( 50,height-wallThickness-120, width-150, wallThickness ) );   // horiz top
        walls.add( new Rectangle( 50,height-wallThickness-50, width-120, wallThickness ) );    // horiz bottom
        walls.add( new Rectangle( 200,height-230, wallThickness, 130 ) );                      // vert on rt
    }
```

continued

```java
public boolean checkCollisionWalls( Rectangle entityAura )
{
        for ( int i=0; i< walls.size( ); i++ )
        {
                if ( entityAura.intersects( walls.get( i ) ))
                        return true;
        }
        return false;
}
public void paintWalls( )
{
        backgroundBuf = createImage( width, height );          // backdrop and walls
        background = (Graphics2D )backgroundBuf.getGraphics( );
        background.setColor( Color.black );
        background.fillRect( 0,0, width, height );
        background.setColor( Color.gray );
        for ( int i=0; i<walls.size( ); i++ )
        {
                Rectangle r = (Rectangle )walls.get( i );
                background.fillRect ( r.x, r.y, r.width, r.height );
        }
}
public void keyReleased( KeyEvent ke )
{
   player.stopMoving( );
}
public void keyPressed( KeyEvent key )
{
   int code = key.getKeyCode( );
   if( code == KeyEvent.VK_UP || code == KeyEvent.VK_8 )
     player.moveUp( );
   else if( code == KeyEvent.VK_RIGHT )
     player.moveRight( );
   else if( code == KeyEvent.VK_LEFT )
     player.moveLeft( );
   else if( code == KeyEvent.VK_DOWN || code == KeyEvent.VK_2)
     player.moveDown( );
   if ( checkCollisionWalls( player.getDimensions( ) ))
         player.undoMove( );
}
public void keyTyped( KeyEvent ke ) { }
public void paint( Graphics g )
{
        g.drawImage( screenBuf,0,0,this);
}
public void update(Graphics g)
{
        paint(g);
}
public void run( )
{
        paintWalls( );
        screenBuf = createImage( width, height );
        Graphics gapplet = (Graphics2D )screenBuf.getGraphics( );
    while( true )
    {
        gapplet.drawImage( backgroundBuf, 0,0, this );   // first draw background on buffer
        player.paintComponent( gapplet );                // then draw player on buffer
```

Walk through ArrayList and check for Rectangles intersecting with either player or other entity's dimensions

continued ⇒

```
                repaint( );                    // draw buffer to applet
                try {
                    Thread.sleep(10);
                } catch( Exception ex ) { stop( ); }
        }
    }
}
```

Now we can have our player move around the dungeon space, with custom graphics based on the direction the player is walking. Now let's add a way for the player to get out of the dungeon. Let's create a fairy flying around the dungeon. When the player runs into the fairy, he gets his wish – to find the door out of the dungeon. We can reuse the Sprite class for the fairy, but we'll have to add some 'brains' to have the computer automatically move the fairy around. We'll also add a check for collisions with the player, and once they collide, we'll display an exit for the player. The exit will be a thing and we'll copy the Sprite class and modify it a bit for all objects in our game (e.g. the exit, coins, food, etc.).

```
import java.awt.*;
import javax.swing.*;
public class Thing
{
    Image image;
    int x, y;
    boolean visible = false;
    public Thing( Image i )
    {
        image = i;
        x = 0;
        y=0;
    }
    public void setLocation( int _x, int _y )
    {
            x = _x;
            y = _y;
    }
    public void setVisible( boolean b )
    {
            visible = b;
    }
    public boolean isVisible( )
    {
            return visible;
    }
    public Rectangle getDimensions( )
    {
            return new Rectangle( x, y, image.getWidth(null), image.getHeight(null) );
    }
    public void paintComponent( Graphics g )
    {
            if ( visible )
                    g.drawImage( image, x, y, null );
    }
}
```

Use the visible variable to determine whether or not to display the item. For the exit, only display after player collides with fairy. For coins, don't display once player picks it up.

```
import java.awt.*;
import java.awt.event.*;
import java.awt.image.*;
```

```java
import javax.swing.*;
import java.util.*;
public class Game extends JApplet implements Runnable, KeyListener
{
        int width, height;              // dimensions of game
        ArrayList<Rectangle> walls;
        Image backgroundBuf, screenBuf;         // screenBuf = draw backgrd then player and entities in layers
        Graphics2D background;
        MediaTracker track;
        Sprite player;
        Sprite fairy;
        Thing exit;
        Thread thread;
        Random random;
    public void init( )
    {
        resize( 300, 300 );
        loadImages( );
        width = this.getWidth( );
        height = this.getHeight( );

        walls = new ArrayList<Rectangle>( );
        buildWalls( );

        player.setLocation( 50, 50 );
        fairy.setLocation ( width-70, height-70 );
        random = new Random( );
        addKeyListener(this);
    }
    public void start( )
    {
        try {
                track.waitForAll( );
        } catch ( Exception e ) { };

        if ( thread == null )
                thread = new Thread( this );
        thread.start( );
        setFocusable(true);
    }
    public void loadImages( )
    {
        track = new MediaTracker( this );
        Image img = getImage( getCodeBase( ), "stand_front.gif" );
        Image back = getImage( getCodeBase( ), "walk_back.gif" );
        Image front = getImage( getCodeBase( ), "walk_front.gif" );
        Image right = getImage( getCodeBase( ), "walk_right.gif" );
        Image left = getImage( getCodeBase( ), "walk_left.gif" );

        track.addImage(img, 2);      track.addImage(back, 6 );
        track.addImage( front, 3 );  track.addImage( left, 4 );
        track.addImage( right, 5 );

        player = new Sprite( img, back, front, left, right );
        img = getImage( getCodeBase( ), "Fairy.gif" );
        fairy = new Sprite( img );
        fairy.speed = 2;
```

continued

265

```java
            exit = new Thing( getImage( getCodeBase( ), "door.jpg"));
}
public void buildWalls( )
{
        // create Polygon or Rectangle objects and store in ArrayList walls
        int wallThickness = 10;
        walls.add( new Rectangle( 0,0, width, wallThickness ) );                      // top
        walls.add( new Rectangle( 0,0, wallThickness, height ) );                     // left
        walls.add( new Rectangle( width-wallThickness,0, wallThickness, height ) );   // right
        walls.add( new Rectangle( 0,height-wallThickness, width, wallThickness ) );   // bottom

        walls.add( new Rectangle( 0,100, 100, wallThickness ) );                      // left
                                                                                      // bottom wall structure
        walls.add( new Rectangle( 50,height-wallThickness-120, wallThickness, 70 ) );       // vert on left
        walls.add( new Rectangle( 50,height-wallThickness-120, width-150, wallThickness ) ); // horiz top
        walls.add( new Rectangle( 50,height-wallThickness-50, width-120, wallThickness ) );  // horiz bottom
        walls.add( new Rectangle( 200,height-230, wallThickness, 130 ) );             // vert on rt

        exit.setLocation( 50+wallThickness,height-wallThickness-50-60);
}
public boolean checkCollisionWalls( Rectangle entityAura )
{
        for ( int i=0; i< walls.size( ); i++ )
        {
                if ( entityAura.intersects( walls.get( i ) ))
                        return true;
        }
        return false;
}
public boolean checkCollisionFairy( )
{
        return player.getDimensions( ).intersects( fairy.getDimensions( ) );
}
public void paintWalls( )
{
        backgroundBuf = createImage( width, height );                         // backdrop and walls
        background = (Graphics2D )backgroundBuf.getGraphics( );
        background.setColor( Color.black );
        background.fillRect( 0,0, width, height );
        background.setColor( Color.gray );
        for ( int i=0; i<walls.size( ); i++ )
        {
                Rectangle r = (Rectangle )walls.get( i );
                background.fillRect ( r.x, r.y, r.width, r.height );
        }
}
public void keyReleased( KeyEvent ke )
{
   player.stopMoving( );
}
public void keyPressed( KeyEvent key )
{
   int code = key.getKeyCode( );
   if( code == KeyEvent.VK_UP || code == KeyEvent.VK_8 )
      player.moveUp( );
   else if( code == KeyEvent.VK_RIGHT )
      player.moveRight( );
   else if( code == KeyEvent.VK_LEFT )
```

continued

```java
            player.moveLeft( );
        else if( code == KeyEvent.VK_DOWN || code == KeyEvent.VK_2)
            player.moveDown( );
        if ( checkCollisionWalls( player.getDimensions( ) ))
            player.undoMove( );
    }
    public void keyTyped( KeyEvent ke ) { }
    public void paint( Graphics g )
    {
        g.drawImage( screenBuf,0,0,this);
    }
    public void update(Graphics g)
    {
        paint(g);
    }
    public void run( )
    {
        paintWalls( );
        screenBuf = createImage( width, height );
        Graphics gapplet = (Graphics2D )screenBuf.getGraphics( );

        while( true )
        {
            gapplet.drawImage( backgroundBuf, 0,0,  this );         // first draw background on buffer
            if ( ! exit.isVisible( ) && checkCollisionFairy( ) )            // exit not yet visible, check if collision with fairy
                    exit.setVisible( true );
            exit.paintComponent( gapplet );
            moveFairy( );
            fairy.paintComponent( gapplet );                                // draw the fairy
            player.paintComponent( gapplet );                               // then draw player on buffer
            if ( exit.isVisible( ) && player.getDimensions( ).intersects( exit.getDimensions( ) ) )
            {
                    gapplet.setFont( new Font( "Serif", Font.BOLD, 42 ) );
                    gapplet.setColor( Color.WHITE );
                    gapplet.drawString( "YOU WIN!", 60, 120 );
            }
            repaint( );                             // draw buffer to applet
            try {
                    Thread.sleep(10);
                } catch( Exception ex ) { stop( ); }
        }
    }
    public void moveFairy( )
    {
        boolean badLocation = true;                         // keep track of whether we found a good location or not
        int numTries = 10;                                  // give up after a while to prevent infinite loop
        while( badLocation && numTries > 0 )
        {
                int newx = random.nextInt( fairy.speed );   // generate a new random coordinate based on speed of fairy
                int newy = random.nextInt( fairy.speed );
                if ( random.nextInt( 2 ) == 0 )             // change direction in x
                    newx = -1 * newx;
                if ( random.nextInt( 2 ) == 0 )
                    newy = -1 * newy;
                fairy.setLocation(fairy.x + newx, fairy.y + newy);
                if ( checkCollisionWalls( fairy.getDimensions( ) ) )
                    fairy.undoMove( );
                else
```

The order in which we draw to the applet is important! Draw the player last to be displayed on top of other things like the exit.

```
                    badLocation = false;
                    numTries = numTries -1;
            }
        }
}
```

Now we've gone through a fundamental structure for building a dungeon game. Here are some hints on how to expand on this game structure. The biggest decision is to decide what we want the purpose of the game to be – is it to collect the most amount of coins? Is it to find a princess and rescue her? Is it to collect all the gems/keys/other in each room before exiting? Can bombs be used to break walls to create doorways out?

If we want to maintain a list of items the user picks up, the ideal data structure is an ArrayList. The ArrayList allows us to add items and remove items from the list quite easily. If each item is of type Thing, we can cast our ArrayList to hold Thing

```
ArrayList<Thing> list;
list = new ArrayList<Thing>( );
```

Even though each 'thing' is quite different (coins vs. gems vs. food vs. keys), we can still use the same Thing class for each. Another option is to extend the Thing class for specific types of things, such as food which is consumable and can be used to maintain health points. This is a good option if we create monsters in a game (use Sprite class) and when the player collides with a monster, he loses some health points (but doesn't necessarily die). To extend the Thing class, we use the `extends` keyword:

```
public class Food extends Thing
```

When we extend a class, we inherit all the methods and variables defined in the parent class. We can also *override* some methods from our parent class that we inherited, by defining the method header the same as the one in the class which we inherited, but write a different body inside the method.

To implement weapons in the game, create a new class that extends the Thing class. Add methods for how many points each hit takes off on a monster (be sure to modify the Sprite class such that each entity loses some health points each time they collide into something). For each Sprite, we could structure it such that they can only pick up one weapon at a time. Instead of maintaining the weapons in an ArrayList, add one instance variable to keep track of the weapon currently in use. We could program it such that when the player picks up a new weapon, he automatically drops his current weapon to replace it.

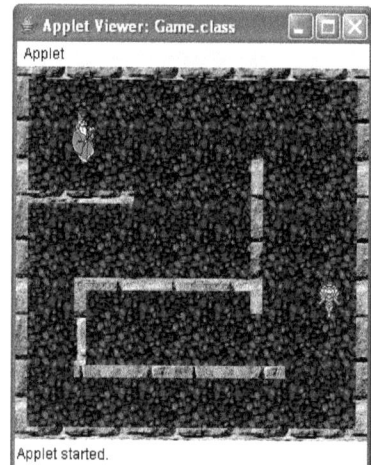

If we have a nice graphics background image for a dungeon, we could easily implement this into the current program. Instead of drawing the walls in the ArrayList, have the background paint the background image. Be sure the walls in the ArrayList match the coordinates of the walls in the image, so that the rest of the code works the same. Create an instance variable at the top of the applet class for the image of the backdrop:

```
Image bkdrop;
```

Read the image in within the loadImages method and add it to the MediaTracker. Then modify the paintWalls method to draw the image instead of drawing each of the Rectangle objects in the ArrayList. Replace the method as follows:

```
public void paintWalls( )
{
    backgroundBuf = createImage( width, height );
    background = (Graphics2D )backgroundBuf.getGraphics( );
    background.drawImage( bkdrop, 0, 0, width, height, this );
}
```

If we want to create a big dungeon with lots of rooms, we should restructure the code to create a Room class that keeps track of each individual room. We could write code to automatically create dynamic room structures, but this takes some serious thought. We would need to ensure that the walls don't completely block off a section (unless we want that). The Room class should maintain the ArrayList of walls and should contain a method to handle collision checks given a Rectangular dimension.

Summary

- Game programming requires the use of threads to continually repaint and handle user interaction events such as key presses.
- To prevent flicker, paint the screen to a BufferImage first before painting on the actual applet.
- Dungeon games can be created as a full maze view from the top, scrolling left to right either top-down view or first-person view.
- Order of painting on the screen is important – the last thing painted will be on top of the rest.
- Games with players and other entities usually maintain information about the entity in a class called Sprite. The Sprite class should maintain all information about the entity – the image, coordinate location, dimensions, speed, direction, objects picked up, weapon, etc.
- ArrayList is a good data structure to maintain a list of items that may be added or removed frequently through the program, such as blocks in a Breakout game and objects picked up in a dungeon game.
- Classes can be extended to add functionality for specific types of objects. Extending a class enables us to reuse the code for multiple other classes that inherit from it.
- MediaTracker is useful for ensuring all images are loaded before starting the applet.
- Start the thread in the start method of the applet.
- The random class can be used to randomly select a number. Calls to nextInt can take a parameter to specify a restriction that the random number be between 0 and the number -1.
- Calls to getImage can only be done inside the class that extends JApplet (method is defined in the JApplet class).
- Check for collisions between two entities/objects by calling the method intersects on two rectangle objects containing the entities/objects' coordinates and width/height dimensions.
- Thread.sleep is used to pause the program for a number of milliseconds. Calls to the sleep method must be inside a try…catch block to catch interrupts that may occur.
- Writing a method with the same method header as a parent class is called *overriding*.

Exercises

1. Modify the Breakout game to use images instead of drawing red blocks.
2. Why should we use an ArrayList instead of an array for each block in the Breakout game?
3. Why should we use BufferedImage instead of drawing directly onto the applet?
4. How do we check for collisions between two entities/objects?
5. True or False: When we write a paintComponent method, we are overriding the method from our parent class.
6. Modify the Breakout game to have two levels – slow and fast. Change the speed of the ball in play accordingly.
7. Modify the dungeon game such that when the game ends, the user cannot move the player anymore and the fairy stops moving. Tell the user they can press the space to start again. If the user presses the space bar, allow the user to start the game over again.
8. Add a monster to the dungeon game. Give the monster a different algorithm for moving around the maze. If the player collides with the monster, end the game.
9. Add a second room to the dungeon game, such that when the user goes through the door, the new dungeon room appears.
10. Expand the dungeon game to enable the player to pick up weapons he finds in the dungeon. Allow only one weapon to be held by the player at a time. When the user presses the letter 'a', have the weapon attack whatever is in front of the player. If the weapon collides with a monster, kill off the monster.
11. Modify the dungeon game to display a nice graphical dungeon (create an image of the dungeon in a graphics program). Make sure the walls match up to the wall coordinates in the image so that the code works as it is.

Chapter 15

Internet Applications

Objectives:

- Internet
- JEditorPane
- Hosting applets on the Internet
- Applet Parameters
- Configuration Files
- Applets and Email
- Writing to a File

Internet

The Internet allows us to share information across the world. We can incorporate our applets on the Internet by embedding them inside a web page. We can also display web pages inside our applet.

When discussing the Internet, there are some key terms used. First and foremost, when using a browser to view web pages we specify the location of the web page by entering the URL. The URL (Uniform Resource Locator) begins with the protocol used (http, https, ftp, telnet, etc.) followed by the Internet address and path to the filename.

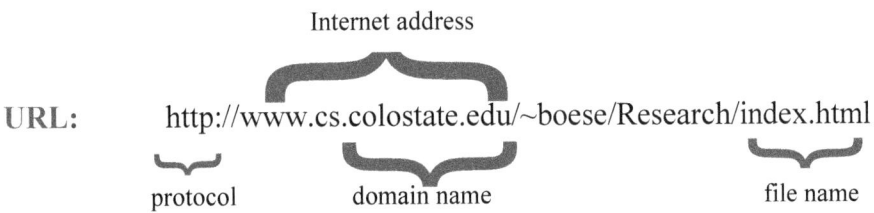

URL

The URL is the full path to some file or directory on the Internet. This includes the protocol, Internet address and path.

Protocol

Protocol is defined as a set of rules. The protocols used in Internet applications determine how to handle the data. The most common protocol is http (HyperText Transfer Protocol). This protocol defines how to transfer web pages between the server and the computer that wishes to display the page. An extension to the http protocol is the https protocol, which is a secure version of http and used frequently for secure credit card transactions and account access. Another protocol is called ftp (File Transfer Protocol) which is used to copy files from one computer to another computer or network.

Domain Name

The domain name is the base of an Internet address that is unique on the Internet. Anyone can buy a domain name that isn't currently registered by someone else.

Internet Address

The Internet address is the full address to a computer or network established on the Internet. The Internet address ends with the domain name, but may have other computers or networks listed before the domain name (e.g. the cs network in the URL above). The Internet address maps to a four-digit IP address that uniquely identifies itself on the Internet.

HyperLinks

Web pages are usually coded in HTML code: HyperText Markup Language. HTML is made up of tags in angle brackets < >. We discussed some HTML tags in previous chapters to incorporate customizaitons of our components. HTML web pages may also have an additional tag which is called a *hyperlink*. This is a tag that enables the user to click on either some text or an image and be redirected to a different web page.

JEditorPane

Want to display an HTML page from the Internet inside your applet? Now we can! The `JEditorPane` is designed specifically for this purpose. Unfortunately, it is a lot more complicated than our other components we've been working with, but if we follow the guidelines it shouldn't be too difficult.

To start off with, let's look at a basic example of displaying my homepage.

```java
import java.io.*;
import java.awt.*;
import javax.swing.*;
import javax.swing.event.*;
public class JEditorPaneEx extends JApplet
      implements HyperlinkListener
{
  JEditorPane pane;
  String sPath;
  JScrollPane scrollPane;
  public void init( )
  {
    setLayout( new BorderLayout( ) );

    sPath = "http://www.cs.colostate.edu/";
    setupURL( sPath );

    pane.setEditable( false );
    pane.addHyperlinkListener( this );
    scrollPane = new JScrollPane(pane);
    add( scrollPane, BorderLayout.CENTER );
  }
  public void setupURL( String url )
  {
          if( pane == null )
                  pane = new JEditorPane( );
          try {
              pane.setPage( url );
          }
          catch( IOException ioe )
          {
              pane.setText ( "Error accessing web page: " + url );
          }
  }
  public void hyperlinkUpdate( HyperlinkEvent event )
  {
    if( event.getEventType() == HyperlinkEvent.EventType.ACTIVATED )
    {
          setupURL( String.valueOf( event.getURL( )) );
    }
  }
}
```

Now let's take a look at the new code. First off, we're working with a `JEditorPane` component.

```
JEditorPane pane;
```

Inside the `setupURL( )` method, we want to create a new `JEditorPane` if one hasn't been created yet. Therefore, we first check to see if it is null (first time we run the applet). If it is null, we can instantiate it:

```
if( pane == null )
      pane = new JEditorPane( );
```

The next step is to set the web page into the JEditorPane. We do this by calling the method `setPage` on the JEditorPane variable, and send it the String for the URL of the web page. *NOTE: The URL MUST begin with http://*

```
pane.setPage( url );
```

However, notice how this method call is inside a `try...catch` block. We won't go in to depth about these coding structures, but we need to understand the basics. Try...catch blocks are Java's way of handling errors which are thrown (yes, Java actually *throws* errors around!). When we want to execute some code that potentially might cause a major error, called an **exception**, we need to wrap the code inside a try...catch block to be able to catch the exception.

In our example, the call to the `setPage` method might cause a major error, so it is inside the try..catch block. If an error does occur, such as the URL is invalid, then the code inside the `catch` block is executed. In our example, an error would result in the text being displayed instead of the web page "Error accessing web page: " and the URL attempted.

```
try {
        pane.setPage( url );
}
catch( IOException ioe )
{
    pane.setText( "Error accessing web page: " + url );
}
```

We also need to store the JEditorPane inside a JScrollPane, which we've worked with before.

```
JScrollPane scrollPane = new JScrollPane(pane);
```

The last thing we need to write is how to handle clicks on links inside the web page that is displayed. To do this, there are four things we need to do (similar to other events we've worked with).

1. First, we need to specify that we are listening for these type of events -

    ```
    implements HyperlinkListener
    ```

2. These events are inside the javax.swing.event package, so we need an import statement at the top of our program:

    ```
    import javax.swing.event.*;
    ```

3. Now we need to specify that we want to listen for HyperLinkEvents on our JEditorPane component:

    ```
    pane.addHyperlinkListener( this );
    ```

4. Lastly, we need to implement the required method for implementing the HyperlinkListener, which is the `hyperlinkUpdate` method

```
public void hyperlinkUpdate( HyperlinkEvent event )
{
    if( event.getEventType( ) == HyperlinkEvent.EventType.ACTIVATED )
        setupURL( String.valueOf( event.getURL( )) );
}
```

Inside this hyperlinkUpdate method, we check to see if the user is clicking on a link. If so, we want to call our `setupURL` method we previously wrote to change the web page in our JEditorPane, based on the URL clicked - event.getURL( ).

 *The URL must begin with http:// when displaying a webpage in a JEditorPane.*

Another example, using buttons:

```java
import java.io.*;
import java.awt.*;
import java.awt.event.*;
import javax.swing.*;
import javax.swing.event.*;

public class JEditorPaneExBtn extends JApplet
      implements HyperlinkListener, ActionListener
{
  JEditorPane pane;
  JPanel toppane;
  String cspath = "http://www.cs.colostate.edu/";
  String csupath = "http://www.colostate.edu/";
  String mepath =  "http://www.cs.colostate.edu/~boese";
  JScrollPane scrollPane;
  JButton cs, me, csu;

  public void init( )
  {
    setLayout( new BorderLayout( ) );

    setupButtons( );
    setupURL( cspath );
    pane.setEditable( false );
    pane.addHyperlinkListener( this );

    scrollPane = new JScrollPane(pane);

    add( scrollPane, BorderLayout.CENTER );
  }


  public void setupButtons( )
  {
    cs = new JButton( "CS Dept" );
    csu = new JButton( "CSU" );
    me = new JButton( "My Homepage" );
    cs.addActionListener( this );
    csu.addActionListener( this );
    me.addActionListener( this );
    toppane =new JPanel( new FlowLayout( ) );
    toppane.add( cs );
    toppane.add( csu );
    toppane.add( me );
    add( toppane, BorderLayout.NORTH );
  }
```

Click on CS Dept

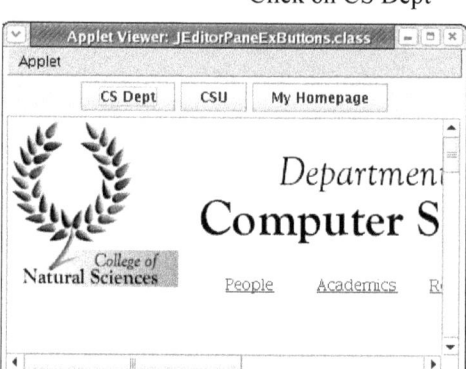

Click on CSU

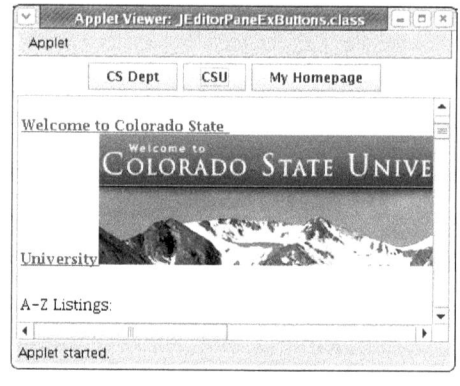

Click on Me

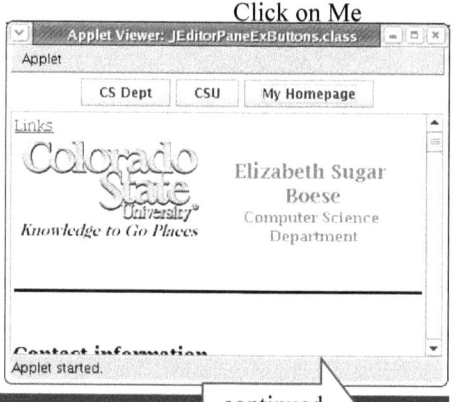

continued

276

```
public void setupURL( String url )
{
    if( pane == null )
        pane = new JEditorPane( );
    try {
        pane.setPage( url );
    }
    catch( IOException ioe )   {
       pane.setText( "Error accessing " + "web page: " + url );
    }
}
public void hyperlinkUpdate( HyperlinkEvent event )
{
   if( event.getEventType() == HyperlinkEvent.EventType.ACTIVATED )
        setupURL( String.valueOf( event.getURL( )) );
}
public void actionPerformed( ActionEvent ae )
{
    Object src = ae.getSource( );
    if( src == cs )
        setupURL( cspath );
    else if( src == csu )
        setupURL( csupath );
    else if( src == me )
        setupURL( mepath );
}
}
```

NOTE: Not all web pages display properly using JEditorPane.

Hosting your applet on the Web

There are several ways to get our applet on the Internet.
First we need to get our applet ready without using an IDE such as Eclipse.

1. **Setting up the HTML file**
    - Create a file (in your text editor).
    - Enter the following line, changing the XYZ to the name of your class.

```
<HTML>
  <BODY>
    <APPLET CODE=XYZ.class WIDTH=500 HEIGHT=500>
    </APPLET>
</BODY></HTML>
```

This needs to be saved in a file named exactly: "index.html" in lower case letters.
Modify the width and height to the size you want in pixels.

When using images, we must first load the image into the applet by calling getImage *before putting into an ImageIcon object; if you try to: ImageIcon icon = new ImageIcon("img.gif")
it will **not** work once you put it up on the Internet!*

2. **Hosting for free** (or buy a domain – see below)
There are many places to put up web pages for free. Check with your school to see if they provide space, or search the Internet for options. Some of the free hosting places such as Geocities will put an advertisement on the upper-right side of you web page. It's a small price you pay to get a free space on the Internet. Here are a few other options to look at:

- University accounts
- Geocities (http://geocities.yahoo.com) Free (but they put ads up on your pages),
- http://www.doteasy.com/
- http://members.freewebs.com/index.jsp

Another option: Buying a Domain Name
If you're really gung-ho about your applets and want to own your own domain name, you can purchase a domain from many different registrars. When purchasing a domain name, ensure that you have full rights to the domain name and you are not merely leasing the name (in case your site becomes famous, you'd hate to have them turn around and charge you more for leasing your domain name!). Many of these places also offer some hosting space for your web site if you buy a domain name from them. If you buy a cheap package it may not have enough space if you have a lot of large image files and/or sound files. Some places you can buy a domain name and host your applet:

- Register.com
- Registar.com
- Aplus.net
- others...

3. **Uploading files**

- Upload the **index.html**, all the **.class** files, all the **images** and **sound** files necessary to make your applet work (do not need to upload the .java files).
- Make sure your code referencing the image file names matches the actual file name (case sensitive!! This is important as Eclipse in Windows has been lazy, allowing any case)

NOTE: if your project reads in from a local file (not a URL) or writes to a file not using CGI, you need to remove that code before it will work on the Internet (see Security section).

Applet Parameters

We can allow easy customization of our applets by initializing our variables through parameters we set in our HTML file. We define each parameter in an HTML param tag with the name attribute identifying each parameter and the value tag containing what the value should be. These tags must be defined between the applet open and close tags. Then we change our applet to read these parameter values.

An HTML file example is listed below, with three customizations: the color of the background, color of the text and text for the title displayed at the top of the applet.

```html
<HTML>
  <BODY>
    <APPLET CODE=XYZ.class WIDTH=500 HEIGHT=500>
      <PARAM NAME=bkcolor VALUE="0000FF">
      <PARAM NAME=textcolor VALUE="AAAA00">
      <PARAM NAME=title VALUE="Lizzie's Playground">
    </APPLET>
</BODY></HTML>
```

Use standard HTML hex values for colors RRGGBB red green blue

Use double-quotes for text with spaces in it.

```java
import java.awt.*;
import javax.swing.*;
public class AppParams extends JApplet
{
        JPanel bkgrnd;
        JLabel heading;
        public void init( )
        {
                bkgrnd = new JPanel( );
                bkgrnd.setBackground( new Color( Integer.parseInt( getParameter( "bkcolor" ), 16 ) ) );
                heading = new JLabel( getParameter("title") );
                heading.setForeground( new Color( Integer.parseInt( getParameter( "textcolor" ), 16 ) ) );
                bkgrnd.add( heading );
                setLayout( new BorderLayout( ) );
                add( bkgrnd, BorderLayout.CENTER );
        }
}
```

Easiest way to parse colors is to read in hex values (commonly used in HTML)

Configuration Files

Another way for us to customize our programs without changing the source code is to make use of configuration files. These are simple text files that contain a "name=value" on each line of the file. Inside our Java program, we can read through this file and set our variables based on the values in this our config file.

An example of a config file using the same parameters as the example above:

```
title=My Favorite Playground
bkcolor=0000FF
textcolor=AAAA00
```

The Java program that reads the config file:

```java
import java.awt.*;
import javax.swing.*;
import java.io.*;
import java.net.*;
public class ConfigFile extends JApplet
{
    JPanel bkgrnd;
    JLabel heading;
```

```java
    Color backcolor, textcolor;
    String titletext;
    String configFilename = "config.txt";              // Name of the file
    public void init( )                                 // – be sure it is in
    {                                                   // the same
        String config = readConfigFile( );              // directory as your
        parseConfig( config );                          // .class files!
        bkgrnd = new JPanel( );
        bkgrnd.setBackground( backcolor );
        heading = new JLabel( titletext );
        heading.setForeground( textcolor );
        bkgrnd.add( heading );
        setLayout( new BorderLayout( ) );
        add( bkgrnd, BorderLayout.CENTER );
    }
    public void parseConfig( String cfg )               // Method to parse the String
    {                                                   // containing the contents of
        String[ ] lines, tokenkey;                      // the config file
        lines = cfg.split( "\n" );
        for( int i=0; i<lines.length; i++ )             // split method on Strings
        {                                               // returns an array dividing the
            tokenkey = lines[i].split( "=" );           // String based on a delimiter
            String value = tokenkey[1].substring( 0, tokenkey[1].length( ) -1 );   // remove newline at end
            if ( tokenkey[0].equals( "bkcolor" ) )
                backcolor = new Color( Integer.parseInt( value, 16 ) );
            else if ( tokenkey[0].equals( "textcolor" ) )
                textcolor = new Color( Integer.parseInt( value, 16 ) );
            else if ( tokenkey[0].equals( "title" ) )
                titletext = value;
        }
    }
    public String readConfigFile( )                     // Read in the entire
    {   String content;                                 // config file
        try {   URL target = new URL( getCodeBase( ), configFilename );   // You shouldn't need
                URLConnection con = target.openConnection( );              // to change this code
                con.connect( );                                            // for reading in any file
                byte b[ ] = new byte[ 1024 ];         // byte array
                int nbytes;                            // num bytes read in
                String retVal = new String( );
                BufferedInputStream in = new BufferedInputStream( con.getInputStream( ), 2048 );
                while( (nbytes = in.read( b, 0, 1024 )) != -1 )   // while there's more data to read
                {   content = new String( b, 0, nbytes );          // get 1024 bytes of data fr file
                    retVal += content;
                }
                in.close( );      // close connection
                return retVal;
        } catch ( Exception e )
        {     return "Error reading config file";
        }
    }
}
```

Applets and Email

Applets have restrictions placed on them to prevent malicious activity. Therefore, in order for us to have our applet email us a message, we will need to make use of a CGI program. CGI programs execute on the server, as opposed to our applets that are executing on the user's computer.

The CGI program we will use in this example is written in the perl programming language. To use this program, we need an account on a UNIX/Linux system (you may need to ask your network administrator how to get the program to work specific to your system setup). The name of the file is also system specific, whether it ends with .pl or .cgi. Many systems require all CGI programs to be in a specific directory, such as the cgi-bin directory.

```perl
#!/usr/bin/perl
use CGI ':standard';

my $outfile = "mailing.out";
my $sendmail = "/usr/sbin/sendmail -t";
my $reply_to = "Reply-to: boese\@cs.colostate.edu\n";
my $subject  = "Subject: Applet Message\n";
my $to       = "To: boese\@cs.colostate.edu\n";
my $content  = param('message');

print header;      # required first set of lines
print "Thanks!";

open(SENDMAIL, "|$sendmail") or die "Cannot open $sendmail: $!";
print SENDMAIL $reply_to;
print SENDMAIL $subject;
print SENDMAIL $to;
print SENDMAIL "Content-type: text/plain\n\n";
print SENDMAIL $content;
close(SENDMAIL);
```

Change to the absolute path to the perl program on your system, and the absolute path to the sendmail program

Change the Reply-to and To email addresses to your own

To make use of our CGI program, we need to encode our message before we send it. We are using the GET protocol (as opposed to POST), which will encode the message at the end of the URL. In the example Java program below, we'll also read a status from the server which is "Thanks!" or "Error" if there is a problem. In our example, we display this in a JLabel to the user.

```java
import javax.swing.*;
import java.awt.*;
import java.awt.event.*;
import java.net.*;
import java.io.*;
public class mailApplet extends JApplet implements ActionListener
{
   JTextArea msg;
   JLabel messageLabel, status;
   JButton submit;
   public void init( )
   {
      messageLabel = new JLabel( "Enter your message: " );
```

continued

```java
      status = new JLabel( );
      msg = new JTextArea(5,20);
      submit = new JButton( "Submit" );
      submit.addActionListener( this );
      setLayout( new FlowLayout( ) );
      add( messageLabel );      add( msg );      add( submit );      add( status );
    }
    public void actionPerformed( ActionEvent ae )
    {
      Object src = ae.getSource( );
      if ( src == submit )
      {
        String message = msg.getText( );
        String s = sendMail( "http://www.cs.colostate.edu/~boese/cgi-bin/mailer.cgi?message=",message );
         status.setText(s);
      }
    }
    public String sendMail( String fullPath, String msg )
    {
      try
      {
        String enc = URLEncoder.encode(msg, "UTF-8");
        URL target = new URL( fullPath + enc );
        String content;
        URLConnection con = target.openConnection( );    // open connection
        con.setUseCaches( false );
        con.setDefaultUseCaches( false );
        byte b[ ] = new byte[ 1024 ];            // byte array
        int nbytes;                              // num bytes read in
        String retVal = new String();
        BufferedInputStream in = new BufferedInputStream( con.getInputStream(), 2048 );
        while( (nbytes = in.read( b, 0, 1024 )) != -1 )        // while there's more data to read
        {
          content = new String( b, 0, nbytes );       // get 1024 bytes of data fr file
          retVal += content;
        }
        in.close( );          // close connection
        return retVal;
      }
      catch( Exception e )
      {
        return "Error " + e.toString( );
      }
    }
}
```

Change the URL to where your CGI program is. Keep the ?message=" part

My e-mail program

PHP is another language for writing CGI programs. It is more platform independent so the code provided should work on any system (UNIX/Linux/Windows/Mac/etc.) The PHP version of the email program is below, where your applet should specify the URL for this file that ends with the **.php** extension:

```php
<?php
    $request_method = $_SERVER["REQUEST_METHOD"];
    if ( $request_method == "GET" )  {
         $query_vars = $_GET;
    }
    elseif ( $request_method == "POST" ) {
         $query_vars = $_POST;
    }
    reset ( $query_vars );
    $emailbody = "New Form Submission: ";
    while ( list ($key, $val ) = each ( $query_vars ) ) {
         $emailbody = "$emailbody \n  $key = $val" ;
    }
    $emailto = 'info@coffeeClubOfTheWorld.com';       // Change to your email address
    $emailfrom = 'info@coffeeClubOfTheWorld.com';
    $subject = "New Form Submission";
    mail ( $emailto, $subject, $emailbody, "From: $emailfrom" );
?>
```

Writing to a File

We can write to files on the server by using CGI programs as well. The following example includes the CGI program that writes to a file. Remember, we need the CGI program to be read, write and execute permissions for the owner (on UNIX/Linux: chmod u=rwx writeFile.cgi).

Note that you can use the exact same Java source code file we used for the email example in this chapter – just change the name of the CGI program.

```perl
#!/usr/bin/perl
use CGI ':standard';

my $outfile = "mailing.out";          # Filename of where to store the information

print header;      # required first set of lines

# Write to file
open(OUT, ">>$outfile") or print("Couldn't open $outfile: $!");   # Use ">" instead of ">>" if you want to rewrite the file – e.g. store a new "High Score"
if (param('message'))
{
   print OUT param('message'),"\n";   # 'message' is the name of the parameter being sent
}
close(OUT);

print "Thanks!";
```

The PHP version is below:

```php
<?php
    $request_method = $_SERVER["REQUEST_METHOD"];
    if($request_method == "GET"){
      $query_vars = $_GET;
    } elseif ($request_method == "POST"){
      $query_vars = $_POST;
    }
    reset($query_vars);
    $file = $_SERVER['DOCUMENT_ROOT'] . "/form_";
    $fp = fopen($file,"a");
     fputs($fp,"---------------------\n");
    while (list ($key, $val) = each ($query_vars)) {
     fputs($fp,"$key = $val\n");
    }
    fclose($fp);
?>
```

We can make use of this CGI program to write to a file, then use the example of reading a config file to read the data file back into our applet. For example, with a little change to the read from a config file example, we could create a voting program that displays the results as a bar graph in our applet. We could also maintain our own bulletin board by recoding the users' messages then reading the file back and displaying the file appropriately within our applet. There are lots of programs we can write now with the ability to read and write files on the server!

Summary

- The URL is the full path to some file or directory on the Internet. This includes the protocol, Internet address and path.
- *Protocol* is defined as a set of rules.
- Internet protocols used determine how to handle the data.
- Common Internet protocols include: http, https, ftp.
- The domain name is the base of an Internet address that is unique to the Internet.
- Domain names can be bought if not currently registered by someone else.
- The Internet address is the full address to a computer or network established on the Internet.
- Hyperlink tags in a web page enable the user to click on either some text or an image and be redirected to a different web page.
- JEditorPane can display HTML tags and web pages from the Internet.
- JEditorPane implements the HyperLinkListener.
- When setting the web page to display in a JEditorPane, the call to setPage must be within a try…catch block in case there is a problem accessing the web page.
- To handle the links within a web page displayed in a JEditorPane, we must listen for the HyperlinkEvent and change the URL of the page being displayed.
- There are some websites that allow people to create web pages (with or without applets) on the Internet for free.
- Applets on the Internet cannot attempt to read local files – files can only be read via http requests.
- The HTML file to embed an applet must define the applet's width and height and include an end tag for the applet tag.
- The HTML file to embed an applet must reference the .class file, not the .java file.
- When uploading files to a website, be sure to upload all required image files and the bytecode (.class file) for the applets.
- CGI programs need to have read, write and execute permissions for the owner.

Exercises

1. Name the URL of a website where you can buy a domain name

2. Given the following: http://www.cs.colostate.edu/~cs150/syllabus.html

   What is the protocol?
   What is the internet address? URL? domain name?

3. What is the .java file? What is the .class file?

4. Fill in the missing blanks in the following HTML code

   ```
   <HTML><BODY>
   <APPLET _____ = "myApplet . _____"
     width=200 height= 200 >
   </_____> </HTML>
   ```

5. True or False. The four parts to a URL include: protocol, hostname, pathname, and filename.

6. Based on the URL   http://www.jujo.uno.com/helpstuff/faq.html
   match the following
   a. ___ domain name   f. www.jujo.uno.com
   b. ___ protocol   g. http
   c. ___ URL   h. uno.com
                                i. com
                                j. helpstuff/faq.html
                                k. www.jujo.uno.com/helpstuff/faq.html
                                m. http://www.jujo.uno.com/helpstuff/faq.html

7. What happens if you don't listen for Hyperlink events and you display a web page in a JEditorPane – does the page display correctly? What happens when you click on a link within the page?

8. Create a JEditorPane in an applet and instead of displaying a web page from the Internet, set the text of the pane with some HTML tag formatting.

9. True or False: When setting the web page to display in a JEditorPane, if the http:// is left off, it will default to use http:// for the protocol.

10. True or False: The try…catch block used for setting the page to display in a JEditorPane is not necessary if you simply set the text of the JEditorPane.

11. True or False: When the user clicks on a link in a web page displayed inside a JEditorPane, a HyperlinkEvent occurs.

12. Create an applet that has four buttons on the left side, one for each of your favorite college football teams. Add a JEditorPane in the center of the applet that correctly displays the main web page for the football team selected.

13. Extend the email example to handle two text fields entered by the user.

14. Write an applet with CGI program that allows users to vote for one of three JRadioButton options. Record each result in a file on the server. Include a button that then reads the data file and displays a histogram or pie chart of all the votes.

Chapter 16

Java

Objectives:

- Java
    - Simplicity
    - Small Language
    - Graphics
    - Object-Oriented
    - Platform Independent
    - Multi-Threading
    - Security
- Modifying and Using Free Applets
- 3rd Party Libraries
- Graphics2D
- Jar Files

Java

Java was originally designed for small appliances, such as smart toasters and cell phones. However, as the WWW came to popularity, Java became one of the forefront languages that could be displayed by web browsers. This has partially led to its popularity. Java started out as a very small language, which also made it relatively easy to learn. It is now growing into a robust language with many complex features.

Simplicity

Java also became popular as a first language in learning programming due to its simplicity. Some of the complex aspects of languages like C and C++ are automatically taken care of in Java. For example, memory management can be a nightmare to figure out in a C/C++ program, where the programmer must allocate and de-allocate memory lest be susceptible to memory leaks, but is automatically handled in Java via object creation and automated *garbage collection*. Java also removed some of the complexity of other languages such as operator overloading, multiple inheritance, and automatic coercions.

Small language – or is it?

Although initially the Java language was quite small and easy to learn the entire thing, it has increasingly become larger and more complex with new versions coming out almost annually. This used to be one of Java's selling points – that it was a small language. However, as the language grows with more spectacular features, it has become a bit disadvantageous as a learning language, requiring more knowledge and programming to make it work. It has also become somewhat problematic keeping students up to date with the current version of Java and a textbook to match it.

Graphics

Java has graphics capabilities, which is easier than C/C++ but still lags behind the ease of languages such as Flash and Visual Basic. The graphics also enable Java to be displayed within a web page.

Object-Oriented

Java is an object-oriented language, meaning that everything (except the primitive data types) is an Object. Objects store data values and methods related to the data together in the same class. Object-oriented languages help facilitate code reuse, either through inheritance or by instantiating several objects. For example, our FontOutline class will work with whatever text we send to it, such that we need not change the Java code but we can instantiate the class several times with different text.

Platform Independent

Java can be compiled on any machine type, then executed on any other machine type assuming they have an interpreter for the machine. This is a huge benefit over other languages, and a fundamental aspect on how applets work over the Internet (review Chapter 1 for more details). However, with platform independence also comes a disadvantage – Java is slow. It's slower than other languages that are compiled directly into machine code, which can then execute right away. Java first needs its *bytecode* to be *interpreted*, where the interpreter translates to machine code and then executes.

Advanced Concept
Although Java usually compiles to bytecode, there are special Java compilers that will compile the source code straight to machine code for a specific machine type. This will not work for applets on the Internet, but can help optimize Java applications that will only be executed on a specific machine type.

Multi-Threading

Multi-tasking is ability to simulate running many processes simultaneously. The CPU which handles computer instructions switches between all running processes fast enough that it appears to the user that they are all being executed at the same time. This prevents one process from holding up all other processes from having a chance to run.

Java supports threads, which allows multiple tasks to be executing at the same time. This is how many animation techniques and processor-intensive code can be executed without freezing the view to the users.

Security

Web browsers that run Java applets impose certain security restrictions to prevent malicious code from wreaking havoc on a system. Some of the restrictions include:
- Applets cannot read or write files on the computer running the applet
- Applets cannot create network connections to other computers
- Applets cannot start a program on the computer that is running the applet
- Applets cannot read system properties on the computer that is running the applet
- Windows that are displayed from an applet are displayed differently than windows from an application, so that the user knows where it came from.

Modifying and Using Free Applets

There are lots of free applets available. Some also provide the source code and allow you to modify it as you like. Be sure to read the copyright, licensing and agreements before you use.

Follow these steps to use an example free applet from the Java Boutique:

1. Go to http://java.internet.com

2. Find an applet you want.
   MAKE SURE it includes the java SOURCE code, NOT just the .class files!

3. Download the files (if it's a .zip file, you'll need to extract the contents of the file)

4. Copy the .java file(s) into your IDE (e.g. Eclipse). The easiest way to do this is to open the file in Notepad (Windows) or Kwrite (Linux), select all the text and copy it, then paste it into a new class inside your IDE.
   Alternatively, you can import the files into Eclipse.

5. Compile and run the Java Applet.

Other Features through 3rd-party libraries

We can enhance our Java applets through the use of 3rd party libraries. Some of these are available for free, and some cost money. The bigger catch is that users that view your website with your applet can usually only do so if they too have downloaded and installed the libraries or a run-time interpreter for these additional functionalities.

Some of the available features include:

- 2D Graphics
- 3D Graphics
- Virtual Reality
- Video
- Accessing Databases
- MP3 playback
- Music manipulation

Graphics2D

Graphics2D is a more advanced and more complex class for drawing. It extends the methods we learned in Chapter 2. We saw an introduction to using Graphics2D in Chapter 4 to enable anti-aliasing to allow us to make our drawing curves more smooth. We can also use color dithering, stroke thickness and stroke patterns, fill patterns, transparency and much more.

To use Graphics2D, we cast our Graphics object to a Graphics2D object then call all our methods on this Graphics2D object. To cast to Graphics2D, we will do one of the following depending if we are using the paint method for a JApplet class or the paintComponent method inside a class that extends JPanel.

```
public void paint( Graphics g )
{
    Graphics2D  g2d = (Graphics2D )g;
}
public void paintComponent( Graphics g )
{
    super.paintComponent(g);
    Graphics2D  g2d = (Graphics2D )g;
}
```

We can create a gradient fill by creating a GradientPaint instance and calling the method setPaint on our Graphics2D object. In the example below we create an ellipse with a gradient fill from blue to white.

```
GradientPaint gp = new GradientPaint(
    x1, y1, color1,
    x2, y2, color2, true );
```

```
import java.awt.*;
import java.awt.geom.*;
import javax.swing.*;
public class Graphics2DEx extends JApplet
{
  public void paint (Graphics g)
  {
        Graphics2D g2 = ( Graphics2D ) g;
        int x = 15, y = 10, w = 50, h = 50;
        Ellipse2D ellipse = new Ellipse2D.Double(x, y, w, h);
        GradientPaint gp =new GradientPaint(50, 75, Color.white, 95, 95, Color.blue, true);
        g2.setPaint(gp);   // fill with gradient
        g2.fill(ellipse);
  }
}
```

To understand how the gradient fill works, it depends on the coordinates you specify for the gradient and where you draw your object. For example, if we set up a GradientPaint object as:
GradientPaint(50, 75, Color.*yellow*, 95, 95, Color.*blue*, **true**);

290

the gradient will repeat over the space, as shown in the figure. Depending on where the circle is drawn will depend on what selection of blue and yellow that appear.

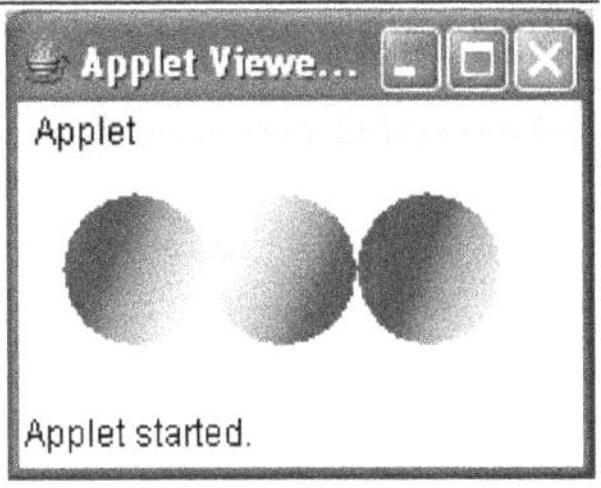

```java
import java.awt.*;
import java.awt.geom.*;
import javax.swing.*;
public class Graphics2DEx extends JApplet
{
  public void paint(Graphics g)
  {
    Graphics2D g2 = ( Graphics2D ) g;
    int x = 15, y = 10, w = 50, h = 50;
    Ellipse2D ellipse = new Ellipse2D.Double(x, y, w, h);
    Ellipse2D ellipse2 = new Ellipse2D.Double(x+w, y, w, h );
    GradientPaint gp = new GradientPaint(50, 75, Color.yellow, 95, 95, Color.blue, true);
    g2.setPaint(gp);   // fill with gradient
    g2.fill(ellipse);
    g2.fill(ellipse2);
    g2.fill(new Ellipse2D.Double( x+w+w, y, w, h ) );
  }
}
```

We can also change the stroke of the shape. We can either add a thickness to it, or use a gradient or textual pattern to fill the shape. The example below creates two circles with varying thickness, both using the gradient fill pattern on the outline stroke.

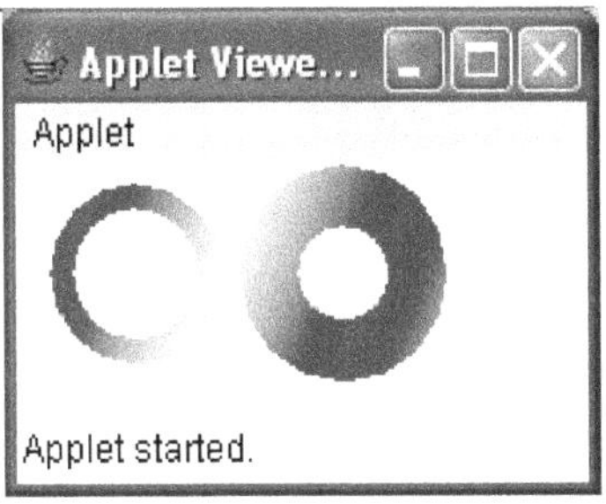

```java
import java.awt.*;
import java.awt.geom.*;
import javax.swing.*;
public class Graphics2DStroke extends JApplet
{
  public void paint(Graphics g)
  {
    Graphics2D g2 = ( Graphics2D ) g;
    int x = 15, y = 10, w = 50, h = 50;
    Ellipse2D ellipse = new Ellipse2D.Double(x, y, w, h);
    Ellipse2D ellipse2 = new Ellipse2D.Double(x+w+20, y, w, h );
    GradientPaint gp = new GradientPaint(50, 75, Color.yellow, 95, 95, Color.blue, true);
    g2.setPaint ( gp );   // fill with gradient
    g2.setStroke ( new BasicStroke( 8 ) );    // outline is 8 pixels
    g2.draw (ellipse);
    // Stroke with a gradient.
    g2.setStroke ( new BasicStroke( 20 ) );   // outline is 20 pixels
    g2.draw ( ellipse2 );
  }
}
```

Jar Files

A useful tool when creating applets with lots of files is to archive them together into a single file. Although we could do this with the zip and tar utilities, we should use the **jar** program provided with our java development kit because we can have our applets reference the jar file and makes it faster for a user to download and run our applet. Our jar files must end with the extension **.jar** and can contain all our .class files, image and audio files to make our applet work.

To create our jar file, go to a terminal window and change directory until you are in the same directory where all your files are located. Type the following to create a jar file:

```
jar cvf   tarFileName.jar *
```

This will create a jar file with all the files in that directory (the '*' is a wildcard for all files). We could also list out each file individually instead of using the *, as in the following example:

```
jar cvf   tarFileName.jar Project.class Logo.class logo.gif sd.au
```

To reference our jar file in our HTML file, we need to add the code: ARCHIVE="jarFileName.jar" as shown in the full HTML file example below:

```
<HTML>
  <BODY>
      <APPLET CODE=XYZ.class ARCHIVE="files.jar"
              WIDTH=500 HEIGHT=500>
          </APPLET>
  </BODY></HTML>
```

Now when you upload your applet for the Internet, you need only to upload two files: your jar file and the html file.

Summary

- Java was originally intended for small appliances, but became popular when they were enabled to be embedded in web pages.
- Java is an object-oriented language. Besides the 8 primitive data types, everything else is stored in an object. This leads to better code reuse and code modularity.
- Some of the complex features in other programming languages were omitted from the Java language to keep it a more simple language to learn.
- Java is platform-independent which means the compiled code (bytecode) can be executed on any type of system. The disadvantage to this is that each machines needs to first interpret to machine code before executing, causing Java programs to run slower than other languages like C/C++.
- Multi-tasking enables a single CPU to handle multiple tasks by swapping between them until each finishes.
- Through threads Java supports multi-tasking to enable many tasks to execute 'simultaneously'.
- Applets have restrictions placed on them to prevent malicious activity on a client computer running the applet.
- There are many free applets available on the Internet that can be downloaded and modified.
- There are additional third-party libraries that can be imported into programs to extend the functionality.
- We could write our own third-party libraries to share with others.

Java Exercises

1. Why can't applets on the Internet write to files?
2. Name the URL of a website where you can buy a domain name
3. What does it mean for a computer language to be object-oriented?
4. Why is Java considered to be easier to program in than other languages such as C++?
5. Why is security an issue for applets on the Internet? How is Java secure?
6. Why is Java slower than other languages?
7. If your computer has only one processor (CPU), how could more than one task be executing at the same time?
8. How does Java enable multi-tasking?
9. What are 3rd party libraries? What are they used for?
10. Go to the website http://java.internet.com and find an applet with source code available. Download the source code and any additional required files and modify it before putting it on your own web page.

Appendix A

Debugging

*The code that is the most difficult to debug
is the code that you know cannot possibly be wrong.*

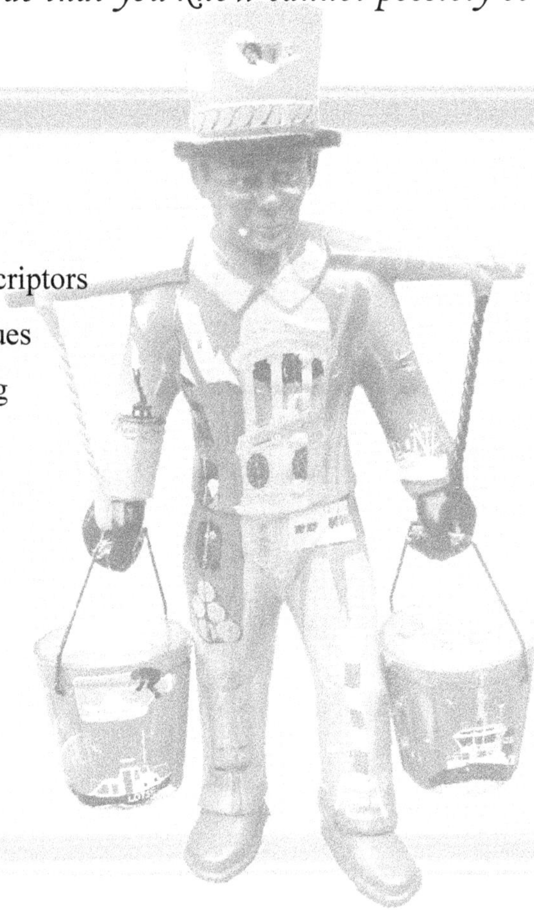

Objectives:

- Errors
- Printing Descriptors
- Printing Values
- Color Coding Components
- Debuggers

Errors

Sometimes when we are working on a project, it's hard to figure out what is wrong with it. Even using an IDE like Eclipse, sometimes it doesn't specify an error or the message it gives us does not help us figure it out. We have lots of methods too, in our bigger programs, and it can be confusing to figure out where the problem is.

When we're trying to fix errors in our program, we are *debugging* our code. There are three types of errors we can have in our code: syntax or compile-time errors, run-time errors and logical errors. Syntax errors are when we violated the Java grammar for programs. This includes when we forget a semi-colon at the end of a statement, leave out a squiggly brace, or try to put a method inside another method. If we're running an IDE like Eclipse, it will usually be able to detect and show us these errors before we attempt to run our program. If there are syntax errors, do not try to execute the program – it either won't work at all or will try to execute an *old* version and will deceive you as to what your code is doing! Always make sure all syntax errors are fixed before proceeding with development.

The second type of error is a *run-time* error. This occurs when the program compiles fine but then crashes when we try to run it. The program may run partly before crashing, and may even run for an hour before it crashes. These are usually more dynamic errors such as a division by zero or an error that is not caught via an exception handler. Check the console window for the location of where the error most probably occurred. There may be many errors listed, so be sure to find the first listing your program name.

The third error type is called a *logical* error. This is when the program compiles and runs fine, but there is an error in the output. Sometimes this is as simple as a misspelled word, but sometimes it's more complicated like a calculation that always results to zero. This is where the debugging techniques below may be very helpful.

There are a couple of methods we can try to debug our code, depending on what is wrong with it. If our code is getting stuck somewhere (e.g. an infinite loop), a helpful method is to print out values to the console window throughout the program. Then we can see where it stops printing and what the last thing was that printed and narrow down how much code we need to look at for the error. If the problem is that the output is incorrect from some calculation we did, we can try printing out all our variables used in the calculation to start narrowing down why the calculation didn't work. This could help us determine whether the variable was not correctly assigned a value from reading a JTextField or whether integer division occurred or a divide by zero. If our problem is that a certain component or JPanel doesn't seem to be appearing on the applet, we could temporarily set the background color of our component and see if it displays and where. A more advanced debugging technique is to make use of a debugger. If we're using an IDE such as Eclipse, there is a debugger built in to the IDE.

Printing Designators

One way to help figure out what's going on in our program, is to use `System.out.println` statements to print out a designator of where we are in our code. For example, we may put a bunch of print statements printing out the alphabet (in expected order) or the name of the method we're currently in or an identifying phrase of what the next statement is about to do. In the following example, we print out the alphabet:

```java
/* Example showing how to loop through a list of items stored in a List object
 * @author : E.S.Boese */
import java.awt.*;
import javax.swing.*;
public class Debugging extends JApplet
{
   JList list;
   DefaultListModel model;
   JTextArea textarea;
   public void init( )
   {
            System.out.println( "A" );
            setLayout( new FlowLayout( ) );
            System.out.println( "B" );
            setupList( );
            System.out.println( "C" );

            textarea = new JTextArea( 5,10 );
            add(textarea);
            System.out.println( "D" );

            addListItemsToTextarea( );
            System.out.println( "E" );
   }
   public void setupList( )
   {
            System.out.println( "F" );
            model = new DefaultListModel( );
            list = new JList(model);
            model.addElement( "Milk" );
            model.addElement( "Cookies" );
            model.addElement( "Eggs" );
            add(list);
            System.out.println( "G" );
   }
   public void addListItemsToTextarea( )
   {
            System.out.println( "H" );
            for( int i=0; i<model.getSize( ); i++ );      // getSize returns the number of items in the list
            {
               System.out.println( "I" );
               textarea.append( (String )model.get(i) );    // grab the item at index i
               textarea.append( "\n" );
            }
            System.out.println( "K" );
   }
}
```

Now when we run our program, we see that it doesn't fully work. The list items are not being added to the textarea. The `System.out.println` statements actually print output to the `Console` window, which is below the code in Eclipse.

The output from our example is as follows:

A
B
F
G
C
D
E

Notice that the print statements H, I and K are never called. This can help determine that the method addListItemsToTextarea is never called. We just need to add a call to this method to fix the problem.

Another example of this use is below which leads to an infinite loop:

```
import java.awt.*;
import javax.swing.*;
public class Infinite extends JApplet
{
  JTextArea textarea;
  public void init( )
  {
      System.out.println( "A" );
      textarea = new JTextArea( 3,10 );
      System.out.println( "B" );
      int i=10;
      System.out.println( "C" );
      while( i<100 )
            textarea.append( i + "\n" );
            System.out.println( "D" );
            i=i+1;
      System.out.println( "E" );
      add( textarea );
      System.out.println( "F" );
  }
}
```

Which prints out:

    A
    B
    C

This can help you realize that the code is in an infinite loop, and that the problem is somewhere after the printing of C and before D or E print statements.

Printing Values

Another use of print statements for debugging is to print out the values of our variables to see if they are what we think they are before we do our calculations.

```java
import java.awt.*;
import java.awt.event.*;
import javax.swing.*;
public class DebugValue extends JApplet
                 implements ItemListener
{
   double cat = 4;
   double dog = 10;
   double horse = 350;
   double costOfItem = 0;
   double quantity;
   JComboBox list;
   JTextField qty;
   JLabel price;
   public void init( )
   {
      setLayout( new FlowLayout( ) );
      qty = new JTextField( 4 );
      list = new JComboBox( );
      price = new JLabel( "0.0" );
      list.addItem( "cat" );
      list.addItem( "dog" );
      list.addItem( "horse" );
      list.addItemListener( this );
      add( qty );
      add( list );
      add( price );
   }
   public void itemStateChanged( ItemEvent ie )
   {
      Object src = ie.getSource( );
      if( ie.getStateChange( )==ItemEvent.SELECTED)
      {
         if( src == list )
         {
            quantity = Integer.parseInt( qty.getText( ) );
            System.out.println( "qty=" + quantity );
            System.out.println( "cost="+costOfItem);
            double totalCost = costOfItem * quantity;
            System.out.println( "total=" + totalCost );
            price.setText( "" + totalCost );
         }
      }
   }
}
```

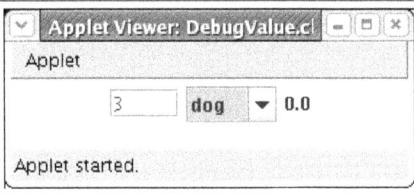

Output to Console window:

```
qty=3.0
cost=0.0
total=0.0
```

Here we can see the variable **costOfItem** is not the correct value. So the total Cost is calculating to zero because costOfItem is zero. Now we can go back and add the necessary code to fix the problem, now that we know what the problem is.

Exercise: Can you fix the code?

Color-Coding Components

Another methodology for debugging our graphical interface is to color-code our panels. When we're having problems with our components not appearing or not appearing correctly, it is sometimes helpful to change the background colors of our components to try to determine where the problem may be. If we make each JPanel a different color, we can see where each panel is being displayed. This can also help immensely when we write a separate class that extends the JPanel class, in case we forgot to set the size of this new component.

For example, in Chapter 7 we covered design. The example of the Library applet had vibrant colors in each section of the applet which helps make it clear where each component is. Although this is probably not how we want our final version of the library to look (prefer to have most if not all regions the same background color), it is a very helpful technique for debugging code when components seem to be in the wrong place or the wrong size.

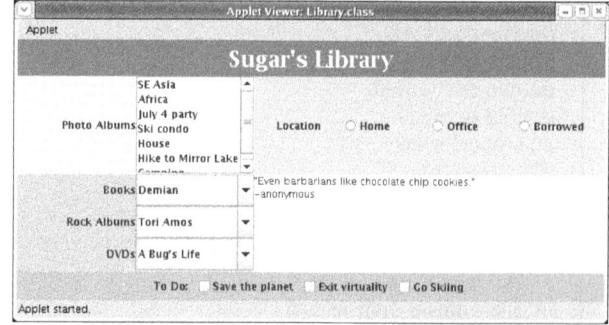

Debuggers

An advanced option for debugging is to use a debugger. These are usually integrated into IDEs, so if you are using an IDE such as Eclipse you can make use of it. Debuggers help you set breakpoints in the code, display values of variables in the code, step through the code line by line or from breakpoint to breakpoint and lots of other features to help us debug our code.

Summary

- Debugging is the process of fixing errors in the code.
- There are three types of errors: syntax or compile-time errors, run-time errors and logical errors.
- Syntax errors are violations of Java grammar rules.
- Run-time errors are errors that cause the program to crash during execution.
- Logical errors occur when the program compiles and runs fine but there are errors in the output produced.
- Use of the System.out.println statement to print locations in the code is one way to figure out where the problems are occurring in the code. System.out.println prints output to the console window.
- Printing out the value of variables helps debug problems where calculations are not correct.
- If components are not showing up or appearing correctly, temporarily change the background color of components to check the size and location of the components and panels.
- For more advanced debugging, make use of a debugger.

Exercises

1. Put an infinite loop into a large program and use the debugging techniques to see how they can help you find the problem.

2. Which debugging technique is best for figuring out why a calculation keeps evaluating to zero?

3. Which debugging technique is best for figuring out why a particular component isn't showing up on the applet?

4. What is a debugger? How do you use one?

5. Write an entire class named **Debug** that keeps track of an `int` value for the level of debugging desired. Create constants for 3 different levels: CLASS, METHOD or VARIABLE where CLASS is the highest level and VARIABLE is the lowest. Create a constructor that initalizes the level of debugging, and a mutator method to change the level. Then create a method called **print** that takes an `int` for the level of the request and a String to be printed. In this method, if the level is equal to or higher than the debugging level (instance variable), then print the String parameter. If not, the method should not do anything. Then integrate this into a program you've written, where you instantiate this class at the beginning of your program and each method calls your print method with the name of the method as a parameter, and each method that changes the value of a variable calls the print method with the value of the variable as the parameter.

Appendix B

Java API

Methods provided are a subset of the standard Java API.

ActionEvent
Constructors
- generated from button clicks

Useful methods:
- Object getSource( )
  - returns a reference to the object that generated the event

ArrayList
Constructors
- ArrayList list = new ArrayList( )

Useful methods:
- Object get(index)
  - returns the element at the specified index – cast to appropriate type
- int size( )
  - returns the number of elements in the list

AudioClip
Constructors
- None – call method getAudioClip on applet

Useful Methods
- void loop( )
  - plays the audio clip continually
- void play( )
  - plays the audio clip once through
- void stop( )
  - stops playing the audio clip

BasicStroke
Constructors
- BasicStroke stroke = new BasicStroke (w)
  - creates a new Stroke object with a stroke width of (w)

Useful methods:
- Stroke createStrokedShape (Shape)
  - takes a Shape as a parameter to define the style for drawing the stroke and returns the Stroke object

BorderFactory
Constructors
- None –

Useful Methods
- Border createEtchedBorder(style)
  - creates an etched border where style is either EtchedBorder.RAISED or EtchedBorder.LOWERED
- Border createLoweredBevelBorder( )
  - creates a lowered bevel border
- Border createMatteBorder(topMargin, leftMargin, bottom Margin, rtMargin, ImageIcon)
  - creates an image border with specified margins
- Border createRaisedBevelBorder( )
  - creates a raised border
- Border createTitledBorder(String)

- creates an etched border where String is the text in the title
- Border createTitledBorder(Border, String)
  - creates a titled border with String as text and Border as the base border
- Border createTitledBorder(Border, String, titleJustification, titlePosition)
  - creates a titled border with String as text and Border as the base border and title justification and position
- Border createTitledBorder(Border, String, titleJustification, titlePosition, Font, Color)
  - creates a titled border with String as text and Border as the base border and title justification and position and title font and color

BorderLayout
Constructors

- BorderLayout layout = new BorderLayout ( );
  - creates a new layout manager instance

Useful Methods

- void add(component, location)
  where location is BorderLayout.NORTH, BorderLayout.SOUTH, Borderlayout.WEST, BorderLayout.EAST or BorderLayout.CENTER
  - adds the component to the next empty cell in the grid

BoxLayout
Constructors

- BoxLayout layout = new BoxLayout (target, axis);
  - creates a new layout manager instance where target is the container that the box layout is to be applied and axis is either BoxLayout.X_AXIS or BoxLayout.Y_AXIS

Border
see BorderFactory

BorderFactory
Constructors

- none

Useful methods:

- Border createBevelBorder (type)
  - creates a Border object with a bevel where the type can be either BevelBorder.LOWERED or BevelBorder.RAISED
- Border createBevelBorder (type, highlightColor, shadowColor)
  - creates a Border object with a bevel where the type can be either BevelBorder.LOWERED or BevelBorder.RAISED and the highlightColor is the color for the outer edge and the shadowColor for the inner edge
- Border createEtchedBorder (type)
  - creates a Border object with an etched look where the type can be either EtchedBorder.RAISED or EtchedBorder.LOWERED
- Border createLineBorder (Color)
  - creates a Border object with the specified color
- Border createLineBorder (Color, thickness)
  - creates a Border object with the specified color and thickness
- Border createTitledBorder (Border, String)
  - creates a border using the style defined in the parameter Border with text specified in the String parameter
- Border createTitledBorder (Border, String, titleJustification, titlePosition)
  - creates a border using the style defined in the parameter Border with text specified in the String parameter where *titleJustification* specifies how the title is displayed and can be one of the following: TitledBorder.LEFT, TitledBorder.CENTER or TitledBorder.RIGHT and *titlePosition* specifies where the title is located with respect

> > > to the component where the values are one of the following:
> > > TitledBorder.ABOVE_TOP, TitledBorder.TOP, TitledBorder.BELOW_TOP, TitledBorder.ABOVE_BOTTOM, TitledBorder.BOTTOM, TitledBorder.BELOW_BOTTOM
> > - Border createTitledBorder (Border, String, titleJustification, titlePosition, Font, Color)
> >   - same as the previous with addition of specifying the Font and Color of the text
> > - Border createEmptyBorder (top, left, bottom, right)
> >   - creates an empty border to take up space based on the number of pixels specified for each region
> > - MatteBorder createMatteBorder (top, left, bottom, right, ImageIcon)
> >   - creates a matte-border based on an image in an ImageIcon that is repeated around the component. Specify how many pixels to display for each region: top, left, bottom, right

BufferedImage
Constructors

> - BufferedImage bi = new BufferedImage (w, h, imageType)
>   - creates a new BufferedImage with a width of (w) and height of (h) and the imageType is one of the following: TYPE_INT_RGB

Useful methods:

> - Graphics2D createGraphics ( )
>   - returns a Graphics2D object to use to draw on the BufferedImage
> - flush ( )
>   - stop optimizing and flush output to the screen

ButtonGroup
Constructors

> - ButtonGroup bg = new ButtonGroup( )

Useful methods:

> - void add (Button)
>   - adds a button to the group such that only one in the group may be selected at a time

Calendar
Constructors

> - none

Useful methods:

> - Calendar getInstance( )
>   - returns an instance of Calendar based on current date/time
> - int get(int)
>   - returns the specified part of date/time where the parameter is one of Calendar.HOUR, Calendar.MINUTE, Calendar.SECOND, Calendar.HOUR_OF_DAY, Calendar.TIME, Calendar.DATE, Calendar.MONTH, Calendar.YEAR, etc.

Color
Constructors

> - Color c = new Color (red, green, blue);
>   - creates a Color object with specified red, green and blue

DefaultListModel
Constructors

> - DefaultListModel model = new DefaultListModel ( );
>   - creates a new model for a JList

Useful Methods

- void addElement(Object)
    - adds the Object (String, ImageIcon, etc.) to end of list
- void add(int, Object)
    - adds the Object (String, ImageIcon, etc.) to position of int in the list
- void clear( )
    - removes all items from the list
- boolean contains(Object)
    - returns true or false whether or not the Object is already in the list
- Object get(index)
    - returns the item at the specified index (parameter), returns the item as an Object (cast to specific type)
- int getSize( )
    - returns the number of elements in the list
- void remove(index)
    - removes the element at the specified index

Double
Constructors

- Double d = new Double(number)
    - creates an instance of Double object with specified number

Useful methods:

- double Double.parseDouble(String)
    - returns a double type of the number stored in the String

FlowLayout
Constructors

- FlowLayout layout = new FlowLayout ( );
    - creates a new layout manager instance with center alignment
- FlowLayout layout = new FlowLayout (alignment);
    - creates a new layout manager instance where alignment is FlowLayout.LEFT or FlowLayout.RIGHT or FlowLayout.CENTER

Font
Constructors

- Font f = new Font(type, style, size) ;
    - creates a new Font where type is "Serif", "Sanserif" or "Monospaced", style is Font.PLAIN, Font.BOLD, Font.ITALIC or Font.BOLD+Font.ITALIC and size is in points (e.g. 12 for 12 pt font)

Graphics
Constructors

- none

Useful Methods

- void clearRect (x, y, w, h)
    - clears the rectangle at coordinates (x,y) with the width (w) and height(h) by filling it with the background color
- void draw3Drect (x, y, w, h, boolean)
    - draws a 3-D rectangle outline that appears *raised* if boolean is true or *sunken* if false
- void drawArc (x, y, w, h, startAngle, arcAngle)
    - draws the outter arc based on where it lies if an ellipse were drawn from the coordinates (x,y) with a width of (w) and height of (h) and the angle based on 0 degrees drawn out from the center of the ellipse directly to the right, and the arcAngle is drawn by going counter-clockwise.
- void drawImage (Image, x, y, this)

- draws the image with the top-left corner at the coordinates (x,y). The *this* keyword specifies that the current class is handling the drawing of the image and will always be *this* for what is covered in this book.
    - void drawImage (Image, xd1, yd1, xd2, yd2, xs1, ys1, xs2, ys2, this)
        - draws the image with the top-left corner at the coordinates (xd1, yd1) scaled to fit within coordinates (xd2, yd2) [bottom-right corner] where the coordinates (xs1, ys1) represent the top-left corner of the *source* image [where to start to draw on the original image, allows for cropping] and the coordinates (ys1, ys2) represent the bottom-right corner of the *source* image.
    - void drawLine (x1, y1, x2, y2)
        - draws a line from the coordinates (x1, y1) to coordinates (x2, y2)
    - void drawOval (x, y, w, h)
        - draws an oval/ellipse whose top-left corner is at coordinates (x,y) with a width of (w) and height of (h) such that the bottom-right corner is at coordinates (x+w, y+h)
    - void drawPolygon (Polygon)
        - draws the figure defined by the sequence of points in the Polygon object. The order of the points added to the Polygon defines the shape, as it connects-the-points in sequential order.
    - void drawRect (x, y, w, h)
        - draws the outline of a rectangle with the top-left corner at coordinates (x, y) with a width of (w) and a height of (h)
    - void drawRoundRect (x, y, w, h, arcWidth, arcHeight)
        - draws the outline of a rectangle with the top-left corner at coordinates (x, y) with a width of (w) and a height of (h) where the corners are rounded based on the number of pixels specified for the arcWidth and arcHeight.
    - void drawString (String, x, y)
        - draws the text specified in the String starting at the coordinates (x, y) where the coordinates define the bottom-left of the text.
    - void fill3DRect (x, y, w, h, boolean)
        - paints a 3-D rectangle that appears *raised* if boolean is true or *sunken* if false
    - void fillArc (x, y, w, h, startAngle, arcAngle)
        - fills the arc based on where it lies if an ellipse were drawn from the coordinates (x,y) with a width of (w) and height of (h) and the angle based on 0 degrees drawn out from the center of the ellipse directly to the right, and the arcAngle is drawn by going counter-clockwise.
    - void fillOval (x, y, w, h)
        - fills an oval/ellipse whose top-left corner is at coordinates (x,y) with a width of (w) and height of (h) such that the bottom-right corner is at coordinates (x+w, y+h)
    - void fillPolygon (Polygon)
        - fills the figure defined by the sequence of points in the Polygon object. The order of the points added to the Polygon defines the shape, as it connects-the-points in sequential order.
    - void fillRect (x, y, w, h)
        - fills the outline of a rectangle with the top-left corner at coordinates (x, y) with a width of (w) and a height of (h)
    - void fillRoundRect (x, y, w, h, arcWidth, arcHeight)
        - fills the outline of a rectangle with the top-left corner at coordinates (x, y) with a width of (w) and a height of (h) where the corners are rounded based on the number of pixels specified for the arcWidth and arcHeight.
    - void setColor (Color)
        - sets the current painting color to the specified color
    - void setFont (Font)
        - sets the current painting font to the specified font

Graphics2D
Constructors

- none

Useful Methods

- void clearRect (x, y, w, h)

- clears the rectangle at coordinates (x,y) with the width (w) and height(h) by filling it with the background color
- void draw (Shape)
    - draws the outline of a Shape where Shape can be one of the following Shape objects: Arc2D, Area, CubicCurve2D, Ellipse2D, GeneralPath, Line2D, Polygon, QuadCurve2D, Rectangle, Rectangle2D, RectangularShape, RoundRectangle2D
- void draw3Drect (x, y, w, h, boolean)
    - draws a 3-D rectangle outline that appears *raised* if boolean is true or *sunken* if false
- void drawArc (x, y, w, h, startAngle, arcAngle)
    - draws the outter arc based on where it lies if an ellipse were drawn from the coordinates (x,y) with a width of (w) and height of (h) and the angle based on 0 degrees drawn out from the center of the ellipse directly to the right, and the arcAngle is drawn by going counter-clockwise.
- void drawImage (Image, x, y, this)
    - draws the image with the top-left corner at the coordinates (x,y). The *this* keyword specifies that the current class is handling the drawing of the image and will always be *this* for what is covered in this book.
- void drawImage (Image, xd1, yd1, xd2, yd2, xs1, ys1, xs2, ys2, this)
    - draws the image with the top-left corner at the coordinates (xd1, yd1) scaled to fit within coordinates (xd2, yd2) [bottom-right corner] where the coordinates (xs1, ys1) represent the top-left corner of the *source* image [where to start to draw on the original image, allows for cropping] and the coordinates (ys1, ys2) represent the bottom-right corner of the *source* image.
- void drawLine (x1, y1, x2, y2)
    - draws a line from the coordinates (x1, y1) to coordinates (x2, y2)
- void drawOval (x, y, w, h)
    - draws an oval/ellipse whose top-left corner is at coordinates (x,y) with a width of (w) and height of (h) such that the bottom-right corner is at coordinates (x+w, y+h)
- void drawPolygon (Polygon)
    - draws the figure defined by the sequence of points in the Polygon object. The order of the points added to the Polygon defines the shape, as it connects-the-points in sequential order.
- void drawRect (x, y, w, h)
    - draws the outline of a rectangle with the top-left corner at coordinates (x, y) with a width of (w) and a height of (h)
- void drawRoundRect (x, y, w, h, arcWidth, arcHeight)
    - draws the outline of a rectangle with the top-left corner at coordinates (x, y) with a width of (w) and a height of (h) where the corners are rounded based on the number of pixels specified for the arcWidth and arcHeight.
- void drawString (String, x, y)
    - draws the text specified in the String starting at the coordinates (x, y) where the coordinates define the bottom-left of the text.
- void fill (Shape)
    - paints the Shape where Shape can be one of the following Shape objects: Arc2D, Area, CubicCurve2D, Ellipse2D, GeneralPath, Line2D, Polygon, QuadCurve2D, Rectangle, Rectangle2D, RectangularShape, RoundRectangle2D
- void fill3DRect (x, y, w, h, boolean)
    - paints a 3-D rectangle that appears *raised* if boolean is true or *sunken* if false
- void fillArc (x, y, w, h, startAngle, arcAngle)
    - fills the arc based on where it lies if an ellipse were drawn from the coordinates (x,y) with a width of (w) and height of (h) and the angle based on 0 degrees drawn out from the center of the ellipse directly to the right, and the arcAngle is drawn by going counter-clockwise.
- void fillOval (x, y, w, h)
    - fills an oval/ellipse whose top-left corner is at coordinates (x,y) with a width of (w) and height of (h) such that the bottom-right corner is at coordinates (x+w, y+h)
- void fillPolygon (Polygon)
    - fills the figure defined by the sequence of points in the Polygon object. The order of the points added to the Polygon defines the shape, as it connects-the-points in sequential order.
- void fillRect (x, y, w, h)

- fills the outline of a rectangle with the top-left corner at coordinates (x, y) with a width of (w) and a height of (h)
- void fillRoundRect (x, y, w, h, arcWidth, arcHeight)
  - fills the outline of a rectangle with the top-left corner at coordinates (x, y) with a width of (w) and a height of (h) where the corners are rounded based on the number of pixels specified for the arcWidth and arcHeight.
- void setBackground (Color)
  - sets the background color
- void setColor (Color)
  - sets the current painting color to the specified color
- void setFont (Font)
  - sets the current painting font to the specified font
- void setPaint (Paint)
  - sets the paint attribute for drawing and filling
- void setRenderHint (RenderingHints.KEY, hintValue)
  - sets the value of a single preference for rendering
- void setStroke (Stroke)
  - sets the stroke for painting

GridLayout
Constructors

- GridLayout layout = new GridLayout (rows, cols);
  - creates a new layout manager instance with specified number of rows and columns

HyperlinkEvent
Constructors

- none

Useful Methods

- getEventType( )
  - returns the type of the event which is one of: HyperlinkEvent.ACTIVATED, HyperlinkEvent.ENTERED or HyperlinkEvent.EXITED
- URL getURL( )
  - returns the URL of the hyperlink

ImageIcon
Constructors

- ImageIcon icon = new ImageIcon(Image)
  - creates a new ImageIcon object with the specified image

Useful Methods

- Image getImage( )
  - returns the image of the icon
- void setImage(Image)
  - changes the image of the icon

Integer
Constructors

- Integer i = new Integer(number)
  - creates an instance of Integer object with specified number

Useful methods:

- Integer.parseInt(String)
  - returns an int type of the number stored in the String

ItemEvent

Constructors
- generated from selecting/deselecting radio buttons/checkboxes/lists

Useful methods:
- Object getSource( )
  - returns a reference to the object that generated the event
- int getStateChange( )
  - returns the type of selection/deselection (e.g. ItemEvent.SELECTED or ItemEvent.DESELECTED)

JApplet
Constructors
- none

Useful Methods
- AudioClip getAudioClip(getCodeBase( ), filename)
  - gets an audioclip from the file system
- Image getImage(getCodeBase( ), filename)
  - gets an image from the file system

JButton
Constructors
- JButton b = new JButton ( )
  - creates a new button with no text nor image
- JButton b = new JButton (ImageIcon);
  - creates a new button with an image
- JButton b = new JButton ("happy");
  - creates a new button with the text "happy"
- JButton b = new JButton ("happy", ImageIcon);
  - creates a new button with the text "happy" and an image

Useful Methods
- void setBackground(Color)
  - sets the background color
- void setBorderPainted(boolean)
  - if boolean is true, the line border around the button is painted
  - if boolean is false, the border is not painted
- void setContentAreaFilled(boolean)
  - if boolean is true, the background of the button is painted
  - if boolean is false, the background is not painted
- void setDisabledIcon(ImageIcon)
  - sets the image to display when the button is disabled
- void setEnabled(boolean)
  - enables (boolean is true) or disables (boolean is false) the button
- void setFocusable(boolean)
  - draws box around component if it has focus (boolean is true) or not if boolean is false
- void setForeground(Color)
  - changes the text color of all text on the button
  - *(use HTML to change only parts of the text)*
- void setHorizontalTextPosition(JButton.POSITION)
  - where should the text be placed with respect to the image
  - POSITION is one of: LEFT, CENTER or RIGHT
- void setOpaque(boolean)
  - sets background as transparent (boolean is false) or solid (boolean is true)
- void setMargin(new Insets(0, 0, 0, 0))
  - sets the buffer between the image/text and the border of the button
  - Inset parameters are ordered as: top, left, bottom, right

- void setPressedIcon(ImageIcon)
  - sets which image to display when mouse presses on the button
- void setRolloverIcon(ImageIcon)
  - sets which image to display when mouse rolls over the button
- void setSelectedIcon(ImageIcon)
  - sets which image to display when button is selected
- void setVerticalTextPosition(JButton.POSITION)
  - where should the text be placed with respect to the image
  - POSITION is one of: TOP, CENTER or BOTTOM

JCheckBox
Constructors

- JCheckBox cb = new JCheckBox( );
  - creates a new checkbox with no text nor image
- JCheckBox cb = new JCheckBox(ImageIcon);
  - creates a new checkbox with an image
- JCheckBox cb = new JCheckBox(ImageIcon, true);
  - creates a new checkbox with an image and initially selected
- JCheckBox cb = new JCheckBox("happy");
  - creates a new checkbox with the text "happy"
- JCheckBox cb = new JCheckBox("happy", true);
  - creates a new checkbox with the text "happy" and initially selected
- JCheckBox cb = new JCheckBox("happy", ImageIcon);
  - creates a new checkbox with the text "happy" and an image

Useful Methods

- String getText( )
  - returns the checkbox's text
  - String theText = cbox.getText( );
- boolean isSelected( )
  - returns whether or not the checkbox is selected
- void setBackground(Color)
  - sets the background color
- void setEnabled(boolean)
  - enables (boolean is true) or disables (boolean is false) the checkbox
- void setFocusable(boolean)
  - draws box around component if it has focus (boolean is true) or not if boolean is false
- void setOpaque(boolean)
  - sets background as transparent (boolean is false) or solid (boolean is true)

JComboBox
Constructors

- JComboBox droplist = new JComboBox( );
  - creates an empty combo box
- JComboBox droplist = new JComboBox(array);
  - creates a list based on the array

Useful Methods
- int getItemCount( )
  - returns the number of items in the list
  - int numItemsInList = combolist.getItemCount( );
- int getSelectedIndex( )
  - returns the index of the selected item
  - int selectedIndex = combolist.getSelectedIndex( );

- Object getSelectedItem( )
    - returns the selected item as an Object
    - String selectedText = (String)combolist.getSelectedItem( );
- void removeItem(Object obj)
    - removes the object from the list
    - combolist.remove("sad");
- void removeItemAt(int index)
    - removes the object at the specified index
    - combolist.remove(2);
- void setBackground(Color)
    - sets the background color
- void setEditable(boolean flag)
    - determines whether the combo box is editable
    - combolist.setEditable(true);
- void setEnabled(boolean)
    - enables (boolean is true) or disables (boolean is false) the combo box
- void setOpaque(boolean)
    - sets background as transparent (boolean is false) or solid (boolean is true)

JEditorPane
<u>Constructors</u>

- JEditorPane pane = new JEditorPane( );
    - creates a new editor pane

<u>Useful Methods</u>

- void setPage(URL)
    - displays the web page at the URL specified
- void setText(String)
    - puts the String into the editor pane (can use HTML formatting)

JFrame
<u>Constructors</u>

- JFrame f = new JFrame( );
    - creates a new frame window
- JFrame f = new JFrame(String);
    - creates a new frame window with String as the title of the window

<u>Useful Methods</u>

- void add(Object)
    - adds the Object to the frame based on the layout manager specified
- void setSize(int w, int h)
    - sets the width (w) and height (h) of the frame
- void setLayout(LayoutManager)
    - sets the layout manager for the frame
- void setLocation(int x, int y)
    - sets the upper-left corner of the screen of where to display the frame
- void setVisible(boolean)
    - shows the frame (boolean is true) or hides the frame (boolean is false)

JList
<u>Constructors</u>

- DefaultListModel model = new DefaultListModel( );
  JList list = new JList(model);
    - creates a list based on a default model, such that we can add items to the model
- JList list = new JList(array);
    - creates a list based on the array

- we haven't done arrays yet…. stay tuned

Useful Methods
- int getSelectedIndex( )
    - returns the index of the item that is selected
- Object getSelectedValue( )
    - returns the object that is selected
- void setBackground(Color)
    - sets the background color
- void setEnabled(boolean)
    - enables (boolean is true) or disables (boolean is false) the list
- void setOpaque(boolean)
    - sets background as transparent (boolean is false) or solid (boolean is true)
- void setVisibleRowCount(number)
    - sets the preferred number of visible rows
- void setSelectionMode(int mode)
    - where mode can be:
      ListSelectionModel.SINGLE_SELECTION
      ListSelectionModel.MULTIPLE_INTERVAL_SELECTION (default)

JPanel
Constructors
- JPanel pane = new JPanel( )
    - creates a new panel with the default layout manager
- JPanel pane = new JPanel(layoutManager)
    - creates a new panel with the specified layout manager

Useful Methods
- void add(component)
    - adds the component to the panel using the layout manager
- void setBackground (Color)
    - changes the background color of the panel
- void setOpaque(boolean)
    - sets whether or not the panel is transparent (boolean is false) or solid (boolean is true – default)

JRadioButton
Constructors
- JRadioButton rb = new JRadioButton(ImageIcon);
    - creates a radio button with an image
- JRadioButton rb = new JRadioButton("red");
    - creates a radio button with the text "red"
- JRadioButton rb = new JRadioButton("blue", true);
    - creates a radio button with the text "blue" and initially selected
- ButtonGroup group = new ButtonGroup( );

Useful Methods
- String getText( )
    - returns the text for the radio button
      String text = radioBut.getText( );
- boolean isSelected( )
    - returns whether or not the button is selected
- void setBackground(Color)
    - sets the background color
- void setEnabled(boolean)
    - enables (boolean is true) or disables (boolean is false) the radio button
- void setFocusable(boolean)

- draws box around component if it has focus (boolean is true) or not if boolean is false
- void setOpaque(boolean)
  - sets background as transparent (boolean is false) or solid (boolean is true)

JScrollPane
Constructors
- JScrollPane p = new JScrollPane(Object);
  - creates a JPanel with scrollbars with Object inside it.

JTabbedPane
Constructors
- JTabbedPane pane = new JTabbedPane ( );
  - creates a text area with a default number of columns
- JTabbedPane pane = new JTabbedPane (location);
  - creates a tabbed pane with tabs at location where location is JTabbedPane.TOP (default), JTabbedPane.LEFT, JTabbedPane.BOTTOM or JTabbedPane.RIGHT

Useful methods:
- void addTab(text, component)
  - adds the component to the tab with text on the tab
- void addTab(text, ImageIcon, component)
  - adds the component to the tab with text and image on the tab
- void addTab(text, ImageIcon, component, tooltip)
  - adds the component to the tab with text and image on the tab and tool tip text when mouse hovers on tab

JTable
Constructors
- JTable table = new JTable(data, colHeadings);
  - creates a new JTable component with the data as a 2-D array and colHeadings as a 1-D array

Useful methods:
- void setBackground(Color)
  - changes the background color of the table
- void setForeground(Color)
  - changes the text color in the table
- void setGridColor(Color)
  - changes the color of the grid lines
- void setPreferredScrollableViewportSize(Dimension)
  - sets the viewable width and height of the table (the rest must be scrolled within a JScrollPane)
- void setSelectionBackground(Color)
  - changes the background color of selected entry
- void setSelectionForeground(Color)
  - changes the foreground color of selected entry
- void setShowHorizontalLines(boolean)
  - show horizontal lines (true – default) or not (false)
- void setShowVerticalLines(boolean)
  - show vertical lines (true – default) or not (false)

JTextArea
Constructors
- JTextArea ta = new JTextArea ( );
  - creates a text area with a default number of columns
- JTextArea ta = new JTextArea (5, 60);

- creates a text area with 5 rows and 60 columns
– JTextArea ta = new JTextArea ("I love JaVa");
  - creates a text area with the text "I love JaVa" inside the text box
– JTextArea ta = new JTextArea ("Java rocks", 4, 10);
  - creates a text area with the text "Java rocks" inside the text box which has 4 rows visible (height) and 10 columns visible (width)

Useful methods:

– void append(String)
  - adds the String to the end of the text inside the text area box
– int getLineCount( )
  - returns the number of lines in the text area box
– String getText( )
  - returns the text that is inside the box
  String theText = ta.getText( );
– void setBackground(Color)
  - sets the background color
– void setEnabled(boolean)
  - enables (boolean is true) or disables (boolean is false) the button
– void setFont(Font f)
  - set the font for the text box
    Font fnt = new Font("Serif", Font.BOLD, 18);
    textField.setFont(fnt);
- void setLineWrap(boolean)
  * sets whether to wrap at edge of textarea box (boolean is true) or not (boolean is false)
– void setOpaque(boolean)
  - sets background as transparent (boolean is false) or solid (boolean is true)
– void setText (String t)
  - enters the text in the string t into the text box (use \n for new lines)
    ta.setText("I like to learn java\nFun");
– void setWrapStyleWord(boolean)
  - wraps at edge of textarea box based on word (boolean is true) or not (boolean is false)

JTextField
Constructors

– JTextField tf = new JTextField( );
  - creates a text field with a default (0) number of columns
– JTextField tf = new JTextField(2);
  - creates a text field with 2 columns (good for states: NC, IL)
– JTextField tf = new JTextField("I love JaVa");
  - creates a text field with the text "I love JaVa" inside the text box
  - size of box will fit exactly to the text
– JTextField tf = new JTextField("Java rocks", 10);
  - creates a text field with the text "Java rocks" inside the text box which has 10 columns visible (width)

NOTE: *A column width is the size of the capital letter 'M' in the current font.*

Useful Methods
– String getText( )
  - returns the text that is inside the box
  String theText = JTextField.getText( );
– void setBackground(Color)
  - sets the background color
– void setEnabled(boolean)
  - enables (boolean Is true) or disables (boolean is false) the button
– void setFont(Font f)
  - set the font for the text box
    Font fnt = new Font("Serif", Font.BOLD, 18);

JTextField.setFont(fnt);
- void setForeground(Color c)
  - sets the color of the text
- void setOpaque(boolean)
  - sets background as transparent (boolean is false) or solid (boolean is true)
- void setText (String t)
  - enters the text in the string t into the text box
  JTextField.setText("I like to learn java");

KeyEvent
Constructors
- generated from keyboard presses

Useful methods:
- int getKeyCode( )
  - returns the key pressed (e.g. arrow keys: KeyEvent.VK_UP, KeyEvent.VK_DOWN, KeyEvent.VK_LEFT, KeyEvent.VK_RIGHT)
- Object getSource( )
  - returns a reference to the object that generated the event

MouseEvent
Constructors
- generated from mouse enter/exit/press/release/click

Useful methods:
- Object getSource( )
  - returns a reference to the object that generated the event
- int getX( )
  - returns x coordinate of mouse
- int getY( )
  - returns y coordinate of mouse

MouseMotionEvent
Constructors
- generated from mouse move/drag

Useful methods:
- Object getSource( )
  - returns a reference to the object that generated the event
- int getX( )
  - returns x coordinate of mouse
- int getY( )
  - returns y coordinate of mouse

Polygon
Constructors
- Polygon p = new Polygon ( )
  - creates a new Polygon object

Useful methods:
- void addPoint (x, y)
  - adds the coordinate (x, y) to the list of coordinates defining the Polygon object.
- boolean contains (x, y)
  - returns true if the coordinates (x, y) are within the boundary of the Polygon or false
- boolean contains (Point)

- returns whether the coordinates (x, y) are within the boundary of the Polygon
- boolean intersects (x, y, w, h)
  - returns whether the region defined by the coordinates (x, y) and width of (w) and height of (h) overlap with the Polygon

Random
Constructors

- Random r = new Random ( )
  - creates an instance of Random based on the current time stamp

Useful methods:

- int nextInt ( )
  - returns the next pseudo-random number as an integer
- int nextInt (num)
  - returns the next pseudo-random number between 0 and (num-1)

Rectangle
Constructors

- Rectangle r = new Rectangle(x, y, width, height);
  - creates a new Rectangle object

Useful methods:

- boolean contains(Rectangle)
  - returns true or false whether the Rectangle is inside the other
- boolean intersects(Rectangle)
  - returns true or false whether the Rectangle intersects with the other

String
Constructors

- String s = new String(text);
  - creates a new String object based on the text
- String s = text;
  - creates a new String object based on the text (shortcut way)

Useful methods:

- char charAt(index)
  - returns a character at the specified index in the string
- boolean equals(String)
  - returns true if the two strings are identical (case sensitive) or false otherwise
- int indexOf(charOrString)
  - returns the index of where the character or String sequence first appears
- String valueOf(number)
  - returns a String object of the number

Stroke
see BasicStroke

Thread
Constructors

- Thread thread = new Thread (this);
  - creates a new thread

Useful methods:

- static void sleep(num)

- pauses execution for num miliseconds
— void start( )
  - begins the thread, calls the run method
— void stop( )
  - stops the thread

Timer
Constructors

— Timer timer = new Timer (delay, this);
  - creates a new timer that triggers after delay in miliseconds

Useful methods:

— void start( )
  - begins the timer
— void stop( )
  - stops the timer

Index

!
!, 117, 118
!=, 115

%
%, 114, 115, 118
%=, 114

&
&&, 117, 118

*
*=, 114

/
/=, 114

|
||, 117, 118

+
+=, 114

=
-=, 114
==, 115

A
abs, 113
ActionEvent, 304
ActionListener, 143
addTab, 198
animation, 172
append, 171, 297
arc, 33
array, 216, 223
array - 2-D, 224
ArrayList, 228, 252, 268, 304
assembly language, 12, 13, 22
audio, 205

AudioClip, 205, 304

B
BasicStroke, 304
boolean, 46, 110
Border, 202, 306
   bevel, 203
   etched, 203
   matte, 204
   titled, 204
BorderFactory, 304
BorderLayout, 90, 305
BoxLayout, 95, 96, 305
BufferedImage, 256, 258, 306
ButtonGroup, 74, 149, 306
bytecode, 13, 14, 19, 20, 22, 288

C
Calendar, 133, 306
Canvas, 155, 188, 242
CGI, 281, 283
char, 46
circle, 41
class, 17, 110
clearRect, 172
color, 29
Color, 306
colors, 227
comments, 16
compiler, 13, 15, 16, 19, 20, 22, 288
container, 87
conversions, 119
coordinate, 17, 26, 31, 41

D
debugger, 300
debugging, 296
DefaultListModel, 75, 306
design, 99, 101
diagnol, 31
do loop, 172
domain name, 273, 278
double, 46, 110, 116
Double, 307
drawArc, 40

drawLine, 31, 40
drawOval, 31, 32, 40
drawPolygon, 40
drawRect, 32, 40, 168
drawRoundRect, 32, 40
drawString, 15, 26, 187, 188, 189

E
ellipse. *See* oval
else, 110
e-mail, 281
equals, 117
error, 173
errors
   compile-time, 296
   logical, 296
   syntax, 296
event, 143

F
file, 279, 283
fillArc, 40
fillOval, 40
fillPolygon, 40
fillRect, 32, 40, 41
FlowLayout, 60, 87, 307
font, 27, 187
Font, 27, 80, 190, 307
for, 110
for loop, 168

G
games, 250, 252
getAudioClip, 205
getCodeBase, 63, 64
getImage, 63
getText, 299
GIF, 37
Graphics2D, 40
GridLayout, 93, 310

H
high-level language, 12, 13, 22
hosting, 278

HTML, 13, 15, 19, 20, 21, 61, 62, 72, 273, 277, 279
HyperLinkEvent, 275
hyperlinks, 273

I

if, 110, 125
if-else, 126
image, 35
ImageIcon, 64, 310
images, 63, 77
implements, 110
import statements, 16, 59
infinite loop, 298
infinite loops, 173
initializer list. See arrays
in-line comment, 17
instance variables, 48, 112, 187
instanceof, 110, 118, 224, 244
int, 46, 110
Integer, 310
internet address, 273
Internet address, 273
interpreter, 13, 14, 22, 288, 289
isSelected, 224
ItemEvent, 311
ItemListener, 143

J

JApplet, 311
JButton, 66, 311
JButtons, 146
JCheckBox, 72, 127, 148, 150, 312
JComboBox, 75, 169, 312
JEditorPane, 273, 313
JFrame, 207, 313
JLabel, 59, 64
JList, 75, 147, 171, 313
JPanel, 87, 91, 180, 187, 314
JPasswordField, 70
jpg, 37
JRadioButton, 74, 149, 314
JScrollPane, 77, 315
JTabbedPane, 198, 200, 315
    tooltips, 201
JTable, 225, 315

JTextArea, 71, 127, 171, 315
JTextField, 70, 316

K

KeyEvent, 317
KeyListener, 143

L

Layouts
    BorderLayout, 90, 305
    BoxLayout, 95, 305
    FlowLayout, 87, 307
    GridLayout, 93, 310
length, 217
line, 31
list. See arrays
    array, 216
    ArrayList, 228
listeners, 143
local variables, 48
loop, 205
loops, 167
    do..while, 172
    for, 168
    infinite, 173
    while, 167

M

machine code, 12, 22
math, 114
Math, 113
method stub, 155
methods, 17, 26, 50, 51, 59, 81, 98, 144
MouseEvent, 317
MouseListener, 143, 156
MouseMotionEvent, 317
MouseMotionListener, 143, 156
multi-line comment, 16

O

object-oriented, 111, 288
oval, 31
overloading, 185
override, 268

P

paint, 15, 17, 26, 31, 32, 49, 50, 181, 190
paintComponent, 180
parameter, 278
parameters, 17, 31, 48, 49, 53, 61
pixel, 38
platform independent, 14, 288
platform-independent, 22
PNG, 37
polygon, 34
Polygon, 317
primitive, 46
primitive data types, 111
problem solving, 99, 101
program, 12, 15, 22, 238
programming language, 12, 22
protocol, 273
public, 17, 110

R

Random, 318
rectangle, 32
Rectangle, 252, 318
relational operators, 115
repaint, 146, 219, 246
reserved words, 110
return, 110
run, 238

S

scrollbars, 77
security, 289
setBackground, 79
setForeground, 79
setHorizontalTextPosition, 65, 68
setOpaque, 79
setPage. See JEditorPane
setSelected, 224
setToolTipText, 201
setVerticalTextPosition, 65, 68
size, 229
sleep, 240
slideshow, 238, 241
sound, 205

321

source code, 13, 19, 20, 22, 63, 289
Sprite, 260
sqrt, 113
square, 32
static, 113
stop, 205
String, 318
stub. *See method stub*
swing, 58
switch, 130
syntax, 12

T

this, 110
Thread, 254, 318
threads, 238, 289
Timer, 172, 238, 243, 244, 246, 319
tooltips, 201
transparency, 40
try, 110
try catch, 238, 275

U

uploading, 278

URL, 273, 275

V

variable, 13, 17, 46, 47, 59, 63, 64, 70, 110, 112
void, 110

W

while, 110, 172
while loop, 167

www.ingramcontent.com/pod-product-compliance
Ingram Content Group UK Ltd.
Pitfield, Milton Keynes, MK11 3LW, UK
UKHW051256180426
11947UKWH00020B/1747